Cases in Middle and Secondary Science Education

The Promise and Dilemmas

Thomas R. Koballa, Jr.
University of Georgia

Deborah J. Tippins
University of Georgia

Merrill
an imprint of Prentice Hall
Upper Saddle River, New Jersey   *Columbus, Ohio*

Library of Congress Cataloging-in-Publication Data

Cases in middle and secondary science education : the promise and dilemmas / edited by Thomas R. Koballa, Jr. and Deborah J. Tippins.

p.   cm.

Includes bibliographical references and index.

ISBN 0-13-082468-2

1. Science—Study and teaching (Middle school) Case studies. 2. Science—Study and teaching (Secondary) Case studies.   I. Koballa, Thomas R. II. Tippins, Deborah J.

Q181.C348   2000

507'.1'2—dc21

99-15331
CIP

Editor: Bradley J. Potthoff
Editorial Assistant: Mary Evangelista
Production Editor: Mary M. Irvin
Design Coordinator: Diane C. Lorenzo
Text Designer: Mia Saunders
Cover art: Elizabeth Zambelli
Cover Designer: Tanya Burgess
Production Manager: Pamela D. Bennett
Electronic Text Management: Marilyn Wilson Phelps, Karen L. Bretz, Melanie N. King
Director of Marketing: Kevin Flanagan
Marketing Manager: Meghan Shepherd
Marketing Coordinator: Krista Groshong

This book was set in ITC Garamond by Prentice Hall and was printed and bound by R. R. Donnelley & Sons Company. The cover was printed by Phoenix Color Corp.

Photo Credits: Photos copyrighted by the companies or individuals listed. Thomas J. Koballa, Jr., pp 1, 41, 65, 81, 135, 155, 181, 241, 269; Deborah J. Tippins, pp. 13, 111, 213; Bonnie Shapiro, pp. 102, 105, 106, 107.

Printed in the United States of America

10 9 8 7 6 5 4 3 2 1

ISBN: 0-13-082468-2

Prentice-Hall International (UK) Limited, *London*
Prentice-Hall of Australia Pty. Limited, *Sydney*
Prentice-Hall of Canada, Inc., *Toronto*
Prentice-Hall Hispanoamericana, S. A., *Mexico*
Prentice-Hall of India Private Limited, *New Delhi*
Prentice-Hall of Japan, Inc., *Tokyo*
Prentice-Hall (Singapore) Pte. Ltd., *Singapore*
Editora Prentice-Hall do Brasil, Ltda., *Rio de Janeiro*

To all the students, teachers, and teacher educators whose stories help us to transcend dominant ways of seeing the world of science teaching and learning and propel us into the 21st century.

Preface

Science teaching is a complex and uncertain endeavor. Today, middle school and secondary science teachers are called on to develop learning environments that facilitate students' construction of science understandings, skills, and attitudes. They must make decisions about curricula, instructional and assessment strategies, and their own professional development. In addition, teachers must be prepared to work with students from diverse cultural backgrounds and consider how their actions in their classrooms contribute to science education reform.

Cases in Middle and Secondary Science Education: The Promise and Dilemmas is about the problematic situations that arise in middle school and secondary science teaching and about dealing with these situations. The science teachers, teacher educators, and scientists who have contributed to this book are experts in many aspects of science and science teaching and learning. In their contributions, they have highlighted many dilemmas associated with middle school and secondary science teaching and have offered suggestions for improving practice and stimulating critical thinking about the science learning environment.

This book is intended for beginning and experienced middle school and secondary science teachers, science teacher educators, science teacher mentors, and school and school district administrators. It is ideal for use as a problem-solving vehicle for preservice teachers. It will assist them in developing an understanding of prevailing instructional practices in science at the middle and secondary levels and current attempts to reform traditional approaches to science teaching and learning. Additionally, the book will be very useful for in-service workshops and secondary education courses at the graduate level. And schools and universities that are collaborating in reform will be able to use this case handbook as a guide in their reform efforts.

The book consists of 12 chapters, with the first chapter serving to introduce the case method and the final chapter describing how to develop cases based on teachers' personal experiences. Chapters 2 to 11 each contain three or four cases, which focus on different dilemmas related to the chapter topic. These range from "Adolescent Learners in Science" and "Reform and Science Curriculum" to "Organizing a Positive Learning Environment," and "Student Teaching and Mentoring." Found among the chapters is a mixture of open cases, those that involve unresolved dilemmas, and closed cases, in which the author is able to resolve the dilemma described. Each case ends with "Questions for Reflection and Discussion." Commentaries that provide possible solutions for open cases and responses to closed cases follow all except for one novel case. "Resources to Consider" are found at the end of each of these chapters.

This book will be particularly valuable to educators who recognize that science teaching and learning occur in a world of uncertainty and that teaching is deeply rooted in our personalities and experiences as learners. Classroom cases provide the problem-posing and dialogical learning environment needed to facilitate reflective and critical thinking about the dilemmas and problematic situations that arise in middle school and secondary science teaching. These situations are embedded contextually and do not have a right answer or tidy solution. This allows individuals to define the problem, identify alternatives, choose a course of action, plan for implementation, and consider possible consequences of the given actions. These activities are often enhanced when several individuals grapple with the same problem at once. A classroom case, as the centerpiece of deliberation, can stimulate reflection among beginning and experienced teachers learning to become better classroom problem solvers.

This handbook should be used interactively and to complement other science teaching and learning resources. It is not intended to be used as a stand-alone science methods textbook. We recommend that individuals read a case and use the "Questions for Reflection and Discussion" to facilitate their reflective thinking and discussion *before* examining the case commentaries. Some commentaries offer reflections on the case's problematic situations by the case author, while others provide an expert's constructive critique of the case. The commentaries shed new light on the case and provide a different perspective from which to consider the problem or the proposed solution. After reading the commentaries, individuals may wish to revisit the "Questions for Reflection and Discussion."

This book is the product of the thinking and experiences of 73 individuals who are dedicated to the improvement of science teaching and learning. We are very much indebted to them for their contributions and appreciate the understanding and flexibility they showed us as we edited the content of cases, commentaries, and abstracts for instructional purposes and consistency of style.

■ Acknowledgments

We wish to express our thanks and appreciation to the following people for their invaluable contributions: Bradley J. Potthoff, our editor extraordinaire at Merrill/Prentice Hall, who believed in the work of this project; Maureen Boyd, for her cooperation, thoughtful perspectives, and attention to detail. We also thank our reviewers for their useful feedback: Richard L. Benoit, University of Houston—Clear Lake; Paul Drotz, City University; Thomas Giles, Cumberland College; George T. Ladd, Boston College; Cheryl L. Mason, San Diego State University; Michael Odell, University of Idaho; Robert E. Yager, University of Iowa; and Edward J. Zielinski, Clarion University.

Finally, we especially wish to thank our families, friends, and colleagues for their support and encouragement during the preparation of this book.

Thomas R. Koballa, Jr.
Deborah J. Tippins
Science Education Department, The University of Georgia

List of Contributors

Sandra K. Abell, Purdue University; Jill Bailer, Jane Long Middle School; Glenda Bell, University of Texas at Austin; Maureen Boyd, University of Georgia; Ava L. Bozeman; Carole Briscoe, University of West Florida; Lynn A. Bryan, University of Georgia; Stephanie L. Cannon, Harlem High School; Eugene L. Chiappetta, University of Houston; Sajin Chun, University of Georgia; Dava C. Coleman, Cedar Shoals High School; Joseph Conti, Oglethorpe County Middle School; Teresa S. Coker; Barbara A. Crawford, Oregon State University; Frank E. Crawley, East Carolina University; Melissa Dunavant; Kevin D. Finson, Western Illinois University; Steven Fleming, Pasadena High School; M. Jenice "Dee" Goldston, Kansas State University; James J. Gallagher, Michigan State University; Yvette Q. Getch, University of Georgia; Julie Gess-Newsome, University of Utah; Belinda Gibson; Shawn M. Glynn, University of Georgia; Kimberly L. Harmelink, Commerce High School; Joseph L. Hoffman, West Bloomfield High School; Elaine R. Homestead; David F. Jackson, University of Georgia; Miriam Jordan, Jasper County High School; Michael Kamen, Auburn University; Andrew C. Kemp, University of Georgia; John Karl Kemper; Carolyn W. Keys, University of Georgia; Pamela J. Kitchens, Harlem High School; Thomas R. Koballa, Jr., University of Georgia; Joseph Krajcik, University of Michigan; Norman G. Lederman, Oregon State University; Gloria "Brownie" Lindner, Northern Arizona University; Julie A. Luft, University of Arizona; Lee Meadows, University of Alabama at Birmingham; Tuller Jan Merrifield, University of Georgia; J. Randy McGinnis, University of Maryland; Gert Nesin, University of Georgia; Sharon E. Nichols, East Carolina University; Morgan B. Nolan, University of Georgia; Michael J. Padilla, University of Georgia; Nita A. Paris, University of Georgia; P. Elizabeth Pate, University of Georgia; Gail Paulin, Tucson Unified School District; John E. Penick, North Carolina State University; Eric J. Pyle, West Virginia University; Jo Quintenz; David L. Radford, University of Alabama at Birmingham; Barbara Rascoe, University of Georgia; Wolff-Michael Roth, University of Victoria; Alice Sampson, University of Georgia; Cherine LeBlanc Schaaf; Lawrence C. Scharmann, Kansas State University; Bonnie Shapiro, University of Calgary; Harry L. Shipman, University of Delaware; Ronald D. Simpson, University of Georgia; Darwin W. Smith, University of Georgia; Elliot Soloway, University of Michigan; Randi Nevins Stanulis, University of Georgia; Mark A. Templin; Norman Thomson, University of Georgia; Deborah J. Tippins, University of Georgia; Kenneth Tobin, University of Pennsylvania; William Veal, Indiana University; Mark J. Volkmann, Purdue University; Melissa A. Warden, Ball State University; Robert C. Wicklein, University of Georgia; Katherine C. Wieseman, Western State College; Rachel Williamson.

Contents

3 Reform and Science Curriculum   41

4 Planning for Science Instruction   65

5 Organizing a Positive Learning Environment   81

6 Learning in the Science Classroom   111

7 Learning in the Laboratory and Informal Settings   135

8

Controversial Issues in the Science Classroom 155

9

The Role of Technology in Science Teaching and Learning   181

10

Assessment in Science   213

11

Student Teaching and Mentoring   241

12

Science Teacher Education: Exploring the Paradoxes and Possibilities of Case-Based Instruction   269

1

Classroom Case Narratives as Pedagogical and Research Tools in Science Education

I n middle and secondary science classrooms, where daily routines are anything but routine and each day brings with it a new set of challenges and issues, teaching is a very complex and demanding process. Middle and secondary science teachers must be well versed in science content; must understand the nature of science, technology, and how students learn; and must be knowledgeable about a variety of instructional strategies, curricula, and assessment practices. More important, these teachers must be able to use and create knowledge in the context of their own classrooms. Teachers ill prepared to deal with the complexity of middle and secondary science teaching often find the demands of the classroom too challenging and quickly become discouraged or adopt a simplistic view of science teaching where "tricks of the trade" serve as a substitute for thoughtful practice.

In recent years, middle and secondary science teacher education has undergone somewhat of a transformation. Prompted by a new understanding of the limitations of professional knowledge to address all the challenges of everyday classroom practice, the focus in preparing science teachers as technical decision makers has given way to preparing reflective practitioners (Anderson & Mitchner, 1994). Rather than allowing their actions to be governed by rules and prescriptions derived from professional knowledge, reflective practitioners, according to Schön (1987, p. 39) construct new categories of understanding and ways of framing problems of practice. More recently, reflection has been situated in the broader context of social justice. Critical reflection undertaken from this perspective considers the assumptions and agendas associated with the traditions and conventions of different social and cultural groups (Nichols, Tippins, & Wieseman, 1997). This reflective focus illuminates the messy nature of science teaching and the teacher's role as a classroom problem solver and dilemma manager (Lampert, 1985). Textbooks and instructional materials traditionally used in middle and secondary science teacher education programs and professional development tend to perpetuate the development of science teachers as technical decision makers. In contrast, classroom cases draw our attention to the dilemmas that characterize the lives of science teachers and serve as a vehicle for reflection and changing practice.

The use of cases in science education resembles conceptions of good teaching advocated in reform documents such as *Science for All Americans* (American Association for the Advancement of Science, 1989) and more recently the *National Science Education Standards* (National Research Council, 1996). These documents call for science teaching that encourages multiple perspectives, critical thinking, and diverse approaches to solving problems. They present a vision for science teaching in which learning takes place best when it can be connected with experience. They also provide a vision for the professional development of science teachers where "becoming an effective science teacher is viewed as a continuous process that stretches from pre-service experiences in undergraduate years to the end of a professional career"

(National Research Council, 1996, p. 55). Widespread dissemination of standards and statewide learning frameworks does not, however, provide total guidance for transformation of curricula, instructional practices, and assessment strategies. Despite the intent of these reform documents to enhance science teaching, teachers, for the most part, must continue to make sense of science teaching and learning in the context of their local schools and communities. In the midst of the standards-based reform movement, classroom case narratives appeal to us as tools that might potentially capture the uncertainty, complexity, variation, assumptions, and purpose that influence the ways in which science teachers construct professional knowledge.

The Need for Cases: Questions of Purpose

Case-based pedagogies in science education have been advocated by many as a useful tool for promoting reflective inquiry, engaging prospective and practicing teachers in learning from their experiences, and strengthening decision-making and problem-solving skills. While theoretical arguments for the use of classroom cases as instructional tools have expanded rapidly, many divergent views exist concerning the definition, purpose, and use of cases in education and science teacher education.

We regard classroom cases, as used in this book, to be examples of the narrative mode of literature. Not to be confused with the term *case study,* which generally refers to a method of research, cases are a particular form of narrative that can be used to explicate and clarify the professional knowledge of teachers. Miller and Kantrov (1998) provide a useful definition in which "case refers to a narrative organized around a key event and portraying particular characters that is structured to invite engagement by participants in a discussion" (p. 2). We also concur with Kagan's (1993) definition of a case as "a description of a real or realistic classroom situation that incorporates all the facts needed to clarify and solve target problems" (p. 705). In this sense, cases are not only vehicles for fostering self-reflection; they represent a way of perceiving and organizing reality (Bruner, 1986; Polkinghorne, 1988). By extension, case narratives can be considered to be a tool through which teachers implicitly express their perceptions and pedagogical beliefs. We use the metaphor of *tool* to emphasize the importance of cases as resources for understanding how teachers think and act within the context of their perceived experiences.

The underlying purpose of case-based instruction can be viewed in different ways, which, in turn, influence how cases are used in science teacher education. Shulman (1986), in emphasizing the substance of the case, suggests that "while cases themselves are reports of events, the knowledge they represent is what makes them cases" (p. 22). For Shulman, the instructive power of the case rests in its structure and substance. By contrast, Welty (as cited in Merseth, 1991) maintains that the substantive value of the case cannot be separated from the class discussion through which students "learn to identify actual problems, to recognize the key players and their agendas, and to become aware of those aspects of the situation that contribute to the problem" (p. 5). Merseth (1991), in *The Case for Cases in Teacher Education,* points out that content and process are inseparable in case-based pedagogies. She emphasizes that "to focus on discussion methods alone, without reference to the material being discussed, is analogous to approaches to teaching that ignore the content that is being taught. Conversely, concern for content alone, without attention to process, denies the reality that how we teach is what we teach" (p. 5).

The cases included in this book are intended to portray dilemmas and contexts that are particular to secondary science teaching and learning. Thus, while the substantive content of each case is critical, its place as a centerpiece for deliberation and discussion is equally important.

Historical Emergence of Cases in Education and Science Teacher Education

Case narratives in education have a well-established history derived from law, medicine, and business, where they are typically used as a context for exploring particular principles or problems (Kleinfeld, 1992; Sykes & Bird, 1992). Kagan (1993) notes that case-based approaches first became a tradition in law with the introduction of the "Langdell" method in 1871. This approach was based on the use of original source materials and doctrines as a context for group problem solving aimed at the extraction of key legal principles. Soon after, case methods were incorporated into the curricula of medical schools, where students would eventually construct complete cases as part of their medical education. Kagan (1993) cites a textbook written by Waples (1927), *Problems in Classroom Method*, as probably the earliest example of the application of case-based pedagogies in education; it contained narratives of classroom dilemmas followed by solutions written by in-service teachers.

Merseth (1991) describes an interesting distinction that can be made to differentiate the use of cases in law and medicine from their use in the field of business. The use of cases in law and medicine is characterized by deductive logic, which is a reflection of the existence of clearly defined knowledge bases in these fields. By contrast, the knowledge base for business might be described as ill-structured, or loosely defined. Merseth notes irony in the fact that the legal model for case-based education has most frequently served as the model for developing cases in education. Given the unpredictable and ambiguous nature of classroom dilemmas, case-based approaches modeled after those in business education may actually be more fitting. In the field of business, case-based instruction is characterized by the presentation of carefully crafted narratives of dilemmas grounded in actual experiences and events.

As the use of classroom cases in teacher education has evolved over the past 50 years, various formats have emerged to illustrate problems or dilemmas in teaching and learning. These formats have included the critical incident, protocols, vignettes, simulations, video cases, and more recently, interactive video cases. Today, as the use of cases continues to gain in popularity, we see the influence of these earlier approaches to case-based education.

■ The Use of Cases: A Question of Context

Just as no exploration of the physical universe is undertaken without an attempt to understand the relationship between the components of the universe, any attempt to make sense of the dilemmas of teaching must be viewed as part of a larger context. Recent conceptualizations of teacher knowledge that acknowledge the complexities of teaching have contributed to an increased awareness of the potential value of case-based pedagogies for contextualizing teaching and learning. The power of cases to represent and be responsive to local contexts and concerns is often viewed as a bridge between theory and practice in education. Abell, Cennamo, Anderson, Bryan, Campbell, and Hug (1996) suggest that cases can "reduce the complexity of teaching into a manageable story situated in a specific context" (p. 138). Case narratives can effectively portray classrooms and dilemmas as they evolve over time, which is an important dimension of context. At the same time, it is important to recognize that context is not a clearly delineated area. Teachers continually negotiate contextual borders as they go about their daily activities. In Clandinin and Connelly's (1995) book *Teachers' Professional Knowledge Landscapes*, Cheryl Craig, a third-grade teacher, vividly describes the tensions that characterize her attempts to negotiate contextual borders:

> As a teacher, I live in two places on the professional knowledge landscape: my classroom where I meet students face-to-face, and places outside my classroom, where I meet all those things that are expected of me. In my classroom, I have a measure of moral freedom as I respond to the dilemmas that present themselves. I am a moral agent who can have a shaping effect on situations. I am in charge of my own response and can influence others' responses to particular situations. But outside my classroom, my experience may be quite different. (p. 23)

While cases can provide knowledge of the histories, social relations, and practices of the communities in which science teaching and learning are carried out, they nevertheless have inherent limitations. Case interpretations and evaluations might be quite different if the reader were to have access to additional kinds of knowledge. Current educational literature provides us with three contexts for considering the use of classroom cases, each based on different epistemological traditions: the use of cases as a context for critical reflection, as a vehicle for instruction, and as a tool for research.

Cases as a Context for Instruction

A basic premise of this book is that case-based instruction can motivate and facilitate science teaching and learning for a wide range of prospective and practicing science teachers. Ertmer, Newby, and MacDougal (1996, p. 720) point out that a general assumption in the literature is that "cases are more motivating than traditional methods for *all* learners, that they promote better transfer in *all* learners, and that they can transform *all* learners into better problem solvers and critical thinkers." While there is a need for further research to examine the intuitive belief in the value of case-based instruction for all learners, it is clear that the instructive value of cases differs from conventional teacher education pedagogies.

The instructive value of cases, as emphasized in this book, rests in their potential to communicate opportunities for teachers to build on prior knowledge and evolving experience to go beyond traditional ways of seeing the world. These cases are intended to present situations that provide a context for teachers to become cognizant of problematic or challenging events, engage in multiple ways of viewing and interpreting these events, recognize their own beliefs, and assess the practical and moral implications associated with each narrative. The cases are not intended to be used in a prescriptive sense that emphasizes the need to clarify or ascertain the best possible approach or solution to a situation. Rather, we view the cases presented in this book as a type of "pedagogical puzzle" (e.g., Harrington, 1991) that brings together teachers' contextual and conditional knowledge to facilitate science teaching and learning.

Cases as a Context for Critical Reflection

Many of the questions we ask about science education and encourage in both prospective and practicing teachers are designed to promote reflection. Reflection, as an active process, is an essential component of professional growth. It compels teachers to make sense of their own practice, students' understandings, and every aspect of science teaching and learning in today's secondary schools. Teachers' reflections on personal experience and reflection in action are starting points for both writing case narratives and responding to the cases of colleagues.

Reflective practice is characterized by opportunities to analyze, both individually and as a group, problematic situations; to evaluate multiple forms of evidence; and to make decisions and recommendations that lead to action. "Practical deliberation," an idea introduced by Dewey (1933) emphasizes the need for conscious and systematic ways of examining the dilemmas and challenges of practice. While most science teacher educators agree on the need for reflective teachers, they do not necessarily share a common understanding of what it means to be reflective. Too often, reflective inquiry is characterized by a technical or procedural orientation that takes the context for granted and leaves unchallenged the accepted traditions of science teacher education. Contemporary educators such as Schön (1987), Smyth (1992), and Zeichner and Tabachnik (1991) have called for reflection that is critical in nature, and thus bound within a system of meaning making that is socially mediated. This type of critical reflection is open to multiple perspectives; considers social, political, ideological, moral, and ethical commitments of one's assumptions; and identifies options, alternatives, and possibilities for future inquiry.

Case-based pedagogies have increasingly been advocated as a means for grounding the questions we ask and dilemmas we pose in a critical system of meaning. Implicit within a critical theory-grounded system of meaning is the need for analyzing hidden and overt curricula, evaluation and pedagogical approaches, and the forces of power embedded within classrooms and schools that ultimately define what we call a problem.

The case authors in this book have independently and uniquely defined the dilemmas and struggles of their own practice. We encourage science teachers and science teacher educators who interact with these cases to recognize how their own assumptions influence the ways in which they make sense of the dilemmas portrayed in each narrative. Additionally, we ask readers to consider the deep social and political structures that surround each case.

Cases as a Context for Research

Teachers' narrative accounts of experience, in the form of classroom cases, are a type of story or coherent system of meaning. In this sense, they can serve as a type of practitioner action research or as data for studying teachers' thought processes and underlying pedagogical beliefs.

Traditionally, educational research has been a university-initiated and controlled endeavor that has been abstract and distanced from the life of the classroom. With the emergence of action research paradigms and the more recent emphasis on teachers as researchers in their own classrooms, what counts as knowledge is being redefined. Against the backdrop of educational reform, classroom cases are gaining acceptance as an interpretive research tool that can assist prospective and practicing teachers in their personal learning processes and provide a vehicle for communicating with the rest of the educational community.

When teachers' written cases and responses are used to infer underlying thought processes and pedagogical beliefs, they support the particular epistemological tradition of narrative inquiry. Narrative modes of inquiry have gained acceptance in recent years with the implicit recognition that "a case reflects the assumptions, beliefs and meaning systems that the teacher/author used to understand and interpret experience" (Kagan, 1993, p. 709).

While case-based instruction has a long history that crosses many disciplines, the evidence in support of this tradition has not been well documented through research. Only recently have research studies attempted to address questions such as the extent to which case-based instruction can facilitate the ability to analyze real classroom problems or the way in which case-based instruction supports or constrains the development of reflective practitioners. An analysis of case-based research of the past several years reveals some of the more common themes that serve as foci of inquiry. These themes include

- Classroom cases as a form of self-study
- The use of cases as an assessment tool
- Cases as a form of curriculum development
- Cases as a tool for professional development and preparation
- Cases as methods for facilitating critical thinking
- Cases as discipline-based teaching methods
- Cases as a tool for exploring ethical dimensions of teaching
- Cases as a tool for examining issues of diversity and family involvement
- Cases as a tool for promoting reflective self-regulation

■ Pedagogical and Philosophical Underpinnings of the Casebook: Epistemological Tensions

A basic premise of this book is that teachers, at all levels, are holders and creators of knowledge, which is reflected in personal and social narratives of experience. These stories of experience are not neat and tidy; they reflect the complexity of teaching and learning science through interwoven scenes and plots. They are stories that are rooted in the lived experiences of children, teachers, and administrators; are mediated by the subject matter; and are situated in diverse communities. These case narratives, as representations of teacher knowledge, are constructed in the classroom through the interaction of teachers' experience with information derived from the discipline of science. Accordingly, knowledge is not considered to exist as an external body of information independent of humans; nor can it be completely codified to the extent that a complete set of consistent principles or scientific theories drive teachers' classroom decisions. Rather, the creation of knowledge can be understood as an inductive process in which teachers make sense of multiple experiences in contextualized settings. Case-based pedagogies are particularly suitable in light of perspectives that view knowledge as "constructed, built on prior knowledge, coupled with experience, transformable, evolving, and sequential and, thereby, provides students with insight into alternative solutions rather than 'correct' answers" (Harrington, 1995, p. 203).

We view cases as tools that can promote discussion, engage diverse perspectives, and explore critical issues of science teaching and learning. We do not approach the use of cases as models of exemplary practice. Rather, we view cases as "windows into science classrooms" (Tobin, Kahle, & Fraser, 1990), where teachers wrestle with the experiences, ideas, issues, and dilemmas of practice. Teachers are confronted with dilemmas characterized by competing and often equally valid solutions. Similarly, cases can be viewed as the mirrors that reflect the beliefs of teachers as they read and discuss case narratives from multiple perspectives.

■ Nature of the Cases in This Book

We use an "open" and "closed" case format to depict the narratives included in this book. While each case is characterized by a central dilemma, multiple story lines interact and bear on one another. Open cases are those that involve unresolved dilemmas of practice. These open cases typically do not include solutions, outcomes, or morals of the story. A second author discusses potential solutions or resolutions to the dilemmas portrayed in each case. In some instances, several respondents offer diverse perspectives for considering the story depicted in each case. We describe closed cases as ones in which the author is able to resolve the dilemma in some manner. A second author provides a personal interpretation of the case and opinions concerning the viability of the solutions described in the narrative. While we use the terms *open* and *closed* to categorize the cases in this book, we recognize that these narratives do not stand alone in isolation from the landscape of professional practice. The readers and users of these cases are participants in dynamic learning communities characterized by changing events and circumstances; each is uniquely positioned in relation to the case narratives that unfold in this book. Readers are encouraged to think of the solutions to open cases and responses to closed cases from multiple perspectives. No one common solution or response is necessary or desirable. Even if prospective or practicing teachers share similar interpretations of cases, these interpretations do not necessarily lead to similar solutions (Nichols et al., 1997).

Each case in this book is followed by a set of "Questions for Reflection and Discussion." We suggest that individuals read through a case in its entirety and respond initially to the questions for reflection individually or through group discussion, before reading case solutions and responses. We provide specific guidelines for using an open and closed case narrative format in the final chapter of this book.

The case narratives, solutions, and responses presented in this book are designed to preserve the insights shared by authors from their unique perspectives. To avoid imposing an interpretation drawn from our own respective worldviews, our editorial work was relatively minor and informed by collaborative dialogue with the authors. The case authors are situated in a variety of positions with respect to science teacher education; secondary classroom teachers, prospective science teachers, student teachers, administrators, graduate students, scientists, informal science educators, and college/university-based science teacher educators all contributed to the development of this book. The authors generally relate case narratives that describe experiences embedded within their unique roles as educators. Their stories are characterized by a variety of writing styles, which we believe ultimately "enrich our understanding and are integral to the personalities of these authors" (Kagan & Tippins, 1995).

Several of the cases in this book offer unique formats. For example, Bonnie Shapiro's narrative, *Creating Objects of Meaning in Science* (see Chapter 5), is organized as a set of key case experiences with accompanying photographs. At the conclusion of each case experience, participants are provided with an opportunity to pause as a group to discuss their goals and the case itself. This case would likely be used in a manner quite different from the other cases in this book. Since it is unlikely that a group would have time to do or discuss all of the experiences that compose this case at any one point in time, facilitators may need to identify points of entry into the case and perhaps create their own sequence for the case experiences.

Layers of commentary build several cases featured in this book. Judith Shulman (1992) initially introduced the idea of building a case with layers of commentary. These cases are accounts of classroom dilemmas, which are followed by commentaries from other teachers or educational scholars who have personal involvement, knowledge, or insight with respect to the situation. The commentaries raise issues in the case but do not necessarily provide solutions or answers. Steve Fleming's case, *A Pressure-Packed Problem* (Chapter 7), and Kenneth Tobin's case, *Social Constructivism: A Referent for Thinking About Teaching or a Way to Teach?* (Chapter 6), are examples that illustrate a layered commentary approach to writing cases. Shulman (1992) suggests that narratives with layered commentaries can link cases to research, provide multiple perspectives on the same issue, or create a context for action.

Written cases are commonly read silently by individuals, with guiding questions acting as a compass to orient or focus the readers' attention. Subsequent discussions that follow the reading of a case are designed to engage teachers in thoughtful analysis and critique. While this is a common approach to using case-based pedagogies, it is not the only approach. Fisch (1997) recommends variations of this approach including: (1) reading aloud portions of the case in group presentations; (2) presenting dialogue embedded in a case as a staged reading; (3) developing interruptive drama presentations of a case, which encourage both readers and listeners to interrupt by asking questions, making suggestions, or clarifying positions; and (4) presenting a case via film or video. In the final chapter of this book, we explore in depth some guidelines for developing written cases and provide suggestions for using them effectively to facilitate group discussion and personal-professional growth.

References

Abell, S. K., Cennamo, K. S., Anderson, M. A., Bryan, L. A., Campbell, L. M., & Hug, J. W. (1996). Integrated media classroom cases in elementary science teacher education. *Journal of Computers in Mathematics and Science Teaching*, *15*, 137–151.

American Association for the Advancement of Science. (1989). *Science for All Americans*. New York: Oxford University Press.

Anderson, R. D., & Mitchner, C. P. (1994). Research on teacher education. In D. Gabel (Ed.), *Handbook of research on science teaching and learning* (3–44). New York: Macmillan.

Bruner, J. (1986). *Actual minds, possible worlds*. Cambridge, MA: Harvard University Press.

Clandinin, D. J., & Connelly, M. F. (1995). *Teachers' professional knowledge landscapes*. New York: Teachers College Press.

Dewey, J. (1933). *How we think: A restatement of the relation of reflective thinking to the educative process*. Boston: D. C. Heath.

Ertmer, P. A., Newby, T. J., & MacDougal, M. (1996). Students' responses and approaches to case-based instruction: The role of reflective self-regulation. *American Educational Research Journal*, *33*, 719–752.

Fisch, L. (1997). Triggering discussions on ethics and values: Cases and innovative variations. *Innovation in Higher Education*, *22*, 117–135.

Harrington, H. L. (1991). The case as method. *Action in Teacher Education*, 7, 2–10.

Harrington, H. L. (1995). Fostering reasoned decisions: Case-based pedagogy and the professional development of teachers. *Teaching and Teacher Education*, *11*, 203–214.

Kagan, D. M. (1993). Contexts for the use of classroom cases. *American Educational Research Journal*, *30*, 703–723.

Kagan, D., & Tippins, D. (1995). Views of American education: The perceptions of non-American professors of education working at U.S. universities. *Educational Forum, 59*, 140–153.

Kleinfeld, J. (1992, April). *Can cases carry pedagogical content knowledge? Yes, but we've got signs of a Matthew effect.* Paper presented at the Annual Meeting of the American Educational Research Association, San Francisco, CA.

Lampert, M. (1985). How do teachers manage to teach? Perspectives on problems in practice. *Harvard Educational Review, 55*, 178–194.

Merseth, K. K. (1991). *The case for cases in teacher education.* Washington, DC: American Association for Higher Education and American Association of Colleges for Teacher Education.

Miller, B., & Kantrov, I. (1998). *A guide to facilitating cases in education.* Portsmouth, NH: Heinemann.

National Research Council. (1996). *National science education standards.* Washington, DC: National Research Council.

Nichols, S. E., Tippins, D., & Wieseman, K. (1997). A toolkit for developing critically reflective science teachers. *Journal of Science Teacher Education, 8*, 77–106.

Polkinghorne, D. E. (1988). *Narrative knowing and the human sciences.* Albany, NY: State University of New York Press.

Schön, D. A. (1987). *Educating the reflective practitioner.* San Francisco: Jossey-Bass.

Shulman, J. H. (Ed.). (1992). *Case methods in teacher education.* New York: Teachers College Press.

Shulman, L. S. (1986). Those who understand: Knowledge growth in teaching. *Educational Researcher, 15*, 4–14.

Smyth, J. (1992). Teachers' work and the politics of reflection. *American Educational Research Journal, 29*, 267–300.

Sykes, G., & Bird, T. (1992). Teacher education and the case idea. *Review of Research in Education, 18*, 457–521.

Tobin, K., Kahle, J. B., & Fraser, B. J. (1990). *Windows into science classrooms: Problems associated with higher level cognitive learning in science.* London: Falmer Press.

Waples, D. (1927). *Problems in classroom method: A manual of case analysis for high-school supervisors and teachers in service.* New York: Macmillan.

Zeichner, K., & Tabachnik, R. (1991). Reflections on reflective teaching. In R. Tabachnik & K. Zeichner (Eds.), *Issues and practices in inquiry-oriented teacher education* (pp. 1–21). London: Falmer Press.

2

Adolescent Learners in Science

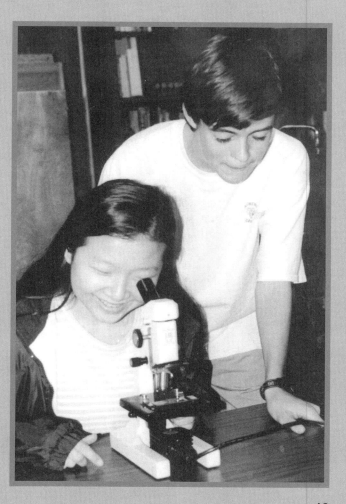

Science teaching occurs in a context that is bound by the nature of the learner. Each student constructs his or her own personal understandings of science. And it is the science teacher's responsibility to guide and facilitate this construction process. But as the middle and secondary student population becomes increasingly diverse, providing the guidance and support needed by individual students has become a real challenge for science teachers. Demographic trends suggest that in the near future all science classes will include learners whose ethnic and cultural backgrounds vary widely. Also to be found among this diverse student group are individuals with a broad range of learning abilities. Science teachers will have to consider the needs of gifted students as well as those with learning disabilities. With recent advances in diagnosing students' special learning needs and the inclusion of these students in regular science classes, teachers are now expected to provide for their needs in the course of day-to-day instruction. More so than ever before, a student's cultural background, ethnicity, gender, disabilities, and multiple intelligences are of concern to science teachers.

The four cases in this chapter provide a glimpse of the dilemmas faced by science teachers as they attempt to meet the needs of today's adolescent learners. The first case highlights how a high school teacher's enthusiasm for making her biology lessons culturally relevant for her Native American students leads to conflicts with their cultural beliefs and practices. In the second case, an earth science teacher describes his frustrating experience of dealing with a special needs student when he has no personal knowledge of the necessary accommodations. In the third case, an international school provides the backdrop for a learning experience that causes a middle school teacher to wrestle with issues of culture and language. An important dilemma in this case centers on how students' culture and language affect their learning about scientists and science. In the final case, a middle school life science teacher tells about her efforts to stimulate very high ability students while at the same time making basic concepts understandable to low ability students.

While the Animals Sleep

Jo Quintenz and Julie A. Luft

As a teacher at a Native American reservation school in the southwestern United States, Jo Quintenz enjoys her professional relationship with Julie Luft, a university professor. In this open case, Jo and Julie describe Jo's attempt to create a more culturally inclusive curriculum in her biology class. Jo develops a unit that includes accounts from different cultures about the origin of life on earth and of the earth itself. In the course of her work, Jo realizes that she has made instructional decisions with little knowledge of her students' cultural backgrounds, and she is left wondering what to do next. The story is told in Jo's voice and followed by a response written by Maureen Boyd and Tuller Jan Merrifield, teacher educators with expertise in culturally relevant teaching and learning.

Over the course of a 25-year career in science teaching, my instructional approach has run the gamut from teacher-directed lessons with verification labs to mastery learning through individualized student learning plans. In recent years, my focus has shifted from a content-driven comprehensive science program designed to produce the next generation of engineers and research scientists to one in which students are encouraged to explore science from a personal and societal perspective. It is my hope that this current approach will motivate more of my students to expand on their experience and understanding of natural phenomena.

This is particularly important for my students, because I teach in a school with a 75% minority population; one that is almost exclusively Hispanic and Native American. I am Euro-American. While it is important that my students understand the Western explanation for scientific phenomena, it is also critical that they not perceive this position as contrary to their own cultural understandings and perspectives.

As a high school biology teacher, I address several topics during the year, including homeostasis, energy transfer, continuity, ecology, and of course, evolution. I try to create a more student-centered and culturally relevant instructional setting by including examples and topics from southwestern biomes and cultures. For example, using Indian corn in genetics lessons has particular meaning for my students. We also draw on indigenous agricultural practices in contrast to modern desert farming techniques in environmental impact studies.

Each year, I begin my course with a unit on evolution. I consider this topic to be fundamental to any course in biology. As an introduction to the unit, I elected to collect stories from different cultures about the origin of life on earth and of the earth itself. My intent was to allow students to develop an awareness of the characteristics of scientific explanations through a contrast of diverse accounts of observed phenomena and at the same time validate the importance of these other explanations.

When I first introduced the readings for my evolution unit, several students commented about the nature of the assignment. Lisa wanted to know if teaching evolution wasn't illegal, and Mario asked "Miss, why are we doing this? We're not in church!" Angie was concerned about how the assignment would be graded. Specifically, she wanted to know if she would be graded on her understanding of each account or her ability to justify one account. I asked the class if there were any other origin stories that they knew about. As there was no immediate response, the students began their reading, and I quietly approached Rhonda, a Tohono O'Odam student. Tohono O'Odam people are thought to have descended from the Hohokam, the original desert dwellers. I asked her if she would like to research and present the origin story of her people. She said she would ask her mother if it would be all right. I was a little puzzled by her response but said I would check with her the next day to see if she or her mother would like to share the story with the class.

As I drove to work the next morning, I planned how to present the various origin stories in class. I decided that each group would share one account with the class. We would then discuss each story and identify common and contrasting elements, as well as attempt to identify what natural phenomena might have contributed to the development of each account. When I arrived at school, I picked up my mail and walked to my classroom. I opened the door, turned on the lights, and set down the canvas tote overflowing with papers. I was ready to begin.

As I wrote focus questions on the board, I overheard two people in a quiet conversation enter the room. It was Rhonda and an older women. "Miss Quintenz, this is my mother, Juana Smith," Rhonda said. We shook hands, and I invited Mrs. Smith to be seated at one of the student tables. While Rhonda made exquisitely detailed observations of her hands, Mrs. Smith began to speak softly but clearly. "I understand that you would like someone to share the Tohono O'Odam origin story with your class. While I am pleased that there is an interest in our story, it isn't possible that either Rhonda or I tell the story at this time." I must have looked puzzled, for she paused a bit and then continued. "We do not speak of some animals when they are awake and might overhear our conversation. We share these stories in the winter when we are inside and the animals are asleep. We could come back and share the stories in a few months," she offered helpfully. As I began an extensive study of my own hands, I wondered how many other times I had forged ahead with the best intentions and little knowledge of other cultures. More importantly, I wondered what I would do next.

Questions for Reflection and Discussion

1. Should a science teacher recognize and teach various origin stories? If so, how could this be done?

2. What should Jo do next with Rhonda and Mrs. Smith? with her science class?

3. What are other science topics that may be sensitive in a class of culturally diverse students?

4. What is meant by "culturally relevant" science curriculum? Should science teachers craft culturally relevant curricula? If so, what strategies could be used to do so?

5. How could you find out if a lesson you plan to teach is incompatible with the beliefs and experiences of your students?

6. Students from diverse backgrounds may look on science taught in school as something that is not applicable to them. How could you help students from diverse backgrounds reconcile the idea that their cultural understandings and perspectives need not be incompatible with accepted scientific explanations for phenomena?

7. Some science philosophers and educators consider science a universal form of knowledge that transcends cultural interpretation, while other science philosophers and educators view science as only one of several possible culturally based frameworks for investigating the natural world. Which of these two positions do you favor? Why?

■ ■ ■

Let Students Propose School–Home Culture Connections

Maureen Boyd and Tuller Jan Merrifield

The importance of a culturally inclusive curriculum is explicitly acknowledged by Jo and Julie. This case illustrates that, while good intentions are insufficient to engender culturally relevant instruction, they can build community connections, which can facilitate culturally relevant and appropriate instruction. Teachers need to affirm student and community "funds of knowledge" (Moll, 1992), but this is best achieved when the students propose the connections to their home culture. The teacher is then cued to acknowledge and build on these student-proposed, intertextual links (Bloome & Egan-Robertson, 1993).

The role of the teacher in this acknowledgment can take two forms: modeling and valuing alternative ways of thinking and facilitating appropriate use of culturally relevant examples. In this case, the role of the teacher is consequential to enhancing or defeating the potential of a culturally inclusive curriculum, and her instructional practices shape and determine the classroom discourse (Boyd, 1996; Cummins, 1989; Guttierrez, 1994; Nystrand, 1997). She can explicitly model and value alternate ways of thinking that are culturally relevant in this classroom and that build on students' prior knowledge. Inclusion of local funds of knowledge not only promotes engagement and enhances cognition but also develops coherence between home and school cultures (Carrel, 1987; Nystrand, Gamoran, & Heck, 1993). However, these connections should be student and community generated, thus ensuring appropriate application and diminishing the potential for teachers' superficial perceptions of the local culture to inadvertently create misunderstandings.

In this case, Jo and Julie actively sought to incorporate local funds of knowledge into the science classroom. Their story reflects a history of respecting cultural practices and beliefs in classroom activities. There is a sense that, in their use of Indian corn and indigenous agricultural practices, Jo and Julie have modeled respect for both the sacredness of corn and the traditions surrounding its planting in some cultures. Indeed, even though the teacher's plan to incorporate the creation stories in her science unit was potentially alarming, her history of cultural sensitivity and her perceived openness to communication with the community enabled Rhonda's mother to approach and explain the cultural conflict and to resolve this misunderstanding in a mutually beneficial way. Ultimately, the teacher and students will learn about the Tohono O'Odam creation story in an appropriate manner and in the process learn about culturally relevant ways of knowing. Talking about such miscommunications can encourage students to articulate similar experiences, can inform the instructional practices of the teacher, and can further enhance communication between the teacher and the local community.

■ ■ ■

Night and Day with Jason

Eric J. Pyle

In this open case, Eric tells of his experiences with Jason, an earth science student whose disruptive behavior demanded special attention. After failed attempts to contact Jason's parents, Eric learns from another teacher that the cause of Jason's behavior is a learning disability associated with bipolar disorder. Eric struggles with the question of how to provide for Jason's special learning needs when he has no personal knowledge of what accommodations are necessary. The case is followed by Eric's reflections years after teaching Jason and by responses from Yvette Getch, a rehabilitation counselor, and from Kevin Finson, a science educator with expertise in special education.

I taught physical science and earth science at Jefferson Mills High School, eventually becoming the science department head. Jefferson Mills is a small school in the center of the largest town in a mainly rural county in North Carolina. At the time, the 51 faculty in the school served approximately 800 students. About 65% of the student body received free or reduced price lunch and breakfast, and the school was rated -27 by the state school report card, an "index of disenfranchisement" ranging from a low of -40 to a high of +40.

My desire to offer earth science as an elective laboratory science course for juniors and seniors stems from my education as a geologist. I was quite pleased when my principal and the school guidance counselors agreed with my arguments for offering the course. They were as proud as I was of being one of only a few schools in the state to offer earth science at an advanced level. My earth science class was offered during the last period of the day. As with any class offered during this time slot, some students were tired, while others occasionally missed class due to extracurricular activities. I found it useful to vary my instructional approach from day to day, providing opportunities for inquiry, hands-on activities, outdoor exercises, and lecture, to maintain student attention and facilitate learning.

About halfway into the second quarter, Jason Murphy was assigned to my class. Jason initially seemed calm and very quiet, preferring to sit in the front row of class. He was captain of the golf team and co-captain of the basketball team. The quiet reserve that Jason displayed for the first week or so, however, was an illusion. Early one week, we began a class dialogue on map reading. I asked Jason several questions related to our examination of local topographic maps. After getting no response other than, "Huh?" several times, my concern for his learning began to rise. The next day, however, Jason was completely different. He couldn't stay on task for more than 2 minutes and kept getting out of his seat. He was talking a mile a minute in a loud voice. One day he was a fence post. The next day he was a ping-pong ball. Jason's seemingly unpredictable behavior changes continued each day, no matter what we were doing or learning, what the weather was, or the outcome of yesterday's golf match or basketball game.

I tried first talking to Jason privately. He was either nonresponsive or gave a response that made little or no sense to me. I tried calling home, to talk to his parents, but they would not return my calls. Calling them at work was equally difficult, as neither of them was available. I spoke to the guidance counselor, who offered little or no information other than stating that there were issues with Jason's learning that his parents did not wish to be widely known, and they had placed severe restrictions on access to his academic records. These issues became more apparent when, after warning Jason about his disruptive behavior, I was forced to write a discipline referral form for him after a particularly unmanageable class session. He was in class the next day, and I was told by the principal to "Give Jason another chance."

Jason's erratic behavior in my class continued. He often missed tests while he was at golf matches. My standard practice was to provide makeup tests on Thursdays after school, and I often provided students with the original test as a study guide, giving them a new test at the makeup session. After several dismal performances by Jason on these makeup tests, I decided to give him a test that was identical to the study guide, with the questions rearranged. After 5 minutes of looking at the test paper, Jason exclaimed, "I don't know any of this stuff!" and handed the test back without having attempted any of the questions.

I mentioned this incident to Louise, the chemistry teacher next door, who closed the door and asked me to sit down. She said that she had had nearly identical problems with Jason the previous year, finally having to call the superintendent to get the parents' permission to access Jason's records, and then only with them present. She learned from the parents and the records that Jason suffered from a mild learning disability associated with decoding complex wording but that problem was second to Jason's severe bipolar disorder, which, according to the National Institutes of Mental Health, is "a mental illness involving episodes of serious mania and depression." Characteristic of the disorder, Jason's mood changed like the movement of a pendulum, swinging from overexcited and irritable to sad and hopeless and then back again. Occasionally, he had periods of normal mood between the two extremes. Jason's condition was being treated with medication, but that medication was not completely sorted out yet. Louise also said that Jason's parents were quite stern in their demands for confidentiality. Louise was taking quite a risk in even telling me about her experiences.

When Jason entered my classroom the next afternoon, I at least knew something about the reasons for his behavior. I felt, however, that I needed more information about his special needs and support from his parents to help Jason succeed in my earth science class. While I don't have a problem with inclusion, nothing in my science teacher preparation or in-service experience prepared me to deal with a student whose needs were so profound.

Questions for Reflection and Discussion

1. How would you suggest responding to the principal's statement of "Just give Jason another chance"?

2. According to the Individuals with Disabilities Education Act, an Individualized Education Program (IEP) must be written for every special needs student placed in a regular classroom. What goals, instructional activities, procedures for evaluating goals, and recommendations for handling behavioral problems would you include in an IEP for Jason?

3. What specific instructional strategies would you suggest to meet Jason's needs in an earth science class?

4. Do you agree with Louise's decision to tell Eric what she knew about Jason's learning disability and mental illness? Why or why not?

5. The Americans with Disabilities Act ensures the civil rights of disabled persons, including guarantees that a child's IEP and other personal records be maintained in confidence. However, this federal law does not maintain that information pertaining to a child's mental illness and associated learning disability be withheld from his or her teachers. How might Eric's knowledge of this law have helped him deal more effectively with Jason?

6. Who would you suggest that Eric turn to for additional support and information about Jason's mental illness and learning disability?

Reflections on My Work with Jason

Eric J. Pyle

I haven't seen Jason in several years now, and I have no idea how he has fared. I haven't heard his name as part of a college basketball team or other prominent sport. I can only hope that he has done well. At best, what I can do now is speculate what I might have done, given what I now know about working with students like Jason who have special needs.

Since Jason's needs were likely to be associated with either his manic or depressive mood, it would be wise to prepare one lesson and a contingency for the opposite mood swing. And since Jason had a learning disability with respect to written language, any lesson or assessment should include modifications that emphasize verbal response first, and any written response should be part of a larger project. Assessment options for Jason would also reflect the fact that he is not held to any lower academic standards than his peers; rather, the path to determining his mastery of the content requires a different approach. Jason's IEP would likely specify, among other things, several items relative to his placement, strengths, and deficits in science learning.

For example, the IEP might specify that Jason will

- Receive services as part of an inclusive educational plan, with no less than 75% of instructional time spent in the regular classroom.
- Use appropriate strategies (key words, mnemonic devices, etc.) for identifying the main ideas of text assignments.
- Demonstrate appropriate verbal responses to questions.
- Ask for additional help as needed from the teacher, an aide, or a peer helper.

Modifications to match Jason's science instructional needs would also be specified. Besides being seated in the front of the classroom, Jason would have his tests read aloud, have an aid or peer tutor assigned to him, be provided with flash cards of important vocabulary, and be given additional time to complete assignments. If Jason is in a visibly agitated mood, he might also be permitted to complete his work separately from other students.

For a lesson on the solar system that involves relative size and distance of objects, two contingencies for Jason could be considered. If Jason were in a manic mode, he might be assigned to tasks in a group where he would collect materials, assist the teacher in monitoring other groups' progress, and once scale models or drawings had been prepared, he would be assigned the task of playing the "role" of an outer planet or comet. The focus on instruction for a manic mode would allow Jason's high energy to be expended in large "orbits" serving both his needs and those of other students.

If, however, Jason were in a depressive mode, or under the influence of his medication, instruction would consist of assigning Jason tasks with clear, definable boundaries that he could complete alone and with a high degree of success. He might be assigned to locate illustrations of or data from planets and other celestial bodies. His results could then be shared with all student groups. He could also pace the distances required for proper scale outside or in the hallway. In a sense, Jason would act as a free agent, completing tasks at his own pace. The tasks, however, would have to be small and discrete so that Jason could see that he could complete them. Other lessons and activities could be similarly modified.

Critical Issues in Working with Jason

Yvette Q. Getch

This case is complicated because several critical issues must be considered. First, it is vital to address the parents' resistance. Although the parents have resisted in the past, I would strongly urge them to participate as members of the student support team. Approaching them with assurance of confidentiality regarding Jason's disabilities, as well as discussing positive outcomes that might be achieved with appropriate interventions, may persuade the parents to disclose needed information about Jason's learning difficulties.

Second, while Jason's bipolar disorder is his most profound barrier to learning, his visual decoding problem should not be overlooked. It should be addressed at all times to ensure Jason has the opportunity to learn the earth science information presented in class. In concert with some of Eric's suggestions, I encourage the use of mnemonics, guided notes, audiotaped lectures, oral tests, graphic presentation of information, and group work to help students with visual decoding difficulties.

Additionally, it is important to recognize that students like Jason are often not self-starters, and they do not ask for additional help even though help is needed. Therefore, being able to recognize when help and support are needed is important to the student's success. Lack of concentration, inability to attend to tasks, and unwillingness to participate in class activities are indicators of a student's need for help. Activities and lesson accommodations for students like Jason need to be age appropriate, academically focused, inclusive to the extent possible, and provide only the needed intervention. Some days, many accommodations, supports, and modifications will be needed, while on other days, relatively few will be needed.

Speaking specifically to Eric's suggestions for working with Jason, I agree that tasks and assignments for Jason when he is depressed should be well defined and designed to ensure success. Additionally, instruction for Jason when he is depressed needs to promote active engagement. On days of depression, participation and movement are likely to be difficult for Jason, and independent work should not be encouraged. When suffering from depression, for example, Jason could be partnered with another student to gather materials to be used that day. The partner could call out the names of materials one at a time, and Jason could gather the materials while the partner checks them off a list. On returning to their work station, Jason should be assigned tasks that keep him actively engaged and serve to further the day's learning objectives.

I disagree that when in a manic mood Jason should be allowed to aid the teacher in monitoring groups and gather materials. When in this state, it is likely that these activities may further exacerbate Jason's behaviors and draw more attention to him. Activities that keep Jason focused while incorporating some movement would be more appropriate. For example, to enable Jason to participate in building a solar system model, the procedure should be broken into several small steps. He could physically construct the model with instructions provided by a partner. This would not require Jason to decode complex written words.

Finally, I recommend that a home group be considered as a long-term intervention for Jason. A home group is nothing more than three to five students who are able to tolerate Jason's mood swings, seem to like him, and are flexible and willing to provide support during assignments. Once up and running, the group can assist the teacher to make many of the accommodations required to meet Jason's learning needs.

■ ■ ■

Trying to Resolve Jason's Problem

Kevin D. Finson

Several steps might be taken to help Jason. First, it is vital that a student support team be convened for the purpose of developing or updating an IEP for Jason and that Eric be invited to be a member of the team. Consistent with the recent amendments to the Individuals with Disabilities Education Act (IDEA) (P.L. 101-476), the team should include a special education teacher, one or more school administrators, a school counselor, Jason's regular classroom teachers, and his parents. I would strongly urge Jason's parents to participate as members of this support team.

When meeting with Jason's parents, I would explain to them that the Americans with Disabilities Act (P.L. 101-336) guarantees that Jason's IEP and other personal records be maintained in confidence by school personnel (Bateman, 1996). I would also stress that this federal law gives them the right to challenge Jason's IEP, but it does not maintain that information pertaining to Jason's mental illness and learning disabilities be withheld from his teachers. In fact, the Family Educational Rights and Privacy Act (20 USC S. 1232g) permits the disclosure of a student's educational records to a teacher without the written consent of parents if it is deemed that information in the student's records would help the teacher meet the learning needs of the student (Bateman, 1996). If Jason's parents feel uncomfortable with this position, I would tell them that under the law they have the right to bring legal counsel to meetings where Jason's IEP is discussed. Unless Louise is a member of the support team, her name need not be mentioned during any team meeting. The essence of the issue, which should be clearly communicated to everyone involved, is that not only is Jason failing to learn, but he is interrupting the learning of other students in the class. Both are unacceptable outcomes, and if providing confidential information to the teacher would help remedy the situation in any way, that course of action should be pursued.

The second step might be for Eric to meet with Jason privately to discuss his perceptions regarding Jason's classroom performance and his concerns for Jason as an adolescent learner. This should be done during one of Jason's calmer days. The nature and details of the discussion will depend on Jason's willingness to listen to what Eric has to say and his agreement to work with Eric and other students in the class to address his special learning needs.

Third, Eric may wish to schedule times to meet independently with the building's special education teacher to discuss the details of Jason's IEP. Eric could describe in detail the problems, difficulties, and behavioral patterns exhibited by Jason during class and his proposal for modifying instruction for Jason. The special education teacher is likely to have experience in working with students like Jason and can suggest strategies that might be employed to help Jason.

Working in concert with the special education teacher, Eric could make modifications to his earth science lessons, activities, and assessments that would make the materials more accessible to Jason. One key here is to make modifications that enable Jason to deal effectively with the materials while at the same time being useful to the "regular" classroom students. Eric should try to avoid having one set of materials for Jason and another for the other students, since to do so would appear to students to be singling out Jason. If done properly, modifications can be every bit as challenging as the original materials were intended, yet their formats are changed so problems resulting from learning disabilities are minimized. In addition, the modifications made to the materials may help other students besides Jason. The teacher should be mindful that students with learning disabilities are typically above average in intelligence.

If possible, Eric may wish to work with the building principal and a counselor in an attempt to place Jason in a science class earlier in the day. By the end of the day, even the best students are fatigued and less attentive, and this characteristic is usually magnified in students possessing learning disabilities. In this situation, the change may mean that Jason would have to select a science offering other than earth science.

■ ■ ■

Scientists Like Me

Katherine C. Wieseman

This closed case describes a teacher's attempt to introduce a culturally diverse class of young adolescents to persons who have chosen careers in science. Katherine Wieseman challenges her students to use their library research skills to identify, learn about, and write reports describing scientists whose cultural or national backgrounds match their own. Through this process, students grapple with their own understandings of *science* and *scientist,* and Katherine recognizes how culture and language affect these understandings. Commentaries on the case are provided by Katherine and by Deborah Tippins, a science teacher educator with expertise in multicultural education.

For 4 years I taught seventh- and eighth-grade science in an international school in northern Belgium with a diverse student population. It was not uncommon to have 10 or more different cultural or national groups represented in a single class. While the language of instruction was English, English was not the mother tongue for most of the students. Hallway conversations were often held in Korean, Japanese, Russian, Gujarati, or Dutch, and several students in each science class also were enrolled in the English as a Second Language (ESOL) classes. Several of my colleagues and I found that communicating with students who had limited English language skills could be challenging, especially given the rigors of the subject area classes and parental expectations for success.

A careers in science project was the first student project of the school year in the eighth-grade science program. The goals of this project were to stimulate student consideration of science-related careers and to hone students' library research skills. The task for the students was to identify and research a scientist whose cultural background matched their own and to construct a brief biography of the scientist to present to the class. Although not a criterion, because so often my students held images of scientists as men, I encouraged them to identify and research women scientists. I left the definition of scientist up to the students but stipulated that the biography needed to include information about the scientist's life and academic history, noteworthy discoveries or research area, and the significance of his or her work.

After I described the task and discussed it with the students, we headed off to the school library. Mrs. Maker, the school librarian, spoke for 5 minutes, refreshing students' memories on the locations of potentially useful information. Toward the end of her remarks, she also named a couple of helpful resources she had located while preparing for our visit, and I piped in with some additional suggestions. Then, the students, most of them eager and intrigued with the task, got to work. Some went directly to the card catalogue, others to the shelves of encyclopedias, and still others to the *Reader's Guide to Periodical Literature*. A couple of students went to Mrs. Maker to ask whether any of the school's videos might be relevant.

A few students immediately approached me. Mohammed spoke first. "Ms. Wieseman, I've never heard of a famous Egyptian scientist. This is going to be hard. All those other kids have it easy. Do I have to find an Egyptian?" "Ms. Wieseman, my English not so good. I not understand the encyclopedia words," said Victor. Matthew asked, "You said scientist, right? What did you mean? My dad says he's kind of a scientist. He helps design ways to recycle plastic, you know, after the plastic is converted into small spheres. Does he count as a scientist? Can I do him?" Neha stood by but did not say anything.

One at a time, I responded to each student's questions. I suggested to Mohammed that he think about what it meant to be a scientist and consider what skills and understandings were required to build the pyramids at a time when the technology we take for granted today was not available. Next, I directed Victor to the elementary section of the library and suggested he start his research by looking under Russia in the *World Book Encyclopedia*. Then, I complimented Matthew on his conception of scientist—how his thinking extended beyond notions of being famous. "There are many kinds of scientists," I said. "Many are not famous and written about in encyclopedias and books. In fact, the parents of some of the students at our school are scientists. I wonder if anyone else will think of this. By all means, do your biography about your father. He'll probably be tickled and honored to have you tell his story." Finally, I turned to face Neha, directing my gaze at her with a questioning facial expression. I waited. After a long pause, she quietly said, "Ms. Wieseman, you said in class how we all come from different cultures. I know you know something about the cultural groups in India. But do you know this? I'll go through twelfth grade, and then my parents will probably send me back to India where I'll get married. My parents will arrange the marriage. Whatever I learn here I will not really use because women do not work except at home. The expectations are different." I listened and said to myself, arranged marriages—still! I was aware of this practice, but never imagined that this situation would be relevant to the lives of my students. How tough this must be for some girls. Is this a problem for the girls, or is this just my issue? At that time in my life, I thought that, for westernized female students, arranged marriages could contribute to internal tension and challenging discussions on the home front, but perhaps this perception was just my Amerocentric perspective. Aloud I responded, "I did not know that these expectations existed for you. Even though the assignment might seem irrelevant to your adult life, I would still like you to complete it. I think it could be an interesting learning experience for you. You might even be surprised by what you uncover. What do you think?"

Questions for Reflection and Discussion

1. Identify a person you consider a scientist. What is it about this person that leads you to label him or her as a scientist? Would you consider this person famous? Why or why not?

2. Work with a classmate to identify two strategies that could be used to help students develop an understanding of scientist that is not limited to famous persons. Share your strategies with others.

3. During the middle school years, teachers often witness students' initial searches for independence and self-identity. How do you think that Katherine's activity might have served to support and challenge students' thinking about their self-identities, especially given the culturally diverse group of students in her class? What are some other ways you might encourage students to think about themselves in science-related careers?

4. How would you have responded to Neha if you had been in Katherine's place?

5. The assignment that Katherine presented to her students required that they have sufficient language skills to independently conduct library literature research. In what ways could this type of assignment be restructured to support students who wrestle with language issues? What are other strategies that a teacher could use to support students who have limited English proficiency?

■ ■ ■

Helping Students Connect with Science

Katherine C. Wieseman

As a middle school science teacher, I continuously searched for ways to facilitate students' efforts to connect science to their personal lives. I also discovered that having students investigate individuals who have chosen science-related careers was one meaningful way to encourage students to ponder the diversity of possible careers in science or related to science. Through these experiences and others, I hoped to satisfy a goal of having my students recognize the importance of science in contemporary society and their personal lives. I also wanted to encourage them to consider professional work related to science. These desires were the basis for having my students write biographies about a "scientist like me." I believed that the assignment supported and challenged students' thinking about their self-identities—an important consideration, given the diversity of this school's student population—and might also encourage students to consider thinking about careers in science or related to science.

Five years later, I still feel good about my challenge to Mohammed to focus on the scientific accomplishments of ancient Egyptians and my suggestion that Victor first consult a resource that would be easier for him to read. My interactions with these students reveal to me how powerful a tool language is and how one's ability to use language facilitates or limits opportunities for success. For Mohammed, his concept of "scientist" influenced his thinking of who might be considered in this role. For Victor, the extent of his English language proficiency constrained his access to the library's resources. Also, I still marvel at Matthew's careful analysis of my charge to the class and feel good about my response to his choice to write about his father. Reflection on this experience has led me in subsequent years to engage groups of students in discussions about what it means to be a scientist. These discussions enable students to clarify their conceptions of scientist, often leading to a realization that living scientists, scientists having the same religious beliefs, traditions, or customs as the student, and scientists not written about in textbooks and encyclopedias could be the focus of their biographies. Furthermore, such discussions provide opportunities for students to consider how personal values, family expectations, and culture can have an influence on their views of science and scientists. The meanings we give to the words *science* and *scientist* are learned from communities of which we are members, which include family, social, and cultural groups. As Lemke (1995) wrote, "We see the worlds our communities teach us how to see, and the worlds we make, always a bit uniquely, within and sometimes just a bit beyond what we've been taught" (p. 4).

To this day, I remain unsettled about the dilemmas I may have created for students like Neha. It is a fact that being female may limit career choices in certain cultures. I still believe it is possible, and probably likely, that students like Neha will experience tension when asked to consider challenging gender role boundaries that are culturally defined. At best, my request that Neha complete the assignment was a temporary fix to an issue steeped in cultural expectations. Other female students I have taught also experienced dissonance as they mentally wrestled with the differences between the gender roles encouraged in science class with those defined by their culture's traditions. Neha was the only one who told me how her adult life would not be of her own choosing. Engaging in learning science can be, after all, somewhat like stepping into a different culture. As a science teacher, I was committed to acknowledging and respecting diverse perspectives. And, I found this process to be indeed a challenge!

Science Is Social and Political

Deborah J. Tippins

The science classrooms of today's schools are full of students much like Mohammed, Matthew, and Neha: students who enter classrooms with a wealth of information, likes and dislikes, values, and untapped abilities. The life stories that these students bring to the classroom reflect social values, epistemological assumptions, and world-views that unconsciously shape their personal beliefs, values, actions, and under-standings of science.

In "Scientists Like Me," Katherine ultimately recognizes the need to examine her instructional goal within a broader social and political context. Her career project was a good starting point for connecting school knowledge of famous scientists with the lived world of students. However, as Katherine soon discovered, we cannot assume that early adolescent learners share a common understanding of what it means to be a scientist, and we cannot assume that they have an awareness of the knowledge of science as a discipline and how it has become legitimate. As Kather-ine's story illustrates, science teaching is a complex task that must begin with the search for student experience in the construction of meaningful science experiences and continue with the uncovering of the tacit infrastructures that shape students' life stories.

■   ■   ■

How Jonah Got Swallowed by the Whale of Apathy While Kip Kept Clinging to the Ship

Cherine LeBlanc Schaaf

This closed case describes Cherine's struggle with providing instruction to a life science class with widely varying ability levels. She initially settles on the approach of "teaching to the middle of the class," advice offered by her veteran mentor teacher early in the school year. As the school year wears on, however, and it becomes increasingly difficult to meet the needs of two students at opposite ends of the class spectrum, this novice teacher comes up with some alternative strategies to create a challenging environment for all students in her classroom. A case response follows by Lee Meadows, a science educator who as a beginning teacher taught students of varying ability levels in a parochial school.

After a decade-long career at home raising small children and a somewhat shorter career before that in laboratory research, I decided to embark on a career in teaching. I felt that my strong academic background in the sciences and my research training would carry over well into this profession. Just as importantly, I knew that skills acquired from motherhood—patience, a sense of humor, and the ability to remain calm in any situation—would be an asset in the classroom. And then there was the fact that I loved working with children.

I was able to easily secure my first teaching position and taught physical science part time that first year. The next year I relocated to the Catholic middle school that my children attend, where I have remained for the past 2 years. I saw stark contrasts between public schools and parochial schools. On the positive side, the discipline problems that I experienced in the public high school where I began my new career have been virtually nonexistent in this parochial school. Then, too, there is tremendous parental support in Catholic schools. On the negative side, teaching resources and funding in general are sometimes much more difficult to attain. The thing that I was least prepared for, however, was the way in which exceptional students (learning disabled and gifted alike) are handled. Or maybe I should say not handled. In public school, I got used to working with the special education and gifted teachers who supported me and provided support for my students who qualified for these resource services. It became clear that in my new school it would be up to me to handle the widely divergent needs of all of my students. I have always loved challenges, but just how great a challenge this would become was not apparent to me until I met a recent memorable seventh-grade life science class!

Before school started, during our preplanning week, I was "briefed" by our school counselor about what to expect from the incoming seventh-grade class. Her expression wore great concern as she explained to me that nearly one-fifth of this class would be outside the range of normal academic ability. But my biggest challenges, she stressed, would be Jonah and Kip. Jonah, she said, had been precocious from infancy. Currently, he was taking math one grade level above his peers. His IQ had been measured around 130 and he was, I was told, "capable of great things." The interesting thing about Jonah, she said, was that he had never excelled in science class, although "it was one of the things he talked most about outside of school." Her hope was that I could draw out the great potential he had for this subject and stimulate him to excel in it. Kip was yet another story. Kip's IQ range, between 75 and 85, put him near the edge of the mildly retarded category. Kip would never be able to make it in our school, the counselor stated, were it not for the tremendous outside support he had from his parents and tutors. Even so, his entry into middle school had been extremely difficult, and seventh grade was likely to bring his greatest challenges yet. Nonetheless, Kip's parents were determined to keep him in the same school that his younger (normal IQ) brother attended.

Had Jonah and Kip been in a public middle school, special resource services would have been provided to meet their individual needs. Jonah would have likely been in all gifted classes or had his instruction carefully supervised by a gifted teacher. Kip would have been mainstreamed in one or two classes only, with the remainder of his time spent in resource rooms with special education teachers. Public schools have the tax base to provide such services. Here I was, though, in a Catholic school without any of these valuable support systems and only 2 years of teaching experience under my belt! Now the job was up to me. I sighed, thanked our counselor for the warning, and prepared myself for a long, grueling year ahead.

When Jonah and Kip walked into class that first week, you couldn't tell that they were far outside the norm. They seemed to fit right in with everyone else, but then all the students were trying hard to just blend in during that first week of school. It wasn't until a few weeks later that the true nature of the class began to emerge.

Jonah always appeared very tired and distant in my class. He usually had his head down on his arms until I asked him to please sit up. Almost every other day, the school nurse had to interrupt my class to bring him his medication for attention deficit disorder (ADD), because he would forget to go to the clinic after lunch to take it. He always wore a sweet smile and was very polite, but I couldn't help but feel that he was somewhere else during my class. During the interesting discussions we had following videos, demonstrations or labs, Jonah would never participate. I knew he was brimming with knowledge on many of the topics we covered, yet his hand would never go up. This was frustrating in itself, but soon I noticed another equally frustrating phenomenon. The apathy that Jonah displayed in class seemed to be catching. Changing seats only relocated the problem to another part of the classroom. This may have had something to do with the fact that in the social context of the class, Jonah was a recognized leader. Academically, Jonah was doing OK, always managing to get a high B or low A, but without any emotional investment in the class. I wanted desperately to light a fire under him, to get him to share his science knowledge with others. I especially wanted him to stop spreading the apathy that seemed to be infecting my class.

Kip, on the other hand, was just the opposite. From the first day of class, his hand was constantly up, and it seemed he had ideas about everything. Many of his answers or comments were way off base, but I noticed that none of the other students reacted negatively to this. It was as if they were impressed that he was so determined. Kip chose a seat at the front of the class next to his friend, Zach, who often helped him to understand things. Kip had great difficulty expressing himself and relating socially to others. When I spoke with him one on one, he would immediately back away to a safe distance and was unable to make eye contact. He had almost no friends (except Zach), and yet I continued to notice an aura of respect around Kip. I began to see that the other students admired his courage and determination in the face of great hardships.

As the school year wore on, I began to feel worn down trying to teach science to this bipolar class of 32 students. It was particularly difficult to go beyond the first stage of learning new concepts (e.g., the modern classification system) to relating and applying concepts (e.g., how do you think the invention of the compound microscope affected the classification system of living things?) Labs were especially difficult. With only one of me and 32 of them, I felt as if I were constantly being torn apart during experiments. Everyone had questions at once. I finally developed the strategy of "Ask three, then me," whereby students must try to get their questions answered by other students first, if I was busy helping others.

By Thanksgiving I knew I needed help. I sought the advice of my appointed mentor teacher, who had 18 years of experience teaching in Catholic schools. Mary Ellen said, "You've got to teach to the middle of the class. There really is no other way to do it." For a while, as I followed this advice, I felt relieved that I could stop trying to be a "superteacher." Yet as the Christmas holidays approached, I was feeling less and less satisfied with the progress of my science class. Nothing had changed with Jonah and Kip either.

Over Christmas vacation, I did a lot of thinking about this situation, and I had a hard time justifying this middle-of-the-road approach. It seemed that no one was winning with this method. I have always felt that students should reach for the high expectations that parents and teachers have for them, and I had certainly not been expecting great things of them up to this point. I resolved, therefore, to raise my sights and try to get *all* students actively involved, to do their very best and to reach for that higher bar. I decided that when we returned to school in January, I would raise my standard of teaching significantly (I would try to teach to the top third of the class). I couldn't help but wonder, though, how Kip would keep up.

When we all returned in January, I spoke to my class about my decision. I began by telling them that they were all capable of being great scientists and that it was now time for them to challenge themselves. I told them that for the remainder of the year the class might seem harder, but I knew they could all do well, and they'd be proud of themselves. I told them that we would all help each other to attain our new higher goals. They all looked worried (especially Kip). I too was secretly worried but had prepared for this moment by drawing up a list of teaching modifications that I planned to use for Jonah and Kip and a few others. I felt that by addressing their needs more individually I could teach successfully on a higher level to everyone. After clearing these modifications with the principal, counselor, parents, and the boys themselves, I began Phase II of my life science class.

The modifications I made for Jonah were fewer and much simpler than those for Kip. Basically, it was a matter of putting more individual challenges in front of him. This was a little more work for me but not as much as I had thought originally, and the results were well worth it. Kip's list was of course longer and more varied. He needed more modifications involving logistical solutions, in order to make him more competitive with the class. Some of the modifications I used with each student follow:

Jonah's Modifications

1. Moved him to the front of the class.
2. Advised him that he would be called on frequently for his unique contributions to science topics.
3. Encouraged him to occasionally research and teach the class about a related topic of interest.
4. Paired him with weaker students in lab, and encouraged him to help them.
5. Made him an honorary student lab assistant (even given a white coat). Asked him to help with the setup and breakdown of labs to stimulate his interest and sense of responsibility.
6. Provided him with challenging enrichment activities. *Example:* When I discovered Jonah memorizing the periodic table one day in class, I assigned the following problem to solve instead, which he should report back to the class on: If a bacterial population doubles every 20 minutes for 24 hours, how many cells will result after 3 days? Show this geometric progression in a chart, and think of a math formula that would give the same results.

Kip's Modifications

1. Paired him with a strong student as a lab partner and as a study buddy. (Jonah filled this position at times.)

2. Gave him much praise, positive feedback, and direct eye contact.

3. Provided him with a copy of each chapter with the important concepts highlighted.

4. Provided him with a small tape recorder and encouraged him to tape himself reading the chapter, reread the highlighted points, and listen to the playback as often as possible. Also encouraged him to tape and listen to class review sessions and important class discussions.

5. Gave him an Alpha Smart laptop word processor to type assignments and notes in class (provided by the school).

Positive results weren't overnight with these two boys. They evolved slowly but surely over time. Kip, despite his learning difficulties, was given the same assignments as the rest of the class, and I saw him rise to the challenge. His determination was unmatched in the class, and his answers were more and more on target. He no longer had to "cling to the ship for dear life" because learning had suddenly become easier. Jonah had joined our class at last and was actually effusive about science. His enthusiasm spilled over to the rest of the class. He especially enjoyed his role as lab assistant and helper to others. It was a happy day for all when Jonah no longer flooded our class with apathy.

By the end of the school year, I felt as though my class had survived the Great Flood—the flood, that is, of mediocrity that comes from mediocre expectations. I had learned one of the greatest lessons of all as a teacher—to believe in myself and the ability of my students.

Questions for Reflection and Discussion

1. Do you feel that this teacher was justified in singling out these two individual students for special treatment? Support your response.

2. How do you think this situation made the other students in the class feel (all those in the middle) both before and after Cherine introduced the changes?

3. To what extent must new teachers let the advice of veteran teachers affect how they teach their classes?

4. What would you have done, had you been the teacher in this situation? How might Gardner's (1993) theory of multiple intelligences be useful in meeting the diverse needs of students?

5. How can you help prepare yourself for the wide spectrum of learning differences found in most classrooms? Can you capitalize on your own individual learning style in your teaching methods?

6. Is it fair that private and parochial schools in this country lack access to public funding for the needs of special education students?

I Taught Jonahs and Kips, Too

Lee Meadows

I saw myself in Cherine's experiences with Jonah and Kip. My first 3 years of teaching were at a Baptist academy in a southern U.S. city, and many of my experiences paralleled those in the case. Just as in Cherine's case, at my school, discipline problems were low, parental support was exceptional, and resources were a real scramble. More importantly, though, I taught Jonahs and Kips.

I had two Kips. Just like Cherine's Kip, my Larissa was eager to please and tried very hard, but understanding chemistry was an impossibility for her. I was told that she had suffered mild brain damage at birth. Reggie, my other Kip, had received head trauma in a sports injury in elementary school. Both Larissa and Reggie appeared to be moving from grade to grade only because teachers passed them out of frustration, not knowing what to do with them for another year. Our college-preparatory academy, including my chemistry classes, offered Larissa and Reggie very little of what they really needed from their education. Also, I taught Reggie and Larissa during my first year of teaching, and I was struggling so hard to figure out classroom management, learn the content as I went along, and patch together a working knowledge of laboratory procedures that I couldn't focus on their exceptional needs.

I also had several Jonahs, but I was more successful with them. Our school did have honors courses that appeared to meet the academic needs of our best students through rigorous expectations. During their junior year, these bright students could take Advanced Placement History and English, Honors Algebra III/Trigonometry, and my Honors Chemistry course. The more I taught, though, the more I began to see a dark side of this honors track. Our school was so small that, due to scheduling, the students basically had to be fully in the honors track with all four courses or fully out. Taking the full complement of all Advanced Placement and Honors courses was extremely demanding at times, and we as teachers often wondered if our students ever had a chance just to enjoy being high schoolers. Many of them seemed to consistently battle burnout. Cherine's struggle with reaching all of her students is a critical dilemma that I consistently hear teachers struggling with, myself included. I wonder, though, how the students other than Jonah and Kip fared with reaching the high standards she set for them all in January. Cherine set high goals for all of her students, but I wonder if she allowed herself to focus mostly on Jonah and Kip.

One strategy that Cherine didn't try was cooperative learning (Johnson & Johnson, 1987), and I think that it would have helped her a lot with bringing all students up to high standards. My experience with cooperative learning, as well as the experience of many teachers with whom I work, has been that cooperative learning is highly successful with increasing the achievement across the whole class. Before I implemented cooperative learning, the top 20% of my chemistry students really grasped the material. The rest memorized their way through to a low B, a C, or a D, and some didn't pass. I've never had a student fail after implementing cooperative learning, and most of them really understand chemistry. I think their success comes from the way that cooperative learning taps the power of peer teaching. Nothing excites me in teaching more than to begin a cooperative learning activity and then hear my students discussing chemistry or chemical problem solving in deep, meaningful ways. I've even found myself having to slow classes down who are well versed in cooperative learning because they're so excited about learning chemistry that they're skipping over some of the fundamentals!

I was also concerned about how Cherine singled Jonah out. Now, obviously in Jonah's case, it worked. I'm skeptical, though, that this strategy would work with most high achievers. They're a funny lot, typically, and their apathy can have many causes. With students like Jonah, my first tack is to pull in close to find out more about them as people. What are their interests? What are their favorite school subjects? What extracurricular activities are they involved in? As I get to know them, I sometimes find really deep questions lurk in their souls. They may be apathetic because in reality they're scared of many of the problems they see in their world, such as environmental destruction, wars, and violence. They often need assurance and hope more than they need another academic challenge.

Also, I've noticed that high achievers often desperately want to be normal in spite of their gifts. Jonah responded to being a peer leader in his class, but I've found that most high achievers want to fit in with their peers and have friends, like almost any other high schoolers feel. I tend more toward encouraging them, using a format where they won't feel embarrassed or set apart from their peers. I may speak to them outside of class or even discreetly write them a note. I try to paint for them a vision of what they can become through their gifts and then offer my help as a resource for pursuing their new dreams in a quiet fashion.

Resources to Consider

Barba, R. (1998). *Science in the multicultural classroom: A guide to teaching and learning.* Needham Heights, MA: Allyn & Bacon.

Roberta Barba provides an overview of critical issues related to multicultural practice in science classrooms. Topics such as motivation in the multicultural classroom, ways of knowing science, and instructional strategies for culturally diverse learners are included in the book.

Bateman, B. (1996). *Better IEPs: How to develop legally correct and educationally useful programs.* Longmont, CO: Sopris West.

In this handbook, educator and lawyer Barbara Bateman explains the IDEA in a meaningful way for regular classroom teachers who work with special needs students and their parents. A three-step process for developing an IEP is presented that focuses on the learner's needs, the role of the school in meeting the learner's needs, and how to assess the effectiveness of the services provided by the school. The text includes example IEPs and addresses numerous issues related to the development and implementation of an IEP, including confidentiality of IEPs, content of an IEP, and the composition and functioning of an IEP team.

Rosser, S. (1997). *Re-engineering female friendly science*. New York: Teachers College Press.

In this book, Sue Rosser proposes a six-stage model for transforming science curricula in ways that make them more inclusive with respect to information on women and men of color. Her model, which is specific to science and mathematics, stems from the work of feminist scholars.

Smith, W. (1998, March). **Native American perspectives**. *The Science Teacher, 65,* 32–36.

In this article, Walter Smith describes several learning experiences that can help students develop a greater appreciation for views of the world's indigenous peoples, including Native Americans. A key point that he makes is that to understand the natural world, science students must also understand the worldviews of different cultural groups. The Western view of the world in cause-and-effect terms is not shared by all people. A list of books and videos useful for linking the Native American perspective with science learning is included at the end of the article.

Special education resources on the Internet. Available: http://www.hood.edu/seri/serihome.htm

This continually modified and updated Web site provides a collection of Internet-accessible special education resources. The topics for which Internet links are provided include legal and law resources, learning disabilities, physical and health disorders, attention deficit disorder, special needs and technology, gifted and talented, parents and educator's resources, and associations and national organizations.

Williams, C., & Hounshell, P. (1998, January). **Enabling the learning disabled**. *The Science Teacher, 65,* 29–31.

Carrie Williams and Paul Hounshell offer practical suggestions for helping high school students with learning disabilities be successful science learners. In the article, they discuss teaching strategies, classroom organization, class assignments and reading, and assessment strategies. Many of the suggestions would also be helpful for students without learning disabilities.

References

The Americans with Disabilities Act 42 U.S.C. section 12101 (1990).

Bloome, D., & Egan-Robertson, A. (1993). The social construction of intertextuality in classroom reading and writing lessons. *Reading Research Quarterly, 28,* 304–333.

Boyd, M. (1996). Negotiating classroom culture. *TESOL in Action, 10,* 13–16.

Carrel, P. (1987). Content and formal schemata in ESL reading. *TESOL Quarterly, 21,* 461–481.

Cummins, J. (1989). *Empowering minority students*. Sacramento, CA: California Association for Bilingual Education.

The Family Educational Rights and Privacy Act (FERPA), 20 U.S.C. section 1232 (1974).

Gardner, H. (1993). *Multiple intelligences: The theory in practice.* New York: Basic Books.

Guttierrez, K. (1994). How talk, context, and script shape context for learning: A cross case comparison of journal sharing. *Linguistics and Education*, *5*, 335–365.

The Individuals with Disabilities Education Act 20 U.S.C. section 1400 (1997).

Johnson, D. W., & Johnson, R. T. (1987). *Learning together and alone.* Upper Saddle River, NJ: Prentice Hall.

Lemke, J. (1995). *Textual politics: Discourse and social dynamics.* London: Taylor and Francis.

Moll, L. (1992). Funds of knowledge for teaching: Using a qualitative approach to connect homes and classrooms. *Theory and Practice*, *31*, 131–141.

Nystrand, M. (1997). *Open dialogue: Understanding the dynamics of language and learning in English classrooms.* New York: Teachers College Press.

Nystrand, M., Gamoran, A., & Heck, M. J. (1993). Using small groups for response to and thinking about literature. *English Journal*, *83*, 14–22.

3

Reform and Science Curriculum

Today we are in the midst of science education reform that is a response to global political and economic pressures. The ultimate goal of the reform is the development of scientifically literate citizens—men and women who possess the scientific and technological skills, understandings, and habits of mind to make wise personal decisions and contribute to the good of society (Rutherford & Ahlgren, 1990). Teachers and other leaders of science education reform view it as a long-term effort that requires systemic change. National documents such as the *National Science Education Standards* (National Research Council, 1996) and Project 2061's *Benchmarks for Scientific Literacy* (American Association for the Advancement of Science, 1993) and state frameworks provide a vision for how the many dimensions of the system should be changed to achieve the goal. The unit of standards-based, systemic reform is typically the school or school district and, by extension, individual teachers and students. Science teachers, school administrators, parents, community and business leaders, and university scientists and educators work together to change the science curriculum and how science is taught and assessed. They may also concern themselves with issues of teacher professional development and school and district policies that affect the teaching and learning of science.

Paralleling this reform are efforts to improve student learning through school restructuring. Restructuring involves making organizational changes to schools to transform them from the learning factories of an industrial age to the learning centers needed for an information age. Block scheduling is only one example of restructuring at the secondary level that offers an alternative to the traditional 50-minute class period, with corresponding changes in science course curricula and instructional strategies. Science teachers must understand the principles, recommendations, and implications of today's reform and restructuring efforts. Only then will they be able to play an active role in changing the educational system that impacts science teaching and learning.

This chapter includes three cases that focus on aspects of today's reform and restructuring efforts. In the first case, a teacher tells of his difficulties in trying to engage students in meaningful scientific inquiry in a biology course shortened by a change to block scheduling. The second case describes a teacher's decision to continue his school's involvement in a statewide project to reform science teaching and learning. His decision is complicated by the allegiance he feels toward his science teaching colleagues. In the third case, the leader of a forum for school administrators narrates the story of two new district-level administrators and how their failure to involve teachers in the early stages of curriculum planning almost derails their efforts to effect change in the district's science program.

■ ■ ■

Too Much Content, Not Enough Time

John Karl Kemper

Karl's student teaching assignment placed him in a school that had recently changed from a traditional six-period day to a 4 × 4 block schedule. His mentor teacher recognizes Karl's enthusiasm for making use of inquiry-oriented activities in teaching biology but discourages him from using activities because she feels that their use takes away from the time needed to cover important content. This leaves Karl facing the dilemma of how to engage 10th-grade students in meaningful scientific inquiry and still cover the content in a course shortened by the change to block scheduling. Karl's story is followed by commentaries from Miriam Jordan, a biology teacher who has worked extensively with block scheduling in high schools, and Dava C. Coleman, a veteran high school teacher with a doctorate in science education.

I student taught at a high school in a rapidly changing community. Historically, the area served by the school was predominately rural, but over the past few years rapid population growth, brought on by urban flight, has changed the demographics greatly. The rural area is experiencing the pains of development that come with population growth. The high school's student body can be generalized as coming from two groups: There are the sons and daughters of farmers who have lived in the area for years, and there are the children of the financially affluent newcomers. The two groups can easily be distinguished.

Brenda Long, the teacher who served as my mentor, holds a doctorate in biology and had less than 5 years of high school teaching experience. Brenda is extremely bright but had no formal preparation in secondary education. She told me that she believes that the schools and colleges of education around the country should be abolished and that all teachers should be required to major in a content field.

The first 3 weeks of my student teaching experience involved primarily observing Brenda teach. During this time, I was able to develop my own opinions about her teaching style as well as insights into the students' thoughts about her teaching. I was astonished at the pace of her instruction. The 4×4 block schedule that the school adopted allows for class periods of 90 minutes. Brenda spent the entire 90 minutes of every day lecturing to her 10th-grade biology students. The students were flooded with content. I witnessed much content being covered but often wondered what the students were learning.

The students' grades were terrible, and the discipline problems in the class were horrendous. I was sure that the discipline problems were arising from the students' sense of hopelessness associated with trying to keep up with all the content covered during the lectures. The metaphor that I associated with this situation is a train. The train of knowledge was going so fast that the students could not jump on, so they decided to throw rocks at it instead.

I talked with Brenda about my concerns about taking over the class based on what I had observed. I told her that I was not comfortable lecturing all the time and preferred to do some inquiry activities with the students. My intention was to make the class more student-centered and increase student participation. I believed that doing this would enhance student learning. Brenda responded coolly to my ideas. She told me that I would not have time to teach this way. She went on to explain that since changing from the traditional six-period school day to block scheduling there was much less time to teach the important concepts and no time for activities. She said that she had to teach 1 year's worth of biology in one semester and there was just no time for "Mickey Mouse" activities.

I felt extremely frustrated on encountering this attitude and was somewhat apprehensive about my future as a student teacher. I had learned about many instructional approaches during my science education coursework, and my university supervisor was expecting to see me do more than just lecture. However, I felt that Brenda wanted me to cover all that she had planned for the weeks that I would be teaching the class. In her thinking, there was simply no time for activities. I was caught in the middle: The students and my university supervisor were screaming at me to do something besides lecture, but Brenda was screaming about wasting time on "Mickey Mouse" activities. What was I to do?

I did what my conscience told me was right. I engaged the students in inquiry activities as often as I could. As Brenda observed my lessons, I could sense her frustration building. She felt that I was not covering enough content. After observing one of my lessons, Brenda described a new educational initiative that she had heard about called "direct lecture." She was told that its use led to higher test scores. "Maybe you should think about using it," she suggested.

After this, I sought help and support from other science teachers in the school to deal with my dilemma. Unfortunately for me, those with whom I talked shared Brenda's views. They reminded me of the time constraints imposed by block scheduling and the need to expose students to all the same topics covered during a year-long biology course. I just couldn't get Brenda's words out of my mind: "We don't have a minute to waste doing activities because there is still so much to be covered."

The 4 × 4 block schedule is designed to allow students to gain more credits toward high school graduation, but it also means that a course previously completed in one school year is taught in only one semester. I feel that 90 minutes is much too long to lecture to high school students, and the block schedule is very conducive to using inquiry activities to teach important biological ideas. How is one expected to do justice to the content of biology in one semester and still make use of student-centered instructional methods?

Questions for Reflection and Discussion

1. What are some advantages of teaching on a block schedule? Disadvantages?

2. Describe some curriculum adjustments that a biology teacher might make when shifting from a traditional schedule to a block schedule. Do the same for a physics teacher and for a chemistry teacher.

3. Time management is an important concern for science teachers when shifting to block scheduling. Choose a science topic familiar to you, and construct a time line of classroom events to show how you would organize your instruction for a 90-minute class period. How would your instructional organization facilitate student learning?

4. Suppose Brenda was your colleague. What information might you share with her to convince her of the importance of inquiry activities to students' science learning?

5. What advice would you give to Karl to enable him to make the most of his student teaching experience? To help him be a successful first-year teacher in a high school on a block schedule?

6. Suppose you have just accepted a teaching position at a school on a 4 × 4 block schedule. You have ninety 90-minute periods in which to teach an introductory biology, physical science, or integrated science course. What topics would you include in your course syllabus? How much instructional time would you give to each topic? Compare your responses with classmates and science teachers teaching at a school on block scheduling.

■ ■ ■

Time and Content on the Block

Miriam Jordan

Block scheduling, in its various formats, is becoming more common in high schools each year. An appealing aspect of block scheduling for many science teachers is the longer class period, typically 90 minutes. Compared with the traditional 50-minute period, these larger blocks of time provide teachers with an opportunity to make use of an expanded array of instructional choices. But because teaching for 90 minutes calls for changes in pedagogy, it also presents challenges for teachers.

Karl's dilemma is not uncommon among student teachers and teachers in the early years of their career. These newcomers sometimes face personal conflicts brought about by differences between what they have learned in their teacher preparation programs and the teaching practices they have observed in schools. Block scheduling, with its longer class periods, often highlights the limitations of some traditional classroom practices. This, in turn, may call attention to issues of curriculum adjustment, time management, and alternative instructional approaches. Unfortunately, the change to block scheduling seems to have had little affect on Brenda's thinking about teaching and learning.

In Brenda's defense, two subtle but powerful influences combine to reinforce the difficulty of enacting the pedagogical changes required when teaching on a block schedule. First, many veteran teachers prefer to use the same instructional and assessment strategies they experienced as students and have used successfully in the past. Lectures, demonstrations, straightforward laboratory activities, and multiple-choice tests all can be completed in a 50-minute period. My guess is that Brenda was an exceptional science student and believes that the instructional practices that brought her success will work equally well for her students, regardless of the length of the class period.

Second, some veteran teachers tend not to be well practiced in some of the instructional strategies recommended for use when teaching on block scheduling. I suspect this is true for Brenda. District in-service sessions and other workshops may introduce teachers to such strategies as cooperative learning, inquiry-based instruction, and design technology. But without practice and encouragement from colleagues and administrators, these do not become the arrows often selected from the teacher's quiver of instructional strategies. For teachers who are not comfortable with these instructional strategies, attempting to make use of them and at the same time help students learn science may be overwhelming. Newcomers to the teaching profession, like Karl, probably have had opportunities to practice these strategies in their teaching methods classes and, as a result, feel comfortable using them.

In my opinion, at the heart of Karl's dilemma is the difference between what he and Brenda believe about how adolescents learn and what they should learn in biology class. Brenda seems to view students as containers to be filled with the knowledge of biology and believes that the best way to do this is to share her knowledge of biology with them, mainly by lecture. She feels an obligation to cover the same content in the semester course as she did during the year-long course. Her reasons for this seem to stem from a school district mandate but may be reinforced by her personal desire to prepare students for future biology coursework, either in high school or college. With total instructional time reduced by approximately 15 hours*

---

*The traditional schedule is 180 days × 50 minutes = 9,000 minutes. The block schedule is 90 days × 90 minutes = 8,100 minutes. 9,000 minutes − 8,100 minutes = 900 minutes, or 18 days × 50-minute class periods.

when shifting from a traditional schedule to a 4 × 4 block schedule, Brenda is under tremendous pressure to meet her own expectation of covering the content. By contrast, Karl's desire to teach with activities that emphasize student interaction and the manipulation of materials seems to support the belief that students construct their own understandings of biology by interacting with the content. As a student teacher, he is somewhat removed from the pressures felt by Brenda. Guiding Karl's actions is his need to survive in the classroom. Curtailing student discipline problems and engaging students in activities that interest them are means to this end.

I think that Brenda and her colleagues should look carefully at their district's biology curriculum and decide what can be left out of the course. *The National Science Education Standards* (National Research Council, 1996) may help them to select the big ideas of biology around which to organize course content. The document may also serve to guide their discussions about the nature of the adolescent learner and desired changes in emphasis in science content and student inquiry. As a student teacher, Karl may wish to use the standards to provide support for his lessons. For example, his lesson plans could be accompanied by a brief explanation of why he would prefer to have students walk to a nearby pond to investigate the behavior of frogs rather than lecturing to them about frog behavior. This action may prompt Brenda to think about her own teaching. In the end, Karl must keep in mind that he is a guest in Brenda's classroom and must follow her instructional lead. Once employed by a school where colleagues support his ideas about teaching and learning, Karl can engage students in what he considers to be enjoyable and meaningful lessons.

■ ■ ■

What to Teach on the Block?

Dava C. Coleman

Karl's case brings to mind my own experiences and those of other teachers at my school as we began to plan for changing from a traditional schedule to a block schedule. From the start, we were struck by two major differences between traditional and block scheduling. First, the class period is longer, 90 minutes rather than 50 minutes. This meant that we would need to consider and try new instructional practices. The second difference is that the total course time is reduced. With up to 900 minutes (about eighteen 50-minute periods) less contact time with students, we knew that we must make decisions about what to teach. There was never any question in our minds that the amount of content in our courses could remain the same. The move to block scheduling would involve reducing the number of curriculum objectives addressed in all our science courses. Some of my colleagues were against the change to block scheduling because they viewed this reduction as watering down their courses. As we visited other schools on block schedules and met with their faculties, our discussions focused more on changing instructional practices than on curriculum modifications. When direct questions were asked regarding changes in their curriculum, the science teachers in these schools responded with a variety of ideas from throwing out 20% of your laboratory work to chopping off your least favorite unit. We were not satisfied with any of these responses, but we knew that trying to cover all the content included in our traditionally scheduled courses was not a realistic option.

Karl's dilemma is not that much different from the one we faced. His concern was for the students, and his desire was to structure the learning experiences so as to help them succeed. As a student teacher, Karl seems to have heard the calls for "less lecture" and is familiar with a list of teaching strategies intended to help teachers make productive use of the longer class periods. The voices of the science education community that Karl may not have heard are those that challenge teachers to look carefully at what they teach in light of state requirements, the needs of learners, and the big ideas of science. This challenge is captured in part by the idea of "less is more," which means that students may actually learn more science and learn it more meaningfully by studying fewer topics but studying them in depth. Karl may have succeeded in encouraging Brenda to view the learning experiences that he proposed to use with the classes if he had used this idea as the basis for his arguments.

Putting "less is more" into practice involves examining course curriculum in light of content standards. Much work has been done recently at the national and state levels to develop content standards based on a broad consensus about what students need to know and be able to do before completing high school. For example, the *National Science Education Standards* (National Research Council, 1996) identify the organizing themes of the cell; molecular basis of heredity; biological evolution; interdependence of organisms; matter, energy, and organization in living systems; and behavior of organisms around which to organize a biology course. Descriptions of these themes within the standards document provide more details about important concepts and theories under each theme.

Karl's description of his mentor teacher's ideas about the biology course curriculum causes me to wonder about the level of support provided by the school district to help teachers think about and plan for the curriculum change that should accompany a shift to block scheduling. Teachers in my school district recently revised our science curriculum K–12 to reflect the Project 2061 *Benchmarks for Scientific Literacy* (American Association for the Advancement of Science, 1993), our state learning framework, and our state high school graduation examination. We, as a K–12 science faculty, felt comfortable with the changes that the new curriculum produced and how our changes reflected the goal of scientific literacy. In our minds, the first hurdle to changing to a block schedule had been cleared with our curricular alignment to national and state standards. However, understanding the standards and translating them into a cohesive curriculum, even for just grades 9 to 12, are time-consuming tasks. They are not completed by a solitary teacher in his or her classroom. They require many hours of discussion and debate involving the entire faculty.

Our second hurdle was to reorganize existing objectives into a new course framework. We realized that although the actual student contact time was less, we would gain what was essentially lost time in a 50-minute period. For example, completing a laboratory activity in one 50-minute period is rare, so there is time lost with start-up and cleanup each day. In a 90-minute period, the entire activity can be completed. Another example is the practice of reviewing a chapter's content the day before a test. This usually requires the entire 50-minute period. In a 90-minute period, the review can take place during the first 30 minutes, leaving the remainder of the period for the test.

The first step we took in reorganizing was to set our basic science course offering and decide on elective science courses. With an opportunity for a total of 32 courses in a 4-year period (on a 4 × 4 block), students would need to have more course options. Because our course content in 10th-grade biology could not be reduced due to the high school graduation test objectives, we decided to add a Biology II course, which would be taken by most, if not all, students. An option such as this, if available in Brenda's school district, would enable her to address the biology content she considers important and still allow time for students to engage in laboratory and other investigative experiences.

The second step was for us to examine our courses for any duplication. We each discovered that we were guilty of including content from chapters in our textbooks that were not part of the curriculum. We all included a unit on metrics and metric conversion because it was one of the first chapters in all of our textbooks from physical science and biology to physics and environmental science. We agreed that the metric unit would remain a part of the physical science curriculum and that instructional time for pretesting and remediating would be provided in other courses. Finally, each teacher examined his or her instructional plan for activities that were extraneous to the course curricular objectives. For example, I love laboratory work and take every opportunity to try out a new activity. I discovered that I did not really need to do three different lab activities dealing with physical and chemical change, no matter how cool they were.

In conclusion, my experiences have told me that both how to teach and what to teach must be considered when planning for teaching on a block schedule. While I believe that Brenda and Karl are both interested in helping students learn about the living world, their ideas about how students learn and what they should learn in biology class differ significantly. Their disagreement highlights the need for district professional development associated with teaching on a block schedule, including activities that focus on curriculum reorganization and alignment. The biology curriculum should be reorganized to reflect the reduction in total course time, and this reorganization should be in alignment with national and/or state standards and state high school graduation requirements. These are tasks that Brenda cannot take on by herself; they require district-level collaboration and time to complete. It is truly unfortunate that as a student teacher Karl finds himself in a situation where the district's lack of attention to curriculum matters makes it difficult to address the needs of learners. This case points out the need for universities and schools to work together to enhance science education at all levels.

Does It Matter Beyond My School?

Michael J. Padilla

As the leader of Georgia's statewide systemic initiative, Mike had the opportunity to work with many science teachers as they struggled with the ideas of systemic reform. In this open case, Mike tells the story of one teacher, Larry, the composite of several teachers with whom he worked. After more than a year of leading the reform effort in his school, Larry must make a decision about his school's continuing participation in the reform initiative. His decision is complicated by the tension he experiences between two competing referents: (1) state reform leaders, who want him to push the reform forward to other schools in his district and neighboring districts, and (2) his science teaching colleagues, who want to celebrate their accomplishments and let others champion the cause. The case is presented in Larry's voice and is followed by commentary from Frank Crawley, a science educator and advocate of systemic reform.

My name is Larry Barnes and I have been teaching middle school science for 14 years. After finishing my master's degree in science education, I began taking on various roles within my school. At first I noticed my fellow teachers coming to me with questions. "Where can I get more information about cold fusion?" "What strategy do you think would be best to use for teaching about polymers?" It made me feel good to be able to help them with both their content and pedagogical questions. I felt valued and an important part of my school's team of teachers. Not long after, I volunteered to give a presentation at the state science teachers meeting with some colleagues. In our workshop, we presented some of the physical science activities we felt worked well with our inner-city kids. From that beginning, I continued to take on leadership and responsibility for science in-service teaching in our school. I attended a state-funded summer leadership workshop, which helped me hone my in-service skills. All of a sudden I was in demand, in my own school, my district, and even by other school districts. The feeling of energy and exhilaration I derived from doing this extra work made me an even better teacher, at least in my estimation.

As a result of the work done at our school, by my colleagues and me, our school was selected to be a special pilot "professional development school for science" when a statewide systemic initiative was funded with federal monies. The entire staff, administrators and teachers, was honored to be selected. What an opportunity! As my colleagues and I began attending the project meetings, the enormity of the task that lay ahead became obvious.

We were not just being asked to be good teachers; rather, we were being asked to change the entire focus of science teaching for the whole school. Our task was to implement systemic reform in science teaching. But what was it? Was it just the new jargon that would soon go away if we ignored it long enough? And I was selected as the team leader! Now what was I to do? As explained in the first few meetings we attended, the *National Science Education Standards* (National Research Council, 1996) took a systemic approach to change of science education. That is, you cannot change just one or even two components of the system if you want to implement significant, positive change. Rather, all components of the system must be aligned and focused on the same goals.

But what were these system components? At our first in-school meeting, that question became the primary focus of discussion. Ms. Jacoby, a veteran science teacher said, "I feel all we need to change is our curriculum and the way it is delivered. That is a big enough system for us to deal with." Mr. Thomas disagreed, "Unless we get the political structure in the school and district behind our efforts, it's foolish to think that science teachers can make dramatic changes." Others pointed out the need to involve parents, community members, and business leaders. Still others felt that the other middle schools in the district must be part of the discussion. In short, our discussion of systemic reform involved two major components: the people who needed to be involved in the change and the parts of the system that needed changing. Once we agreed on this focus, we began to brainstorm actual people and system components. As shown in Table 3.1, our initial lists included many groups of people and system components. But, we were sure there were missing pieces.

In subsequent meetings, we continued to refine our lists and extend invitations to a broader sample of people. We made sure that at least one representative from each of the groups we identified attended our biweekly meetings. We felt that getting them involved early was critical to our success. Then we began to devise a set of priorities and a plan to implement them. After weeks of struggle, we decided to attack the science curriculum, assessment, and instructional practices components of the system within our school. Our rationale was that these needed to be in place before the other parts could be meaningfully changed.

We decided to break into grade-level teams to study the *National Science Education Standards* and our state's curriculum framework in after-school meetings. We continued our biweekly meetings, discussing the results of our study efforts. We

TABLE 3.1   People and system components.

People	System Components
Science Teachers	The science curriculum
Principal and school administrators	Science teaching strategies
Parents	Assessment practices
Community leaders	How we view diversity
Business leaders	District and school policies that affect science education
Professors from the local college	Direct support for science education
Community scientists	District and school professional development plan

were surprised that it took many months to come to philosophical agreement on the direction we should take. I expected that there would be some difference of opinion between some parents and business and community leaders, but I didn't expect to find so much disagreement among my fellow science teachers. Most of us have been teaching together for more than 10 years! This was the most frustrating and disappointing part of the process. During some meetings, it was painfully obvious that we were taking steps backward. The frustration levels of everyone rose, but we rationalized that everybody needed an opportunity to say his or her piece. The endless talk had a purpose: to get all of our ideas onto the table and to tear away all of our clichéd thoughts and ideas.

Between meetings, many of my colleagues came to me to vent their frustration. "Why can't we just ignore what Mr. Mills says, he's such a dinosaur." "These younger teachers don't really understand how the school works. They are so idealistic." "Why put so much effort into something that will probably fail anyway?" I found myself the lightning rod for everyone's complaints. With thoughts and feelings like these, why were we continuing? Yet I became convinced that even with the apparent frustration, we were making progress. To help everyone focus more on issues and less on personalities, we decided to engage a neutral facilitator for biweekly meetings. We also began inviting science content and pedagogical experts from the college. The addition of these individuals raised the level of discourse to a new high. My colleagues began listening more and trying to understand the point of view of others. After months of haggling, we began to emerge speaking with a common voice. It was obvious that we needed to begin building our new science curriculum and associated teaching strategies and assessments.

With the help of the local college professors, we wrote an Eisenhower Higher Education grant, which was funded. The grant paid us to work in the summer to create draft documents that present a vision of our science curriculum and instructional and assessment practices. It also paid for consultants to help us think through some of the toughest issues. During an early brainstorming session, we created the following list of topics for in-service sessions:

Potential In-Service Topics

National curriculum standards

Performance and portfolio assessment

Diversity issues

Inquiry teaching

Using community resources

Leadership skills

The nature of the early adolescent learner

Interspersing in-service and work sessions, we began to make progress. Slowly but surely, a new schoolwide science curriculum, with associated teaching and assessment strategies, took life. With extra grant funds, we hired an editor with science teaching experience who was able to smooth out our drafts. By the end of the summer, everyone was exhausted but pleased that what we had produced, while not as polished as national or state documents, was professionally done. We were all so exhausted—thank God for the 2 weeks of free time at the end of summer! We needed the rest to be ready to try to put our ideas into practice during the next school year.

During preplanning at the beginning of the new school year, we reviewed our efforts. Mr. Thomson, our principal, summarized the feelings of all when he said, "Wow, I guess we did make some progress last summer. I can't believe how difficult it was and how far we have come." As a group, we then made some minor changes and developed a plan for testing our ideas.

We are now in the middle of the year, still testing and changing what we wrote during the summer. We are continuing our biweekly meetings, sharing results, and discussing issues. It is becoming obvious that our work has not led to all the changes we had hoped for. But, we are mostly proud of our efforts and knowledgeable of what we must do next summer and in the coming school year to get closer to our goals.

As I reflect on all that we have accomplished in our small system—our middle school—it is becoming clear to me that if our moderate success is to be sustained, the larger system must also change. The state reform leaders want us to push forward the reform to other schools in the district and neighboring districts. They want our school to serve as a model for systemic change and show others how it can be done. But my science colleagues who stuck with me through all the tough times are tired. They recognize the value of systemic change, but feel other needs competing for their time and attention. Attendance at our biweekly meetings has gradually dropped. And with our draft documents revised and being used to guide our science classroom practices, most feel that our work is done.

Tomorrow I meet with the state reform leaders, but this afternoon we meet as a school team. The state folks will want to know our decision. Do we agree to involve our school in the larger system change, or do we celebrate our accomplishments and let others champion the still unfinished business of reform? As a result of our work, I realize that the decision is not a simple one and that it is not mine alone to make. The issues surrounding the decision are much more involved than I believe my colleagues think they are. How can I help them understand the complexity of the decision? One thing's for certain: I know I won't sleep easy until this matter is resolved.

Questions for Reflection and Discussion

1. What should Larry do? Support your response.

2. Is there a compromise decision that would satisfy Larry's colleagues and the state reform leaders?

3. Why is it important that Larry and his colleagues carry their reform work beyond their school's science program?

4. What strategies should Larry use to convince his colleagues to continue their participation in the reform effort?

5. How should other middle schools in the district be involved in the reform process? How could high schools be involved?

6. What are characteristics of systemic reform?

7. Is there a danger that momentum made will be lost, or that Larry's school will be required to follow the district policies in the near future, if the project does not spread to the rest of the schools in the district? Explain.

■ ■ ■

Does It Matter Beyond My School?—Indeed It Does!

Frank E. Crawley

Larry Barnes and his middle school science teacher colleagues truly reflect the long-standing adage regarding reform, namely, "the teacher is the key." I salute them for the hard work, perseverance, and leadership they have shown in tackling the tough task of reforming their science teaching practice. They now have reached an interesting, unavoidable juncture in the reform process regarding the next step. On the one hand, state leaders recognize the leadership that Larry and his colleagues have exhibited and want to enlist their experience and expertise in the service of science education reform on a large scale. Their call is to "Scale-up!" Some of Larry's colleagues, on the other hand, lack interest in the bigger picture and are content to "celebrate their accomplishments and let others champion the still unfinished business of reform." These teachers advise Larry, "Scale-down!" Does it matter beyond my school?—Indeed it does! The problem that Larry and his colleagues face is one of scale. Richard Elmore (1996) provides timely insights regarding the problem of scale that Larry and his colleagues face in an article titled "Getting to Scale With Good Educational Practice," which serves as the basis for this commentary.

My advice to Larry is "Scale-up while scaling-down." To do less than act on two fronts is to put at risk the progress that Larry and his colleagues have made up to now. So, in a sense there is sage advice in Ms. Jacoby's comments uttered early on in the reform process, "I feel that all we need to change is our curriculum and the way it is delivered," and in Mr. Thomas's counter admonition, "Unless we get the political structure in the school and district behind our efforts, it's foolish to think that science teachers can make dramatic changes." The tasks for Larry and his colleagues are to change the core of their practice while they create a framework of incentives in their school and district that support them to act in the ways that they value. The following paragraphs describe the scale-up and scale-down tasks, as I see them.

Larry and colleagues started the reform process at the right place, with the development of new curriculum, assessment, and instructional practices. Teachers can't stop here. The scale-down question is "Will reform on paper become reform in practice?" Will the core of teachers' educational practice be changed, or will traditional views on teaching and learning remain intact? Ms. Jacoby might be a good candidate to lead the effort to reform science teaching and learning in practice—just what's called for in the *National Science Education Standards* (National Research Council, 1996). The *Standards* challenge science teachers to rethink the relationship among student, teacher, and science knowledge. A new epistemology of practice is called for, in which students are helped by teachers to construct scientific knowledge rather than expected to receive the knowledge that their teachers have constructed and transmitted to them. As part of their agenda as a professional development school for science, Ms. Jacoby and her colleagues have the unique, exciting opportunity to systematically study the learning that takes place in their science classes as students engage in new forms of instruction and to develop the professional knowledge so needed to assist and sustain them and other science teachers in the reform of science instruction. In the process of studying the outcomes of middle school science curriculum reform efforts, how diverse groups of students come to understand science, and under what conditions learning takes place, Larry and other science teachers will engage in challenging new forms of professional development. These opportunities are clearly connected to the improvement of their practice as advocated in the *National Science Education Standards* for professional development. However, transforming the practice of a few science teachers is not enough.

Reform in isolation is quickly displaced by other new ideas, particularly if the core of science teaching practice is left unchanged and incentives are lacking for other science teachers to transform their teaching. The scale-up question is "Will reform in practice remain an isolated event?" Lacking incentives, only a few science teachers—Larry for one—who truly value, believe in, and are committed to the goal of universal scientific literacy, the goal of current reform efforts, are likely to work to bring it about even without incentives to do so. Other science teachers are likely to view the successes of Larry and his colleagues as the product of near-heroic efforts of a few highly talented, energetic individuals—feats that can't be expected of every teacher. Unless these accomplishments are captured and institutional incentives provided, other teachers are unlikely to change their day-to-day teaching practices. (Here is where Mr. Thomas's leadership is needed.) Teachers are part of a school culture that provides them with incentives to act in certain ways, and they respond to these incentives by testing them against their values and their competence. With an institutional reward structure in place, other science teachers who value universal scientific literacy and who are provided with time and support are more likely to implement professional practices that transform the nature of science teaching and learning; in the process they will learn from their efforts.

In summary, Larry and his colleagues must work on two fronts. They should scale down and change the core of their teaching practice, or the reform they value will become superficial and short-lived. At the same time, they need to work with school and district administrators to create institutional incentives and expectations for teachers to transform the core of their instructional practices, or Larry, Ms. Jacoby, Mr. Thomas, and colleagues risk isolating themselves from and being ridiculed by other science teachers.

■ ■ ■

Fixing the Engine While Driving 65 MPH

Gloria "Brownie" Lindner

In this open case, Brownie tells about the efforts of two newly employed district-level administrators to revise a school district's science curriculum and instructional materials selection process. Participation in an Administrator's Forum serves to raise their awareness of critical issues surrounding their work, including the role of the *National Science Education Standards* (National Research Council, 1996) in supporting science education reform. As they move quickly to build the momentum needed to effect change in the district's science programs, the administrators come to realize that they have failed to involve teachers in their planning, and they are left wondering what to do next. Following the case is a response written by Gail Paulin, a science resource specialist with expertise in science reform.

This past summer brought several new faces to Sunshine School District: a new District Superintendent (Dr. Tom Anderson), an Assistant Superintendent for Curriculum and Instruction (Dr. Claudia Perez), and a relatively new Coordinator for High School Curriculum (Dr. Barbara Lawrence). One of the first priorities of the new superintendent was the revision of district science curricula and the instructional materials selection process.

In the past, the previous Assistant Superintendent for Curriculum and Instruction organized yearly committees to revise and update district curricula for a different discipline each year. The standard process involved recruiting both a curriculum-writing committee and a textbook selection committee. The committees operated independently of each other, with the products of the curriculum-writing committee used to guide the textbook selection committee's work. No one in the present administration could remember exactly why this configuration was used.

The process led to great variability among the district's schools in terms of what science materials were adopted and how the district's science curriculum was implemented. Not surprisingly, the two district high schools favored quite different approaches to science instruction based on the materials chosen for individual courses. Science teachers at Foothills High School maintained a traditional set of course offerings, commencing with either physical or earth science for ninth graders and continuing with a sequence of biology, chemistry, physics, and advanced placement courses in all three science areas. In contrast, the science faculty of River View High School chose a nontraditional approach to meet the needs of an academically less successful inner-city student population. The offerings included an interdisciplinary 2-year science course plus a variety of other new courses based on current science issues and problems.

At the direction of the new superintendent, an ambitious plan was drafted to revise curricula district wide. Being new in their positions and armed with great enthusiasm, Drs. Perez and Lawrence forged ahead and created curriculum and textbook groups for the different subject areas, as their predecessors had done in the past. The science curriculum committee met to consider how to distribute the newly drafted state science standards and devise a scope and sequence. And the science textbook selection committee met to discuss what materials they would like to review and how they were to proceed.

About the same time the committees were beginning their work, Drs. Perez and Lawrence read about a forum for administrators to be held at one of the state's universities, entitled *Using Standards for Curriculum Planning and Selection*. The description of the forum sounded like it might be useful for their work: understanding the role of the national standards for science in developing local standards-based programs, examining selection criteria for evaluating and comparing science curricula that support standards-based programs, and learning strategies for planning and implementation processes to help effect change in school systems.

The forum was a positive experience for the two new administrators, and they both participated in all the activities with a great deal of enthusiasm and interest. As they investigated the national standards, they came to realize that there were some significant differences between the state standards for science and the *National Science Education Standards (NSES)* (National Research Council, 1996). In particular, they discovered that the *NSES* presented a clear framework of unifying concepts that provide linkages, coherence, and connectedness for the other content standards. These unifying themes had not been included in the new state science standards. Dr. Perez and Dr. Lawrence both agreed that that was a grievous omission and started thinking about how they could build the state standards and these unifying themes into the science curriculum they were about to help develop. They worked on an activity that helped them articulate this discovery into a poster, which later served as a framework and organizer for the action plans starting to emerge in their minds.

As the forum continued, Drs. Perez and Lawrence used evaluation tools developed by the National Science Resource Center and the National Science Foundation to determine the degree of alignment between local curriculum materials with the national standards. Through these activities, they were introduced to a selection of nontraditional middle and high school science programs, including the American Chemical Society's (1993) *Chemistry in the Community, Science Education for Public Understanding Program* (SEPUP), developed by the Lawrence Hall of Science (1992), and the Biological Sciences Curriculum Study's (1997) *BSCS Biology: A Human Approach*. Both Drs. Perez and Lawrence saw these materials as quite different from traditional textbook-based programs, and noted that some of the more issue-oriented and multidisciplinary materials articulated well with the school-to-work and technical preparation initiatives in place at River View High school.

The close of the 2-day forum brought with it many questions for Drs. Perez and Lawrence about the implications of what they had learned. Why were there separate curriculum revision and materials selection committees? Should the district curriculum be a framework or more prescriptive? How could they infuse more study of the *NSES* into the curriculum revision process? Is it possible to find common ground among schools with a history of strong site-based management? Could their understanding of the change process be used to affect the expectations of teachers and principals about curriculum revision and materials selection? In particular, how could better articulation between the high schools and their feeder middle schools be achieved? Do the two high schools need to have more similar science courses and philosophies? Were students in the two high schools currently offered equitable experiences? How could the old paradigm be changed?

Perez and Lawrence reflected on their dilemma. It was apparent to both that, since the previous curriculum adoption cycle in the district, there was very uneven implementation of district curriculum and use of adopted materials. The district curriculum document reflected changes geared toward science literacy envisioned by *Science for All Americans* (Rutherford & Ahlgren, 1990). However, it had apparent deficiencies and was not reflected as intended in science classrooms across the district.

Drs. Perez and Lawrence returned to their district with renewed energy. They called an administrative team together to consider some possibilities: Should they consolidate the two committees? Should the district curriculum be a framework or more prescriptive? How much latitude will individual schools be given in materials selection? The team discussed and debated these and other questions. By the end of the meeting, the team had reached a consensus about changes all wanted to implement in the science curriculum and selection process: They would initiate professional development activities; they would seek instructional materials from sources other than traditional textbook publishers; and they would conduct pilot tests of different instructional materials to inform adoption decisions. While there was no movement to change the two-committee structure, the team agreed that the district needed a significant change in science teaching and learning; the district needed movement from a fairly traditional textbook-based approach to a more active process aimed at science literacy for all students.

As Drs. Perez and Lawrence walked back to their offices after saying good-bye to the members of the administrative team, they talked about how pleased they were with all that they had accomplished in only a couple of months.

"Participating in the Administrative Forum really helped jump-start our efforts to initiate district reform," said Dr. Lawrence.

"Yeah, I agree," responded Dr. Perez, "Dr. Anderson and the other administrators seem to really like where we're headed, but we really need to get some input from teachers. What do you think the science teachers at Foothills and River View will make of our plans?"

Questions for Reflection and Discussion

1. How did participation in the Administrative Forum change Drs. Perez and Lawrence's thinking about reforming the district's science program?

2. Do you think that Drs. Perez and Lawrence made a wise decision to redirect the district's science curricula revision and materials selection processes once they were underway? Why or why not?

3. The *NSES* unifying concepts and processes include

   ■ Systems, order, and organization
   ■ Evidence, models, and explanation
   ■ Change, constancy, and measurement
   ■ Evolution and equilibrium
   ■ Form and function (National Research Council, 1996, p. 104)

   How might the use of these concepts and processes as unifying themes for the district's science curriculum affect the development of common ground between the two high schools? Articulation between the high schools and their feeder middle schools?

4. Drs. Perez and Lawrence chose to maintain the existing organizational structure of separate curriculum and materials adoption committees. What do you see as the advantages of this arrangement? What are some disadvantages?

5. If you were a science teacher in the Sunshine School District, how would you respond to the administrators' plan for reforming the district's science program? How might the plan be different if teachers had participated in the administrators' planning meeting?

■　■　■

Change Happens With Buy-In

Gail Paulin

This case appears to be a classic example of top–down decision making, exacerbated by the fact that these newly appointed administrators haven't had much time to establish rapport and assess the readiness level of the teaching staff. They are unaware of the staff's concerns regarding science education reform and past science performance of students at both Foothills and River View High Schools. Given this context, the proposed curriculum developed and materials selection processes will likely be met with mixed reactions from teachers.

However, many science teachers at the two schools may welcome the superintendent's support of science reform (since there are superintendents who don't consider science a priority at all) and may be encouraged that the administration has made the effort to understand national standards and science reform efforts, as evidenced by the participation of Drs. Perez and Lawrence in the administrators forum. While these administrators appear to share an enthusiasm for and commitment to reform, their proposed changes are rushed and clearly ignore or discount the necessary buy-in process for classroom teachers, students, parents, and community.

The bilateral committee approach to curriculum revision and materials selection does little to ensure a good fit between the curriculum and instructional materials. By using this old paradigm, there will probably be little incentive to bring about truly meaningful change. The proposed reform does not appear to be truly systemic and, thus, will probably not be fully implemented. In addition, there will be some teachers who will resist the proposed change (status quo), particularly if they don't know the new administrators well and trust is not clearly established.

Assuming Drs. Perez and Lawrence are sincerely motivated toward meaningful change in science education (not just making change to impose their own stamp on the system), they should use their own positive experience at the administrators forum to develop similar sessions for all the science teachers from both high schools. Topics that could be addressed at these sessions include the similarities among and differences between the state standards and the *National Science Education Standards* (National Research Council, 1996), student needs, and the supports and barriers for change. Similar sessions could be held for parents and community groups who might be called on to provide support for the change process.

After all these groups have met and a shared vision and framework have been drafted, these same groups, or representatives from each, should proceed to develop guidelines to adequately assess materials for adoption. Pilot tests of potential choices that meet the goals of the district framework should be conducted, and teachers should look at the effectiveness of these instructional materials in terms of student achievement of the goals outlined in the framework. In-service support will then be needed to ensure effective implementation. This support should address the content and pedagogical needs of the teachers and continue until it is clear that all students have access to effective science instruction and can achieve at the levels identified in the established assessment goals.

This plan is workable for several reasons. First, it demonstrates trust, respect, and awareness of all stakeholders of a reform effort. It also occurs in incremental stages, with time for reflection after each phase. Additionally, it encourages buy-in and supports curriculum implementation far beyond the purchase of materials. It also is built on the premise that the change process cannot be exclusively top–down or bottom–up. Meaningful change takes time, involves the active participation of many parties, and requires a clear vision of the desired outcomes. If the framework is clear about what students should know and be able to do, then the two high schools may vary their approach as long as students have equal access to science learning opportunities. Science instruction must be meaningful, engaging, and challenging, if the needs of students at both high schools are to be met.

Resources to Consider

Educational standards and curriculum frameworks for science [On-line]. Available: http://putwest.boces.org/StSu/Science.html

This part of the *Developing Educational Standards* Web site maintained by Charles Hill and the Putnam Valley Schools of New York is of particular value to teachers interested in learning about organizational, state, and international efforts related to the development and use of science educational standards and curriculum frameworks. The annotated list of Internet sites includes links to numerous documents, including those developed by the American Association for the Advancement of Science, the U.S. Department of Education, the National Science Teachers Association, most of the 50 states, and Canada.

Louden, C., & Hounshell, P. (1998, September). **Student-centered scheduling**. *The Science Teacher, 65,* 51–53.

As many high schools shift from traditional 50-minute schedules to block schedules, making the most effective use of time in the classroom has become a topic of increasing interest. In this article, Cynthia Louden and Paul Hounshell report on a study in which they found that higher levels of student achievement occurred in classes where teachers stressed student-centered learning, regardless of scheduling arrangement. The authors discuss the potential benefits of block scheduling, which provides greater opportunities for student-centered instruction.

National Science Teachers Association. (1996). *NSTA pathways to the science standards—High school and middle school editions*. Arlington, VA: Author. (National Science Teachers Association, 1840 Wilson Boulevard, Arlington, VA 22201)

These two volumes provide concrete suggestions and examples for implementing the National Science Education Standards. The High School Edition is for teachers of grades 9 to 12, and the Middle School Edition, for teachers of grades 7 and 8. Sections of these books address changes advocated by the standards in the areas of teacher professional development, science program, and school system as well as in the content domains of life science, physical science, and earth and space science.

Wasley, P. A. (1991). *Teachers who lead: The rhetoric of reform and the realities of practice*. New York: Teachers College Press. (Teachers College Press, 1234 Amsterdam Avenue, New York, NY 10027)

P. A. Wasley explores in depth the dilemmas associated with the current rhetoric of reform and the everyday realities of classroom teachers. The author uses cases to illustrate the dilemmas of three teachers who are participants in the reform process.

References

American Association for the Advancement of Science. (1993). *Benchmarks for scientific literacy*. New York: Oxford Press.

American Chemical Society. (1993). *Chemistry in the community.* Dubuque, IA: Kendall/Hunt.

Biological Sciences Curriculum Study. (1997). *BSCS biology: A human approach.* Dubuque, IA: Kendall/Hunt.

Elmore, R. F. (1996). Getting to scale with good educational practice. *Harvard Educational Review, 66,* 1–26.

Lawrence Hall of Science. (1992). *Science education for public understanding program.* Berkeley: University of California at Berkeley, The Regents of the University of California.

National Research Council. (1996). *National science education standards*. Washington, DC: National Academy Press.

Rutherford, F. J., & Ahlgren, A. (1990). *Science for all Americans*. New York: Oxford University Press.

4

Planning for Science Instruction

Teacher planning serves to link teaching and learning. When planning for science instruction, the teacher must consider many things, including the content, instructional strategies, teaching materials, learning objectives and goals, and, of course, students. An important aspect of planning is the teacher's ability to make science content relevant and appealing to students. Consistent with a teacher-directed view of instruction, planning in science has traditionally focused on the organization and delivery of the lesson. Planning based on this view of instruction stresses the science content to be learned by students and the teacher's skill at controlling the sequence and pace of instruction.

Recently, the teacher-directed view of instruction has given way to a more student-centered view. This shift has been greatly influenced by constructivist thinking and the desire to provide students with authentic science experiences. The effect of this shift on science teacher planning has been profound. When planning for instruction, teachers must consider content sources other than the textbook and the fact that students enter our science classrooms with a variety of understandings and experiences that influence what and how they learn. Teachers must organize learning experiences that enable students to construct, apply, and test their developing science understandings. Teachers' planning must also recognize the needs of students to engage in explorations and make mistakes, as well as to negotiate their science understandings and challenge the knowledge claims of others. In this context, the ideal instructional plan is one that emerges from the interactions of teacher and students, where students participate as partners in the planning process.

Planning of this type is very complicated and involved. Some teachers may find it frustrating not knowing how instruction will proceed. To lessen the cognitive and emotional demands associated with planning, many teachers will engage in collaborative and interdisciplinary efforts with other educational professionals and perhaps make use of technology to access the assistance and support not readily available at their school. Today, the outcome of planning is no longer a script to be followed by the teacher, but a dynamic learning environment with the focus clearly on the needs of students. Science teachers must always be mindful of the fact that how they plan will determine what their students learn.

The three cases in this chapter describe various aspects of science teachers' planning. A teacher's struggle to balance the benefits and limitations of interdisciplinary planning for middle school science instruction is highlighted in the first case. The second case explains how the absence of student textbooks led a biology teacher to shift the focus of her planning away from content delivery and toward student-centered learning experiences. And the final case illustrates how the on-line support provided by colleagues in different schools helped a teacher change her views of planning as she engaged her classes in student-directed, problem-based learning.

The Enemy of Understanding Is Coverage

Elaine R. Homestead and P. Elizabeth Pate

This closed case portrays two educators' attempts to address planning and the issue of depth versus breadth, through curriculum integration. Elaine, a veteran middle school teacher, and Elizabeth, a professor in middle level education, have collaborated on progressive education for the past 9 years. They utilize each other's strengths and knowledge as they seek to make schooling at the middle school and university levels more meaningful. This case illustrates the importance of collaborative planning, as students and teachers together learn science by engaging in curriculum integration. Commentary on the case is provided by Gert Nesin, a veteran middle school teacher and administrator, who also values planning for science through curriculum integration.

As soon as Elizabeth read the article, she knew she had to phone Elaine. "Elaine, listen to this newspaper article addressing state-mandated curriculum:"

A curriculum covering too many topics without depth is being blamed as the primary reason for the low showing of American 12th graders in a recent Third International Mathematics and Science Study report ("Study Gives Georgia Curriculum Mixed Grades," 1998)

Elaine responded, "I wish that had been printed before I had that conversation about depth versus breadth with my administrator."

Middle school teachers are often in mental turmoil over this dilemma. They ask themselves, "Do I teach for understanding or for coverage?" We maintain that understanding is of greater importance. And we believe that depth of understanding is an inherent part of curriculum integration. Curriculum integration is a philosophy that helps many teachers solve the dilemma of planning for understanding. In curriculum integration, subject boundaries are dissolved, and students and teachers collaborate on what is taught, why it is important to learn, and how something is learned and assessed.

Last year, Elaine was on a two-teacher sixth-grade team. On paper, she was assigned to teach social studies and language arts. However, Elaine chose to focus on her students' needs and concerns rather than dividing the content into subject areas.

"I began our curriculum planning process by asking students to write what questions they had about themselves and what questions they had about their world. Next, we [students and teacher] grouped and labeled these questions. One set of questions focused on the environment," reflects Elaine.

The students were worried about their environment and their future lives. Since our state-mandated curriculum included studies of Europe, we focused on that geographical area. After their general study of Europe, students wanted to learn more about the physical environment of the area. Specifically, they wanted to know about environmental problems in Europe. They were interested in finding out if Europe had some of the same environmental problems as the United States. They also wanted to know how countries in Europe were solving their environmental problems.

Students brainstormed specific environmental concerns they were interested in learning more about. Some wanted to know about problems associated with nuclear power. Some wanted to find out about the causes and effects of acid rain. Others wanted to know about landfills and the process involved in their construction. And still others wanted to know about toxic waste and the associated disposal problems.

For 3 weeks, students were involved in researching their particular group's concern. They began the process by developing a list of appropriate researchable questions. They divided up their questions and began the search for relevant information. During this process, they learned to locate, read, and synthesize information. They learned to take good notes and write an accurate bibliography. They also learned to develop plans, individually and as a group. During this process, they gained practice in being discriminating readers and listeners.

It was at this time that, during a conversation with an administrator, a discussion took place about how long it was taking for students to research and report on their research. The administrator asked, "But, do you think you are going to have enough time to cover the curriculum?"

Elaine answered with one of her favorite quotations, "To quote Howard Gardner, 'The enemy of understanding is coverage'" (Gardner, 1997).

After the research process was completed, each group spent the next 3 weeks planning and then presenting their findings to the class. Teachers and students together developed a rubric that guided both planning and evaluation of presentations. Students learned to develop their own lesson plans, using a "design-down format" (Pate, Homestead, & McGinnis, 1997). For example, the group that was interested in pollution problems associated with nuclear power initially wanted to know two things. They wanted to know what happened at Chernobyl and how Europeans handled the disposal of nuclear wastes. As a result of their in-depth research, they learned how a reactor works; differences between the reactor at Chernobyl and reactors in the United States; the materials used by different countries to fuel their reactors; different kinds of radiation; materials that stop radiation; radiation sickness; the half-life of different radioactive materials; nuclear waste disposal; nuclear waste storage; the ways in which different countries dispose of nuclear waste; and the legacy of Chernobyl.

These sixth-grade students understood what they learned. They were engaged in meaningful learning relevant to their needs as young adolescents. Through collaborative curriculum development, the students learned not only science, mathematics, social studies, and language arts content, but personal and social skills as well. They were actively involved in the planning process because the curriculum came from their own questions.

Even so, the dilemma associated with planning for breadth versus depth remains. Recently, Elaine phoned Elizabeth and said, "Guess what? You won't believe this. . . . The other day I was in class at the university and had just finished describing our environment curriculum, when someone asked me, 'Why would you want to go to all that trouble with curriculum integration when you already have a textbook that outlines everything a student should know in science?'"

Questions for Reflection and Discussion

1. Traditional models of planning are teacher-centered. In Elaine's classroom, students and teacher plan the curriculum together. What are some of the benefits of this constructivist-oriented approach?

2. It is clear that Elaine and Elizabeth have strong convictions regarding the issue of depth versus breadth in the curriculum. How does an educator come to feel strongly about an educational issue? How would you justify your stance on the issue of depth versus breath?

3. How would you answer the question "Why would you want to go to all that trouble with curriculum integration when you already have a textbook that outlines everything a student should know in science?"

4. What do you think Howard Gardner meant when he stated, "The enemy of understanding is coverage" (Gardner, 1997)?

5. Write a question about a contemporary science-related issue that you think would be of interest to middle grade or high school students. Then, decide how you might go about helping students find an answer to this question. What science concepts or principles could be addressed by answering your question? How would planning for instruction based on students' questions differ from planning for instruction guided by a school district's curriculum framework?

6. This case illustrates curriculum integration in a middle school setting. What might curriculum integration look like at the high school level?

Vital Context for Science Vigor

Gert Nesin

Many educators assume that planning for curriculum integration builds on student interests and concerns at the cost of academic rigor. I have heard this particular criticism from science teachers and other educators. As this case illustrates, curriculum integration when properly executed exceeds and broadens academic expectations beyond the traditional separate subject approach. Elaine's sixth-grade students learned about the construction and functioning of nuclear reactors as well as the benefits and hazards of nuclear energy. These science concepts were explicitly connected to social, political, and environmental issues in the context of the students' concerns. Furthermore, her middle school students had an active role in planning their own curriculum.

Elaine allowed her students time, and she helped them develop sufficient research expertise to explore their questions in depth. If we expect young people to understand not only concepts but how those concepts impact real situations and living beings, time is essential. Although students may not "cover" as many topics in an academic year, they will be more likely to truly learn the concepts and facts they do cover. More importantly, they will better understand how to be collaborative scientists and learners. They also discover how their own serious queries can lead them to academic skills, knowledge, and understanding.

As educators, we often state that one of our primary goals is for our students to become lifelong learners. Yet we drag them along behind an impersonal, minute, overstuffed curriculum, and, to exacerbate the insult, tell them how they will be dragged—lesson by lesson. We certainly make educated (but frequently incorrect) guesses at how the students will best learn and most enjoy the numerous facts and skills they must digest, but we rarely question the bulk of the underlying curriculum or the way in which it is delivered. If students are to be lifelong learners, they must not depend on teachers to be the sole planners and deliverers of knowledge; instead, students must be given the opportunity and guidance to participate in the planning process and to seek answers to their own questions. Curriculum integration offers a philosophy and vehicle to meaningful, rigorous student involvement and lifelong learning.

Many science teachers strive to make their classrooms alive with activity and scientific inquiry. As this case illustrates, curriculum integration can provide a much more meaningful context for this important learning while providing a vehicle for depth of understanding.

■ ■ ■

Creative Planning Carried the Day

Thomas R. Koballa, Jr.

Jake Chasman faced many obstacles as a first-year physical science teacher without his own classroom. In this closed case, Tom describes how Jake worked through the dilemma of having no textbooks for his class of physical science students, all of whom had failed the course and were taking it for the second time. The unavailability of student textbooks caused Jake to shift the focus of his planning from the delivery of physical science information to the development of an instructional environment that matched the learning needs of his students. Jake Chasman is a composite of teachers with whom Tom has worked. The case is followed by commentary from Barbara Rascoe, a science education graduate student and former high school teacher.

I began my teaching career as a roving physical science teacher in a large, suburban high school. The student body was 1,500 strong and included adolescents from rich and poor families representing all ethnic groups. The teaching faculty numbered about 75. The physical plant consisted of a two-story main building, with three single-story wings extending to the south, east, and west. In the middle of the central building was an open atrium where students would hang out during lunch or in the morning before the beginning of classes.

The science department consisted of nine teachers, including me, with classrooms located on the first and second floors of the main building. As a floating teacher, my office was in the laboratory prep room between the classrooms of the department chair and one of the biology teachers on the second floor. I was assigned to teach physical science in one science room on the first floor and one on the second, as well as a mathematics classroom and a home economics classroom, both located in the west wing. I moved my teaching materials from room to room on an old battered cart with squeaky wheels.

My sixth period was a class of 16 boys and 12 girls who had previously failed physical science. This class of repeaters included students with family problems, learning disabilities, and some real trouble makers. It was not uncommon for one or more students to be absent each day for fighting, cutting class, or smoking in the restroom. To make matters worse, the number of physical science books needed that year was underestimated, so as the "new kid on the block," I had no books to distribute to this class. Having no books became a point of contention for these students. My temporary fix for the problem of no books was to come to class with overhead transparencies for the purpose of presenting the information covered in the book. The few reinforcement activities I could provide for these students were those I prepared myself the night before or on the weekend. Only the one biology teacher who befriended me was willing to let me borrow her teaching aids, but because I taught physical science, they were of little help to me. I spent quite a few dollars out of my own pocket for consumables that year.

A few days into the second month of school, I received a note from the office informing me that the long-awaited textbooks had finally arrived. I was so excited. Finally, the students would have books to read, and I wouldn't have to prepare overhead transparencies every day just to present the information in the book. I hurried down to the office as soon as the final bell rang to get my books. As I tore away the packing material from the box, I saw the book covers. Someone had ordered the wrong books! My excitement quickly turned to frustration and anger. I rushed to my principal's office to inform him of the error. He was very apologetic and said that new books would be ordered immediately. As I left his office, he added that the district shipping department worked at a snail's pace and I shouldn't expect the right books anytime soon.

As a new teacher who had always believed that the textbook was at the heart of science teaching, there I was with the wrong books. I tried to use these "wrong" books, but my students' interest in learning physical science did not improve. They knew which textbook physical science students were using in other classes and were upset about being told that they had to use "the wrong books." At this point, I recognized that I had to plan some different learning experiences for this group of students. So, I stopped teaching physical science by the book and literally threw out my lesson plans and transparencies. I starting showing videos and doing demonstrations that had even the remotest relationship to what I felt I should be teaching. The demonstrations were ones described in Janice VanCleave's (1991) *Physics for Every Kid*, Brenda Walpole's (1988) *175 Science Experiments to Amuse and Amaze Your Friends*, and several other books. My nights were spent developing guided-viewing assignments for the videos or gathering materials and trying out demonstrations to see how they worked. My intention was to get students to think about particular physical science concepts and principles while enjoying the videos and demonstrations. After a couple of weeks of this type of teaching, my students began to suggest videos from Blockbuster for us to view and even started to look through the various science activity and demonstration books that I brought to school. They recommended several demonstrations that we try in class, and five students volunteered to gather materials and present a couple of the demonstrations while I watched. Their mimicking of my questioning strategies and typical behaviors drew laughter from their classmates and me. When we did not watch videos and do demonstrations, we talked about physical science in our daily lives. Our discussions were often prompted by articles from the newspaper and popular magazines, TV news broadcasts, and students' experiences outside of school. In any way I could, I tied in the science understandings that I felt my students should learn. My video selections and demonstrations became so popular that other physical science teachers in the school asked to borrow them to use with their classes.

The week after the Thanksgiving holidays, my books finally arrived. I wasn't sure I wanted to use them, since I had now taught without books for 3 months. As I loaded the boxes of books on my old battered cart and started pushing it down the hall, I thought about my initial anger when the wrong books arrived and reflected on the changes in my planning and teaching that resulted as a consequence. I recognized how, as a result of this experience, the focus of my planning had shifted away from my delivery of lessons and toward my students and the environment I was establishing to foster their learning. I came to understand my students and how they made sense of my lessons; I realized that my planning had a direct effect on what they learned.

I did distribute the books that week, and the students were pleased to get them. But, we never used them as I had initially intended. We continued to watch videos, do demonstrations, and make use of other media. The books served as one of many class resources. To this day, the central element of my planning continues to be developing successful learning experiences for my students.

Questions for Reflection and Discussion

1. How would you describe Jake's goals for student learning in science?

2. What are some obstacles a teacher faces when moving to different classrooms during the school day?

3. How would you have planned instruction for Jake's class of repeaters? Should repeaters be grouped together in a single class?

4. Do you agree with Jake's decision to show science-related videos to his students and engage them in physical science demonstrations and discussions about science in daily life? Explain your position.

5. How effective was Jake in creating a coherent science curriculum?

6. How did Jake's experience with this class of repeaters influence his thinking about planning and instruction? How are planning and instruction related?

I Empathize and Agree with Jake

Barbara Rascoe

As a former roving teacher, I empathize with Jake and agree with how he used his creativity to reformat the design of his physical science class for the following reasons: (1) Variety is the spice of life; (2) teachers cannot teach beyond the experiences of their students; and (3) students frequently fail not because of their inability to construct science understandings but because they do not achieve all of the objectives for success in a particular science classroom setting. The mediation and negotiation of the teaching process should be determined by the students that make up the class. The science teacher should focus on how to mediate the teaching and learning of science in situations that may not be ideal.

Frequently, teachers become chattels to the textbook. Textbooks should be used as condiments that enhance the flavor of the classroom environment. For most teachers, especially first-year teachers, texts are used as the central core, or meat, of the teaching process. A diet that contains meat as well as a variety of items from the other food groups is healthier than a diet of meat alone. One must also consider that some instructional resources and strategies, like some foods, are more easily digested than others. Texts in the classroom better serve the teaching process when used as part of a vast array of resources, including old textbooks, magazines, and the World Wide Web. Dieters eat foods according to ascribed rules, but dieters become bored and opt out of diet plans when they are required to overeat one particular food. Science teachers use a set of guidelines to help their students make sense of science content. There is a limit to how much teachers should use any single resource in the classroom.

Jake's textbook dilemma is particularly significant in light of current constructivist views of science teaching and learning. Constructivism is a set of beliefs about knowledge that begins with the assumption that a reality exists but cannot be known as a set of truths, in that human experience is fallible (Tippins, Nichols, & Tobin, 1993). Tippins and her colleagues further assert that teaching should be a meaningful learning activity in a classroom environment where participants can engage in the construction of new knowledge. This construction of new knowledge is both individual and social. The coordination of science content with the experiences of the students is the work of the science teacher. The students in Jake's classroom are not atypical but present dilemmas for first-year teachers depending on their experience and confidence in using approaches to teaching science that are based on constructivism.

The objectives for success in a particular classroom should embody interactions and discourse that emphasize ideas and evidence, with students as equal participants (Shepardson, 1996). Jake's teaching strategies included these characteristics. These teaching strategies were effective because, to teach science to special populations of students, the teacher must initially find mechanisms to divert students' attention from the reveries of personal problems.

Be Prepared!

Sandra K. Abell

In this closed case, Sandra tells about Chris Baca's struggle with planning for science instruction when student-directed, problem-based learning is the goal. Chris works through the dilemma with the on-line support of Anna and Jackie, two veteran teachers with whom she attended a summer science teaching institute. Through reflecting on the summer institute as well as on their science teaching experiences, the three teachers develop a way to be prepared for their science teaching while simultaneously engaging students in defining and investigating science problems. Toward the end of the experience, Chris reflects on how her views of planning have begun to change through this collaboration. Chris, Anna, and Jackie are pseudonyms and represent teachers with whom Sandra has worked over the years. The case is followed by a response prepared by Thomas Koballa Jr., a science educator with experience in science teaching and planning.

"Be prepared!" was the phrase that rang in Chris Baca's ears. She remembered her grandmother using that phrase repeatedly to admonish her while growing up; the phrase recurred during her scouting experiences in grade school; several of her college professors had used the phrase on the eve of her student teaching experience. It was a phrase that fit Chris well; in fact, she had dubbed it her motto. In her daily life, she always tried to be prepared and keep herself organized. In her teaching, Chris's "be prepared" motto inspired her to write detailed plans for new units of science instruction as well as weekly lessons. But this August, preparing for her fourth year of science teaching at Montaño Middle School, her motto was causing more frustration than inspiration.

75

On the one hand, she was excited about the new school year. "I can't wait to try this problem-based learning approach I learned this summer," she had proclaimed to Dr. Sanchez, her principal. When Dr. Sanchez probed for more information, Chris was exuberant. She recounted her 3 weeks at SIPS, the Summer Institute for Problem-Based Science, in a nearby school district. "We examined inquiry in science by carrying out our own investigations. We asked questions, collected and interpreted data, and presented our findings just like scientists. It was a blast, and I learned so much. I just can't wait to try it out with my students." Dr. Sanchez nodded and smiled. This exhilaration about science teaching was the very reason she had hired Chris 3 years ago.

Yet for all of her enthusiasm, Chris was becoming more frustrated daily. Her "be prepared" motto haunted her. She was eager to plan her first problem-based learning experience for eighth-grade science. However, she wanted the experience to be student-directed. She wanted the students to select researchable questions, design investigations, and collect data. How could she plan something that was to come from the students themselves?

Chris remembered that some teachers at SIPS had asked a similar question. Maybe by now they had an answer. Chris leaped to her computer and fired off e-mail messages to several SIPS participants: "Help! I'm in a panic! I want to plan my first problem-based unit, but planning seems to undermine the whole SIPS philosophy. What have you tried????"

By afternoon several responses had arrived. Marty, a veteran teacher of 19 years wrote, "Don't worry. Go with the flow. Forget planning. Let it happen. Be happy!"

This response did not exactly satisfy Chris. Then she read the responses from Anna and Jackie, also teaching veterans with 24 years of experience between them. Anna wrote, "I've been struggling with that, too. Let's talk more."

Jackie's response was the most promising of all: "I've been thinking about a few ideas. Let's talk."

Soon Chris, Anna, and Jackie were e-mailing daily, discussing what they had learned in SIPS and what they wanted to happen with their students.

First, they reflected on their learning goals for the students. After sharing her goals and hearing from the other teachers, Chris started to feel more relaxed. The conversation soon shifted as the teachers reflected on past experiences with their students and inquiry. "Here's where my students always have problems," wrote Anna, and she listed common hurdles for students. Her list included developing researchable questions, team planning, and keeping track of observations. Jackie added a few of her students' problem areas to the list: narrowing the research question, learning necessary lab or field techniques, and data analysis. Chris, who had never tried student-directed inquiry, was awed by this rich repertoire of experiences. How could she use these experiences to inform her own teaching? The conversation next turned to teaching strategies for helping students through these problem areas. Together the three teachers reflected on strategies they had experienced in SIPS and how these might need modification for middle school students. Chris finally saw a plan begin to take shape. "I've got it!" she wrote late one night. "Our plans don't have to be daily outlines of what we'll do. They could be more flexible. We could have plans for different phases of the problem-based learning experiences that focus on different contingencies." By morning Jackie had responded, "Yeah, we'll call it the CP—contingency plan."

By the time the school year started, Chris was charged with excitement, eager to try the instructional strategies in her CP. She was still a little nervous that her plans did not contain a step-by-step set of actions as in the past. However, the CP did give her confidence. She felt prepared to manage the learning environment and facilitate student investigations.

After the teaching began, Chris's support group persisted. Through daily e-mail messages, Chris, Anna, and Jackie reflected on the day's instruction. They discussed what worked and what did not. Often they were stumped by how to proceed. Their reflections helped them plan for the next day's contingencies.

However, even with her support group, Chris sometimes felt as if she was going into a lesson blindly and wished she had a more concrete plan of action. Some days the lesson proceeded very smoothly, and the students themselves were able to figure out the next steps. Other days Chris felt as if she and her students were floundering together. Chris was accustomed to a lot of activity in the classroom; she had often used laboratories to help science come alive for students. But this was different. To have students developing their own questions and research plans meant giving up some of the control and order that Chris was used to. Chris enjoyed seeing the excitement of student teams and hearing the buzz of their teamwork. Yet some days she felt drained of energy and unsure of what the next lesson should look like. That's when Chris started recording her feelings of frustration and success in a personal teaching journal. Her writing helped her recognize that her old views of planning for instruction and of science teaching were changing. One evening she wrote, "I didn't realize change would be quite so difficult for me."

At the end of the unit, Anna suggested that they celebrate their collaboration by writing an article in the SIPS newsletter. In the article, Anna described their teamwork, and Jackie discussed the CP they developed. Chris tried to explain her changing views of planning, "I used to think planning was something I did before a unit to prepare for the teaching. Now I realize planning occurs throughout a unit of instruction as you adjust your teaching ideas to the students. I used to think planning meant having a script prepared for each day. Now I realize that students can do some of the planning, too. I used to think planning was something I did alone on Sunday night. Now I realize the value of a planning team."

Before long, Chris was contemplating her next eighth-grade science unit. She thought about the difficulties she'd had in changing her planning and teaching styles and wondered if she could handle that kind of stress for another month or more. Since Anna and Jackie were teaming with the social studies teachers in their buildings for their next unit, Chris would not be able to share her thinking with them as before. Chris decided that she would feel most comfortable going back to her old way of planning for science, which also meant going back to more teacher-directed lessons. After all, she could always come back to planning for problem-based science after she'd had a bit of time to think about her recent classroom experiences.

Questions for Reflection and Discussion

1. How important do you think planning is to science teaching? What do you think of Marty's comment, "Forget planning. Let it happen."?

2. How can teachers plan for student-directed, problem-based learning?

3. What do you think of Chris's decision to go back to her old teaching strategies? What prompted her decision? How do you think her decision will influence her participation in student-directed, problem-based learning in the future?

4. Do teachers need a support group of other teachers in order to reflect on their practice? Explain your response.

5. When the e-mail group with Anna and Jackie broke up, what alternatives might Chris have pursued to get the support she needed to continue engaging her students in problem-based learning?

6. "By planning well, a teacher can eliminate instructional surprises and classroom management problems." What is your reaction to this statement? How do you think a teacher who favors student-directed, problem-based instruction would react?

■ ■ ■

Change Is Not an Easy Thing

Thomas R. Koballa, Jr.

Sandra's case highlights two important aspects of educational change. The first is the benefits of collaboration when changing existing practices (Texley & Wild, 1996). And the second is the importance of support for maintaining change (Fullan & Steigelbauer, 1991). Chris, the central character in the case, saw planning as something that the teacher does to be prepared for instruction. Her plans functioned as scripts to guide her actions and those of her students, and they provided the sense of control that she desired. Chris's experiences in the summer institute caused her to think about science teaching differently. Her notions of her role as science teacher shifted from that of giver of science information to the facilitator of student inquiry. In her mind, teaching science as inquiry, where students ask questions and design and carry out their own investigations, was incompatible with her ideas of good planning. How could she be prepared when she was not totally sure what the students would be doing and learning in her class? Chris's feelings of discomfort were lessened when Anna and Jackie responded to her e-mail for help. Their electronic exchanges served to bolster Chris's confidence in teaching by inquiry and calmed her fears associated with not being able to control all aspects of instruction and student learning in her class. In a sense, it could be said that based on her summer institute experience, Chris was poised at what learning theorist Lev Vygotsky (1978) called the "zone of proximal development," where significant strides in learning can occur when proper guidance is provided. Anna and Jackie provided the guidance that Chris needed in order to learn how to plan for student-centered instruction.

The true disappointment in the case was Chris's decision to return to her past planning practices when her curriculum no longer matched that of Anna and Jackie. Lacking the critical support provided by these two teachers, it is not surprising that Chris returned to her old ways. Chris had not reached the point where she felt comfortable planning for student-centered instruction by herself. However, because of her positive experiences with Anna and Jackie, I was surprised that Chris did not attempt to identify other collaborators via e-mail or even in her own school. Unable to find teacher collaborators, Chris could have turned to her students to play an increased role in planning. At the very least, her students could have served as sounding boards for her planning decisions. It is likely that Chris viewed her return to her old way of planning as easier because it was less time-consuming, did not rely on the involvement of others, and meant that she was in control. In returning to the old ways, Chris's focus was clearly on herself as the teacher and not on her students as learners. Questions that Chris likely grappled with in the weeks following the return to her old ways were: "How are my students dealing with my return to teacher-centered planning? How is it affecting their learning?" I wonder how she answered.

Resources to Consider

AskERIC lesson plans-science [On-line]. Available: http://ericr.syr.edu/Virtual/Lessons/Science/Index.html

This Web site is part of the personalized Internet-based service provided by the Educational Resources Information Center (ERIC) Clearinghouse on Information and Technology. It contains lesson plans on 12 science-related topics including biological and life sciences, careers, earth science, instructional issues, physical science, space sciences, and technology. As an example of the materials available, the biological and life sciences list contains 75 sets of lesson plans on different topics.

Lubber, J. (1994). **The process of planning for science learning.** In L. Schafter (Ed.), *Behind the methods class door: Educating elementary and middle school teachers in science. Association for the Education of Teachers in Science (AETS) yearbook* (pp. 47–53). Columbus, OH: ERIC Clearinghouse for Science, Mathematics, and Environmental Education.

In this chapter, James Lubber describes a model for lesson planning that highlights student-centered instruction. Undergirding the model are the epistemology of constructivism and assumptions about teaching and learning presented in the National Science Education Standards. Questions about science content, student understandings, instructional approaches, and assessment help to guide the reader through the maze of issues related to planning for student-centered instruction.

Peterson, C. (1997, November/December). **Why am I teaching this?** *Science Scope, 21,* 18–21.

> Planning extends far beyond preparing lessons in accordance with the district's curriculum guide, according to author Cyndie Peterson. Rather than teaching about atoms, as recommended by her district's curriculum guide, she questioned her students about their understandings. What she learned helped her think about how to structure her science curriculum to achieve the desired outcomes. Peterson describes the questions she asked students as well as details about how her planning changed to meet her students' learning needs.

Science Learning Network [On-line]. Available: http://www.sln.org/info/index.html

> Supported with funding from the National Science Foundation and UNISYS Corporation, this Web site is organized under four different headings and has a wealth of information for use in lesson planning. *Visit Our Museum* contains science inquiry resources developed by six science museums; *Connect with Schools and Educators* facilitates students' involvement in collaborative projects; *Check Our News and Links* provides linkages to science "hot lists" developed by museums, including San Francisco's Exploratorium; and *Exploring Our Resources* provides a wealth of inquiry-based resources on different science topics.

References

Fullan, M. G., & Steigelbauer, S. (1991). *The new meaning of educational change.* New York: Teachers College Press.

Gardner, H. (1997, November). *Multiple intelligences.* Keynote address at the annual conference of the National Middle School Association, Indianapolis, IN.

Pate, P. E., Homestead, E. R., & McGinnis, K. L. (1997). *Making integrated curriculum work: Teachers, students, and the quest for coherent curriculum.* New York: Teachers College Press.

Shepardson, D. P. (1996). Social interactions and the mediation of science learning in two small groups of first-graders. *Journal of Research in Science Teaching, 33,* 159–178.

Study gives Georgia curriculum mixed grades. (1998, March 11). *Athens Banner-Herald*, p. 10A.

Texley, J., & Wild, A. (1996). *NSTA pathways to the science standards.* Arlington, VA: NSTA.

Tippins, D. J., Nichols, S., & Tobin, K. (1993). Reconstructing science teacher education with communities of learners. *Journal of Science Teacher Education, 4,* 65–72.

VanCleave, J. (1991). *Physics for every kid.* New York: Wiley.

Vygotsky, L. S. (1978). *Mind in society: The development of higher psychological processes.* (M. Cole, V. John-Steiner, S. Scribner, & E. Souberman, Eds.). Cambridge: Harvard University Press.

Walpole, B. (1988). *175 science experiments to amuse and amaze your friends.* New York: Random House.

5

Organizing a Positive Learning Environment

I t is widely recognized that the learning environment plays an important role in the science teaching–learning process. Traditionally, the learning environment has been viewed in terms of physical space and the teacher's arrangement of facilities within the space (Loughlin & Suina, 1982). The size and shape of the classroom, the position of laboratory benches, adequate storage, and access to the out-of-doors establish the basic learning space. Within this space, the teacher arranges the active elements of the environment, such as furniture, displays, and materials, to make them responsive to students' learning needs. The teacher's strategic arrangement of the environment is a deliberate instructional decision, much as the selection of textbook and curriculum, and may encourage safety consciousness, indicate how materials are to be used, and lead to specific learning outcomes. Recently, this view of the learning environment has been expanded to encompass aspects of school and classroom climate, including the interactions among students, between teachers and students, and between teachers and their colleagues (Fraser, 1986). This expanded view recognizes the importance of fit between students' preferred learning environments and their academic success in science and feelings toward it (Fraser, 1994), and acknowledges that multiple types of messages are conveyed in the school science learning environment (Shapiro & Kirby, 1998).

Teachers' efforts to understand the science learning environments they create and the messages these environments send to students and classroom visitors have been greatly facilitated by semiotic interpretation. Semiotic interpretation involves critical analysis of messages conveyed by the signs and symbols present in the science learning environment (Shapiro, 1998). Central to this perspective is a consideration of how the science learning environment conveys meanings about science and science learning that are tied to and tend to perpetuate the beliefs and values of the dominant culture. To be sure, students construct different science understandings in a traditional science learning environment where text reading and verification laboratories are the norm compared to a constructivist-oriented one in which group problem-solving and community connectedness are important features of the culture. Whether the focus is the physical setting, arrangement of learning materials, or patterns of social interaction and support, teachers have much to consider when attempting to create positive and productive science learning environments.

The three cases included in this chapter emphasize different aspects of the science learning environment. The first case highlights how social interaction and support among teaching colleagues is central to a healthy learning environment. Specifically, this case illustrates what can happen when a middle school teacher's beliefs about what constitutes good science teaching are inconsistent with the beliefs held by teaching colleagues who represent the dominate culture in the school district. The second case shows how a beginning high school teacher's failure to attend to certain physical and managerial aspects of the science learning environment almost resulted in a serious chemical accident. The third case makes use of a novel format to introduce semiotic interpretation of the science learning environment. This case is organized as a set of eight key activities that focus on aspects of the science learning environment ranging from messages conveyed by the architecture of the school building and classroom to the rituals of student and teacher interactions. This case is best experienced not in its entirety at one point in time but as a personalized sequence of adventures into the many dimensions of the science learning environment.

Where's the Science?

Mark J. Volkmann

This closed case describes a dilemma faced by Juan Verde, a beginning teacher who uses student-centered, problem-posing pedagogy to teach seventh-grade science. Mark presents the case from the point of view of Luke Andrews, a teacher who is responsible for evaluating Juan's teaching performance. As revealed in the case, Juan helps students examine local issues by encouraging them to choose questions, design investigations, gather information, and develop creative presentations. Luke visits on the day students are giving their presentations. He likes what he sees but is troubled by what appears to be the absence of a school board-approved science curriculum. This case demonstrates how power and control issues impact curricular and pedagogical decisions and that beliefs about what constitutes good science teaching are philosophically and politically constructed.

L uke Andrews walked briskly out of the Winona Middle School central office and headed toward Juan Verde's classroom. Luke taught high school chemistry, but today he was visiting Juan's seventh-grade science classroom in his capacity as Chair of the Winona Community School District's Science Department. Part of the Chair's responsibilities include serving as a member of the evaluation team of all nontenured employees. This was Juan's first year of teaching, and Luke was assigned to head Juan's evaluation. Juan taught seventh-grade science in the newly erected science wing of Winona Middle School. The science wing consisted of three classrooms that opened into a shared conference/computer space, called the pod, which connected to the school library through a short hallway.

As Luke walked through the library, the fifth-period bell rang. Students poured out of the adjacent classrooms into the hallways. As he walked, he recalled that the last time he had visited the middle school was during Juan's job interview last summer. Three applicants had been chosen from a pool of 45 for the final round of interviews. Juan was selected as a finalist because he had excellent credentials and because the district wanted to increase the ethnic diversity of its faculty. The final decision was based on which applicant had the most potential as demonstrated by his or her teaching expertise. The three applicants were given a choice of topics and asked to develop a lesson to teach at the job interview. Juan chose the topic of water pollution. He furnished photocopies of a newspaper clipping about nitrate contamination of Winona's drinking water to each member of the committee. Then he initiated a series of activities to help participants clarify the problem by listing what they knew about the quality of their drinking water and what they wanted to find out. By the end of the demonstration, each participant had written a question he or she wanted to address.

Luke enjoyed the investigation of a local issue; however, he had wondered how well Juan's approach would work in a middle school classroom. Luke approached teaching more traditionally: He encouraged students to read the text and perform laboratory experiments associated with scientific principles. Luke also wondered how well Juan would get along with Jackie Finn and Warren Olson—the two veteran members of the middle school science staff. The committee chose Juan in spite of Luke's reluctance because they believed Juan's problem-posing approach would stimulate the science department to grow professionally. Luke believed that their choice also had a lot to do with the recent increases in the Latino population of Winona.

As Luke entered the pod, he surveyed the four new computer stations located along the walls between the classroom doorways. The one nearest Juan's door was occupied by students. Seeing no teachers in the pod, he wondered how their activities were being monitored. Just as Luke was about to enter the classroom, the door opened with a jerk and out popped a seventh-grade girl, who side-stepped Luke and dashed down the hallway to her locker. Luke, regaining his balance, entered the classroom. The room was nearly empty. One of the remaining students said Mr. Verde had taken a phone call. Luke made his way to a desk in the back. He surveyed the classroom and noticed how different Juan's room was from his own. The teacher's desk was in the back, instead of the front; student desks were arranged in small clusters, instead of neat rows; and the walls were covered with student drawings, posters, and charts, instead of the periodic table and posters of famous scientists. The drawing nearest him read: "United States bridges are in poor shape! What's the condition of the Winona suspension bridge?" Luke chuckled to himself at the drawing that showed snapped cables and crashed cars on the Winona suspension bridge.

Students began to enter the classroom and talk in small groups as Luke waited for Juan to appear. As he waited, he read the file he had picked up from the central office. It contained four documents: Juan's lesson plan for the week, a note from a university scientist, a complaint lodged by Finn and Olson, and a letter from a parent:

■ Today's lesson plan was brief. It read "presentation of student air and water pollution projects."

■ The note was from a scientist at the local state university. It was an e-mail response to questions asked by students from Mr. Verde's class about air and water standards.

■ The complaint dealt with noise and constant activity in Mr. Verde's class. According to Finn and Olson, Verde's students occupied the conference area and library more than they occupied the classroom.

■ The parent letter stated:

Dear Mr. Verde,

   I was truly surprised when you called last week and informed me of my son Mike's progress. It's the first time I've received *anything* positive from the school. With only one adult in the house, Mike has had to grow up fast. He fixes breakfast for the family (me and his younger brother, Alex). After school he looks after Alex and fixes dinner (I get home about 7:00). I know I depend on Mike more than I should, but Mike likes to be in charge, and I think that's why he likes your class. He told me that he's the leader of a team that's investigating the widening of Lindberg Road. He's very proud of that. I'm glad you're teaching at Winona Middle School. You've made a difference for Mike.

   Thanks,
   Pete Anderson

Luke looked up from the folder as the bell rang and Mr. Verde calmly entered the classroom. Students took their seats as the PA squawked announcements and Mr. Verde took roll. Juan introduced Mr. Andrews, then asked Lisa (the student who had earlier rushed out of the room) to introduce her group and their project. Mr. Verde sat at his desk as Lisa and her team assembled in front of the class:

LISA: (Standing) The question my group decided to investigate is "Why does the city want to widen Lindberg Road?" We chose this problem because everyone on my team either lives on Lindberg Road or lives near the wetland that Lindberg crosses. We have decided to have a mock hearing conducted by the city manager. Mike plays the role of the city manager, Lou is a conservationist, and I'm a home owner.

MIKE: The city is talking with state and federal agencies to get money to make improvements to Lindberg Road. The reason we are holding this meeting is to find out what the community thinks about this project. Lindberg Road is in lousy condition. It's got potholes and it's too narrow, and in the place where it crosses the wetland, it's sinking. Besides that, the number of cars on Lindberg Road is going to increase from 5,000 to 10,000 cars per day in the next 10 years. Unless we improve the road, it will not be safe.

LISA: What makes you think the number of cars will double in 10 years? Right now, our population is increasing at a rate of 2%. A 2% growth rate doubles the population every 35 years, not every 10 years. Why do you think the number of cars will increase by that amount?

MIKE: Because the state is planning to connect Highway 39 with Interstate 56. In 3 years, the traffic on Lindberg Road will increase because of this connection.

> LOU: As a resident of Winona, I agree that Lindberg Road should be repaired. But as a conservationist, I do not understand why the city wants to double the width of the road. This will damage the wetland.
>
> MIKE: If the city gets a grant from the federal government, they will pay up to 80% of the cost. But the federal government will only help if we're building a four-lane road. Federal assistance is unavailable for the repair of two-lane roads. The feds require us to replace every square foot of damaged wetland with 3 square feet of new wetland.

Luke was pleasantly surprised at how well these three understood the issues. Lindberg Road passed right by Luke's front door, yet these students understood the situation better than he did. However, Luke was somewhat dismayed because these students appeared to be learning more about social issues than they were about science. He wondered if Mr. Verde ever used the textbook.

Luke spent the remainder of the class observing groups present their investigation of local problems. Each group had chosen a different problem to investigate. Topics included Winona's superfund waste disposal site, nitrate contamination of the local water supply, failing bridges, wetland preservation, household carbon monoxide poisoning, household radon poisoning, and the future merchandising of electric cars by local car dealers.

After class, Luke interviewed Juan. He began by complimenting him: "The quality of the students' projects was fantastic, and their attention span and respect for one another were better than I have seen anywhere. However, I must tell you that I am deeply troubled by the absence of the district's science curriculum from these projects. Are you covering the topics?"

Juan responded, "Thank you for the compliments for my students. I have tried to teach them how to investigate questions that are interesting to them and important to the community. I have also worked on how they show respect to one another. I am sorry that you question what my students are learning. I feel that students learn science best when what they learn is connected to their own lives. I believe that, as students understand more and more about their community, they become more sophisticated and their understanding of the world and of science increases. I do not think that science can be taught solely from texts; furthermore, I believe that laboratory science is meaningful only when the experiment is relevant to the students' experience."

Juan's words burned in Luke's ears. Everything he valued about science teaching was being challenged by Juan's philosophy of science teaching. Luke thought to himself, if only the job committee had listened to me in the first place.

Later that night, as Luke wrote his observation summary, he neglected to repeat the compliment he had made to Mr. Verde about the quality of the student projects. Instead, he questioned the apparent absence of the district science curriculum from Mr. Verde's lesson plans. In addition, he cited the note from Finn and Olson, his near collision with a student before class, Mr. Verde's last-minute arrival to class, and the general commotion in the classroom as evidence of poor classroom management. He suggested that Mr. Verde work closely with Ms. Finn and Mr. Olson to develop better classroom management strategies. Furthermore, he recommended noise level checks outside of Mr. Verde's classroom and follow-up observation sessions to make sure Verde conformed to district science curriculum guidelines.

Questions for Reflection and Discussion

1. Juan does not use a textbook but focuses his instruction on local issues. Are students learning science in Juan's class? Support your response.

2. Examine The National Science Education Standards (National Research Council, 1996) for grades 5 to 8 (pp. 143–172). In what ways is Juan's teaching representative of these standards? As you reflect on Luke's visit and his conversation with Juan, how would you edit Luke's evaluation of Juan?

3. Compare the way Luke taught science and the way Juan taught science. What kinds of students might be advantaged and disadvantaged in each teacher's classroom? Is one approach better than the other? Is one approach better for certain "types" of students than the other? Should both approaches be used in the same classroom? School? School district?

4. What are the qualities of a good science teacher? While reflecting on this question, imagine you are Juan, and describe the qualities of a good teacher, then imagine you are Luke, and describe the qualities of a good science teacher. What qualities are present in both descriptions? Can one teacher embody both approaches?

■   ■   ■

Important Goals of Project-Centered Teaching

James J. Gallagher

This case has special relevance to me, as I have been part of a project to initiate the form of teaching that is represented, and we have had to answer the question "Where's the science?" many times. As in Volkmann's case, the conflict often arises between people in authority, such as Luke Andrews, with strongly held, traditional views of what should constitute science, and people who recognize that traditional approaches have been effective with only a small proportion of students. Moreover, innovators like Juan Verde base their approach on the premise that students actually learn and retain more from engaging in meaningful activities that allow them to use science in addressing real problems than from traditional, text-centered approaches.

How can we justify the form of teaching and learning that Juan Verde is providing for his students? What do students actually learn from approaches like these? The answer lies in clarity of goals in the teachers' mind. Studies we have done in classrooms where teachers are using project-centered approaches to teach about environmental issues show great variations in clarity of teachers' goals (Wheeler, Gallagher, McDonough, & Sookpokakit-Namfa, 1997). For some teachers, the purpose is mainly to engage students in problems of local interest. Other teachers go beyond this basic goal to have students collect information and then use it to foster understanding of the problem and possible solutions. Still others include these two goals and add a third goal: to comprehend the problem and each of the alternative solutions from a scientific and social perspective. To reach this third goal requires understanding of, and the ability to apply, the science that pertains to the problem and the proposed solutions. This is a tall order, since most practical problems are complex, demanding interdisciplinary understanding that is uncommon in our culture.

From the brief description in this case, it is probable that Juan Verde has a clear understanding of the first two goals, and it appears that he has helped his students realize them. However, it does not appear that he has addressed the third goal. Thus, Luke Andrews's concerns are valid, even though achievement of the third goal is difficult.

In our work with 23 experienced middle school teachers (Wheeler et al., 1997), we found a range of development across these three goals. We also found change with time, as teachers learned more about the substantive content of the environmental questions contained within the project, and as they became more confident in their ability to implement the new teaching methods. In this project, middle school students and their teachers studied forest-related environmental problems by collecting data in their local communities, often by interviewing adults and working with them to find and implement solutions to the problems.

What did students learn from this work? We interviewed more than 100 students about their answer to the question, and the common responses were as follows:

- We learned how to ask questions that would give us sound information about forests and forest-related problems in our community.
- We learned to organize information and make presentations to large groups of adults at community meetings.
- We became more confident in our ability to talk with adults individually and at group meetings.
- We understood school subjects better and learned how to apply what we learned in our own community.
- We found school more useful and interesting.
- We were motivated to learn more than we had learned in the past and to apply that knowledge to resolve our community's problems.

Students attained the confidence and these abilities even though not all of the teachers reached the third goal. However, we continue to strive toward helping teachers and students attain greater understanding of the science that underlies the problems and possible solutions. Importantly, in our project, we were very careful to focus only on forest-related problems, in spite of the temptation to add a range of other concerns that faced the communities. We did this to allow teachers and students to develop the scientific knowledge needed to understand the problem more thoroughly and to avoid superficial treatment of it.

Juan Verde's students show promise of attaining achievements similar to those in our study. He certainly has affected their interest and motivation in ways that are not common in traditional science classes. However, he could be more effective if he were to give greater attention to helping students become more knowledgeable and articulate about the scientific principles that underlie the problems he is addressing. To improve the focus on the science, he will need to work with each specific environmental problem and address each environmental problem in a more detailed way. Taking on six very different problems may have motivational benefits, but the range of scientific principles that pertain to these problems makes for an unmanageable task for both teacher and students.

■ ■ ■

Help Can Sometimes Lead to Problematic Situations

William Veal

In this closed case, William describes a situation in which Herman Jackson, a new teacher, seeks help from a more experienced colleague to select a chemistry laboratory for his class. Herman is a composite of many high school teachers William has taught alongside over the years. In the process of determining that one particular laboratory is better than another for ease of preparation and completion, Herman fails to consider appropriate safety measures. His oversight almost results in a student being seriously injured. Commentaries are provided by William and by Darwin Smith, a university chemist and chemical educator.

At the end of a long week, Herman Jackson was looking through his notes to plan and prepare for the next chapter. He had just finished teaching the chapter on equations and mass relations and was beginning to organize his ideas for the next section on gas laws. As a first-year teacher with three preparations, Herman did not have much time to think about labs. He was familiar with the content of the next chapter and recognized the importance of engaging students in laboratory experiences but had not identified labs that he felt would help his students learn about gases. Since the chapter test for chemical equations and mass relations would be given on Tuesday of next week, Herman had only 5 days to prepare. He wanted to plan some good yet simple laboratory experiments that were easy to set up and did not take a great deal of class time.

As he thought about the concepts addressed in the chapter, Herman remembered that carbon dioxide could be generated by heating copper (II) carbonate ($CuCO_3$). He remembered doing labs in college in which oxides were burned or heated. Another lab Herman remembered from college centered on the determination of the gas constant R. These were good labs and left an impression on his understanding of the concepts of gas laws and stoichiometry. He wondered if he could use some of the same labs with his general chemistry class.

Herman felt that he needed some help to find the right labs for his students. Since he did not have the college lab manuals, he consulted Clarence Norton, a chemistry teacher in the classroom across the hall. Clarence had been teaching for more than 25 years at the same rural high school and had collected and saved a myriad of chemistry laboratory manuals. Some of these manuals dated back to when the school was built in 1964. Herman asked Clarence whether he had any good, easy labs to help his students understand properties of gases and gas laws. With a big grin on his face, Clarence said, "Sure Herman, let me show you an experiment that I have been using since I began teaching."

Clarence went to his reference bookcase and found some laboratory manuals for general chemistry. The first manual was *Laboratory Manual of General Chemistry* by C. H. Sorum (1963). He had done many experiments from this manual in past years and thought that he could find a lab on gases for Herman to use. Experiment 16 involved heating different oxides to determine the rate of oxygen release and the creation of molecular oxygen from solid compounds. "Here is a pretty good one, but you have to check to see if we have the supplies and chemicals," offered Clarence as he put on his reading glasses. "You will need ring stands, clamps, test tubes, and Bunsen burners."

"The equipment is easy to find," responded Herman, "but finding mercury (II) oxide (HgO), silver oxide (Ag_2O), and lead (II) oxide (PbO), might present some problems."

While Herman looked for the chemicals in the stockroom, Clarence decided to look for another possible laboratory on gases. The second manual he consulted was *Laboratory Experiments for Brown and Lemay* by Nelson and Kemp (1985). Clarence was familiar with the textbook by Brown and Lemay (1990) because he had used it with his advanced placement chemistry class several years ago. Experiment 12 is entitled *Determination of R: The Gas-Law Constant*. Clarence thought that this would be a good laboratory to help students understand the significance of the gas constant *R*. It involved heating a mixture of potassium chlorate ($KClO_3$) and manganese oxide (MnO) to generate molecular oxygen (O_2). Herman noticed the warning label about not touching the solid mixture to the rubber stopper, because it might cause a "severe explosion," but he thought that it would not be a problem as long as the students were careful.

Not only did Clarence have a good reference library of chemistry books and laboratory manuals, he also had a stockpile of chemicals. Many of the bottles of chemicals had been purchased 15 years earlier during the renovation of the east wing and science area. As Herman searched the shelves of Clarence's storeroom, he found all the chemicals he needed for Sorum's Experiment 16 and Experiment 12 from the Nelson and Kemp book. The bottle containing the potassium chlorate ($KClO_3$) was dusty, and the lid was ajar, and the one containing the mercury (II) oxide (HgO) had a faded label, which was barely readable, but the contents of both bottles looked okay.

After collecting needed chemicals, Herman spent the next couple of hours preparing trays and apparatuses for the two labs. He inserted all of the glass rods into the rubber stoppers so the students would not have to spend time on this task. On his way home from school, he reflected on the labs his students would soon be doing. They were easy to set up and clean up would be a breeze with the students' help. He was happy with his choices. Yes, there were always safety concerns, but he had done these exact same experiments in college.

The following Thursday arrived. The students were coming into class for first period. All of the equipment and chemicals were ready in the laboratory area. Herman had briefed the students on the particulars of the lab the day before, and the students had prepared their lab books for recording data.

Sharon, a junior, entered the room talking with her friends. She was not prepared. She had forgotten to read the laboratory procedure for homework, including the part about safety precautions. The lab that they were doing was the *Determination of R: The Gas-Law Constant*. Although Herman had introduced the gas laws the day before, he emphasized once again that the purpose of today's lab was to investigate the origin of the gas constant, *R*.

He went on to explain, "To determine the gas constant, oxygen (O_2) is to be prepared by the decomposition of potassium chlorate ($KClO_3$), using manganese dioxide (MnO_2) as a catalyst. By using the ideal-gas law and van der Waals' equation with measured values of pressure, temperature, volume, and number of moles of an enclosed sample of oxygen (O_2), the gas constant can be determined."

After explaining the purpose of the lab, Herman reviewed the relevant procedures and safety precautions. He emphasized that the solids should not come into contact with the rubber stopper, goggles were to be worn at all times, and solids should not be heated quickly or at high temperatures. Sharon was busy copying her friend's prelab exercises and did not hear the review.

As the students began the lab, Sharon's lab partner, Karla, weighed the potassium chlorate ($KClO_3$) and placed the sample on the lab bench. Sharon's attention was elsewhere, and when she turned she inadvertently knocked the weighing tray, resulting in some solid being spilled on the lab bench. While Karla was not looking, Sharon decided to quickly pick up the spilled solid by pinching the small amount in her fingers. Karla slowly added the solid into the test tube. After the potassium chlorate ($KClO_3$) was added, Sharon added a small amount of manganese oxide (MnO). As Karla began to heat the mixture in the test tube, Sharon felt a burning sensation on her fingertips. She quickly called for Herman, who wasn't quite sure what to do except to wash her hands. After washing her hands for 5 minutes with soap and water, the burning Sharon felt in her fingertips began to subside.

Questions for Reflection and Discussion

1. What could Herman have done to ensure that Sharon was not burned?

2. How did the help provided by Clarence possibly contribute to Sharon's injury?

3. How and when should science teachers learn about the safe handling, storage, and use of chemicals?

4. Who should be responsible for monitoring the safe storage and use of chemicals in secondary schools? How might this monitoring occur?

5. What kinds of information might a beginning science teacher seek from a more senior colleague?

6. If a beginning teacher is uncomfortable with the suggestions offered by a veteran teacher, where might he or she go for a second opinion?

■ ■ ■

Laboratory Safety Is Every Teacher's Responsibility

William Veal

Many experiments that have been stalwarts in the chemistry laboratory have recently been replaced by ones that use less harmful and dangerous chemicals. The reason for this is an increased awareness of the safety hazards associated with certain chemicals and laboratory procedures. Two factors of safety awareness seem to have contributed to the problem Herman encountered in this case. One, veteran teachers may not be familiar with recently introduced laboratory safety regulations and precautions. Second, it is often assumed that beginning teachers, having studied or majored in science, are knowledgeable about all aspects of chemical safety.

I believe that there are two possible solutions to the case. First, schools and school districts should establish means of communication to ensure that all science teachers learn about new regulations and standards put out by Occupational Safety and Health Administration (OSHA). This must involve more than just learning how to file Material Safety Data Sheet (MSDS) papers into a three-ring binder and alphabetizing the chemicals in the storeroom. Updated laboratory experiments should be made available at locations in the schools accessible to science teachers. Also, with the multitude of Internet resources currently available, teachers should learn how to access MSDS information at various chemical supply houses. For example, through the Fisher Scientific Web site *(http://www.fisher1.com/catalogs/index.html),* teachers can access the MSDS for almost any chemical by simply typing in the chemical name and clicking a button.

Second, beginning teachers should become familiar with safety concerns that they may encounter in teaching. One way to do so is to make use of cases that address chemical safety, and another is to invite university safety and disposal personnel to speak with beginning teachers about such topics as standard laboratory safety procedures, proper chemical disposal, and handling of chemical spills in the laboratory. Safety is a topic that teachers cannot know too much about. Many schools have old and potentially dangerous chemicals stored in science classrooms and storage areas. All science teachers should become aware of the potential dangers associated with the chemicals stored and used in their schools.

Beginning teachers also should carefully consider the advice and experiments passed down from veteran teachers. Some experiments used in the past may not be considered safe for school use today. For example, a very popular experiment used to simulate a volcanic eruption involves combining ammonium dichromate, potassium permanganate, and a small amount of glycerin. The glycerin is dropped on the potassium permanganate, which causes a flame, which then ignites the ammonium dichromate. New safety warnings state that these chemicals are carcinogenic and advise teachers of the possibility of explosion when they are mixed together.

Chemical safety is an important part of any science teacher's education. Most beginning teachers can benefit from additional instruction on chemical safety. When planning laboratory experiences, teachers need to spend the extra time required to become familiar with the safety precautions that may prevent an injury like the one suffered by Sharon or a more serious injury.

■ ■ ■

Thoughtful Science Safety

Darwin W. Smith

William's case illustrates the need for better safety training for chemistry teachers. Mandt (1993) and Moore (1990) reported several years ago that very few of the high school teachers in their states had received any formal safety training. While the situation has probably improved in recent years due to OSHA's increased emphasis on laboratory safety (Geriovich, 1992), there is a continuing need for those of us who teach chemistry to upgrade our practices. Older teachers were trained when much less emphasis was placed on safety practices in college and high school labs, and old laboratory manuals leave much to be desired. This increased awareness of safety issues in recent years has resulted in better training for new teachers and the use of safer chemicals in laboratory experiments.

The following checklist may help teachers reflect on the issues raised in the case and to clarify their own thoughts about labs. The key factor is to recognize that it is the duty of everyone involved in the education of teachers and the teaching of students at all levels to develop good habits and attitudes toward safety.

1. Prepare a one-page list of safety precautions for your students, and hold them responsible for following it. See, for example, the safety rules used at the University of Kentucky and available at their Web site (www.chem.uky.edu/Courses/che450g/safety/).

2. Become familiar with the laboratory safety standards and procedures of your school and school district. If these are absent or incomplete, take action to remedy this situation.

3. Supplement your school's regulations by reading articles on safety. For example, see the safety tips section in the annual index of *The Journal of Chemical Education* for articles such as that written by Hunsley (1995).

4. If selecting demonstrations or experiments from lab manuals, be sure that they incorporate up-to-date safety procedures.

5. Read the MSDS for the chemicals you are using. Pay particular attention to safe storage, handling, and disposal. Links to Internet sites containing MSDS information can be found at www.ilpi.com/msds/index.chtml.

6. Review procedures for accidents and emergencies. Know the emergency telephone number for your site.

Creating Objects of Meaning in Science

Bonnie Shapiro

In this novel case, Bonnie introduces semiotic interpretation as a way of looking at what goes on in science classrooms based on an understanding of the values and beliefs of the dominant culture within a society. Then, through eight activities, she shows how semiotic interpretation can be used to create science learning environments that give significant lessons to learners about the meaning and value of science. The first three activities ask the participant to identify important science learning goals and consider how the goals might be communicated to students within a science learning environment, while the last five activities engage the participant in constructive critique of the signs and symbols of science learning environments, as described and captured in photographs.

As a science teacher educator, I work with colleagues to help beginning and veteran teachers learn new ways to engage learners in understanding the nature of science, the ideas of science, and the meaning of science in their lives. With a reduction in the number of hours we are able to spend with student teachers in our teacher-preparation program, we have been faced with a dilemma:

How can we maximize the impact of the science learning experience by creating environments that speak significant messages to learners about the meaning and value of science?

I have discovered that my own efforts to address this problem with colleagues in the university setting have been very similar to work that student teachers and practicing teachers do in their school setting. This work has led to discussion, research, and analysis of learning settings to better understand how the science learning environments we create function as *message-giving systems* that speak to learners about the nature of science, about how learning science proceeds there, and about the meaning of science in our daily lives. I have found that both practicing teachers and teachers in preparation have benefited from considering classrooms and the activities that occur within using a perspective called semiotic interpretation.

The particular way of looking at what occurs in classroom settings that semiotics offers is based on the recognition that the values and beliefs of the dominant culture within a society influence the organization of its educational systems. For example, the ways that school buildings are designed and constructed serve our culture's need to establish the rules and standards of behavior within those settings. The buildings themselves exemplify cultural values. The buildings are also places where we attempt to perpetuate those values through the organization of what takes place within the walls. Cultural values and beliefs are embodied in the artifactual world of the classroom but also through the ways that we organize the conversations, discussions, and interactions that take place in those settings. From the ways that we organize desks and seating arrangements to the rituals of interaction we engage in, to the placement of posters on bulletin boards, we are using resources from our language and culture that send messages and meanings about science to learners. It is not only through the physical spaces of the classroom that we send meaning to learners; the ways that we encourage them to speak with us and with one another also send powerful messages about the subjects we are teaching.

Through this case narrative, I attempt to engage you in thinking about the value of approaching planning for teaching and learning through a critique of learning goals and environments. The case presents an introduction to the field of semiotics and offers a consideration of the value of using a semiotic interpretive perspective through the insights and developing understandings of several student teachers. Through these student teachers' eyes, I hope that you will consider some of your own experiences in science learning settings and will, through the activities integrated into the case, discuss some of the important messages of science learning that exist in the environments that we create for students.

Through recognizing how the environment exists as a text of learning for students, you may be inspired to make greater use of this learning medium to more powerfully organize signs and symbols of science into messages within the environment so that they become *objects of meaning* in the learning setting. This insight also allows a critique of science learning environments.

When we engage in a critique of learning, we look critically at what educators do and suggest alternatives—better ways of doing things and new ways of thinking about what we do. Looking for ideal approaches can make us critical of what we see happening, and this is a good thing for anyone's developing practice. It is also important when we apply new ideas to what occurs in school settings to distinguish constructive critique from destructive criticism. The purpose of this critique is to learn new ways of thinking about how the goals of science learning are embodied through the sign and message systems learned in our culture that are lived out through our behaviors and the kinds of learning settings that we create.

What Is Semiotics?

Recognition of the need to study sign systems and understand the meaning of systems of signification is a relatively recent phenomenon. It is helpful to begin by considering how our culture is a reserve of ideas and information that serves as a resource for actions that are used daily to communicate with one another. To the semiotician, all cultural phenomena are essentially processes of producing and interpreting signs and symbols. Semiotics asks questions about meaning, knowledge, and knowing through the use of signs and sign systems.

We often engage in research and thinking about what goes on in classrooms by asking the question, "What are the particular ways that teachers and students work together in the construction of knowledge?" A semiotic view adds an additional perspective by asking the question, "How are the ways that teachers and students work together in learning communities representative of the values and activities of the larger culture?" The values and beliefs of the dominant culture within a society serve to establish the rules and standards of behavior within those settings. These values and beliefs are *embodied* in the artifactual world of the school setting. Within this world are *objects* of significance and meaning, from the organization of students' desks to the ways that the teacher interacts with students and they with her.

Consider the student who comes into the classroom from another culture. This learner not only must learn new subject matter but also must master the language of the culture and the daily customs and rules of social interaction taken for granted by students who grow up in the dominant culture. But even students who have been born into the dominant culture are usually unfamiliar with a scientific perspective on the world. Despite this, they are expected to integrate, if not wholly adopt, scientific views about phenomena.

Among the important goals of schooling are not only the consumption of the sign and symbol systems of the culture but the development of the ability to create and use sign and symbol systems. When we grasp the complex ways that we use sign and symbol messages, we gain powerful insights into the ways that we communicate with and expect learners to communicate with us. The school setting itself is an expression of forms of action and of the ideas about how action will proceed. When viewed semiotically, the science classroom can be analyzed as interweaving sets of sign, symbol, and signification systems that students learn as texts of science. The approach used to analyze these systems is called *semiotic interpretation*. It is based on the recognition that the learning environment that we create and even the way we are with our students speak a significant message about what science is, about how it proceeds, and the extent to which it is accessible to the nonscientist. Through thinking semiotically, and as we examine the nature of these messages, we will consider ways that we might extend and enhance the messages of science in your own classroom.

Activity 1: Goals of Science Teaching

Get together with a small group of colleagues to create a list of 10 of the most important goals of science teaching that you believe should be conveyed to middle-school students. To help you get started, here are some examples written by groups who completed this exercise:

> "Science is an active process involving observation and the development of problem-solving skills."

> "The male and female and members of any race may make equally significant contributions to investigations in science."

> "There are certain ideas in each field of science that must be grasped by learners."

Objects of Meaning in the Science Learning Environment

It is important to keep in mind the goals of science learning, such as those that you have identified as you begin to consider creating science learning environments of your own. As part of my own work to explore the nature of school science learning culture, I have entered a variety of school settings to document the types of messages conveyed in school science learning environments.

Some settings have science laboratories set aside exclusively for science teaching and learning. In other school buildings, science takes place in an assortment of settings within the school, conveying a message about the interdisciplinary nature of science and science learning or about the lack of emphasis given to science learning.

Another kind of message in the learning environment is in the patterns of interaction carried out by teachers and students. Many forms of interaction are repeated as regular patterns of discourse behavior in classroom settings. For example, in our culture, students learn to raise their hand when they want to speak. The performance of this ritual signals an acceptance of this form of interaction and speaks messages to learners about who may talk and when in the classroom. In the science learning setting, patterns in rituals indicate to learners who has the answers in science, who is allowed to ask the questions, and whose ideas and thinking are valued. Patterns that we see in discourse and interaction in a classroom also deliver powerful messages about science. For example, is there a pattern of question asking and response giving in the classroom in which the teacher is the only one with the questions and the answers, or do pupils ask and have an opportunity to answer questions of their own?

The enactment of policy decisions speaks about the importance of science in the school curriculum. This message is conveyed not only to students but to teachers, parents, and other members of the community. Policy decisions at the national, school board, and local school level determine the amount of time and money that is spent on science, delivering another message about the importance of the subject to teachers, students, and members of the community.

To help further understand what is meant by a semiotic interpretive study of the messages of learning, it is worthwhile to consider ways that room arrangements speak about how learning will take place in a setting. Messages are spoken through the furniture and architecture of the learning setting. Desks organized in groupings or individually and separate from one another speak, for example, about whether discussion is to be encouraged or discouraged, whether equipment is to be shared, or whether the focus will be on the teacher or on students and their activities. Another example involves a consideration of the ways that bulletin boards and wall space are used. Are posters placed on walls to fill an empty space, or is material carefully selected for the messages it conveys about science?

Activity 2: Message Forms

Now that you have completed your own list of science learning goals in Activity 1, describe some of the forms that messages might take by developing a set of categories of messages using the following headings:

> Architectural messages
>
> Text and curriculum messages
>
> Social/behavioral messages
>
> School policy messages

For example, under the heading *architectural messages,* you might state "Organization of the building—special space for science instruction." Under the heading *text and curriculum messages,* you might list "The presentation, images from textbooks, or people engaged in scientific activities."

Which of the goals that you identified in Activity 1 might be conveyed through architectural messages? Which might be conveyed through text and curriculum messages? social/behavioral messages? school policy messages?

Activity 3: Creating Objects of Meaning

For each goal identified in Activity 1, offer a specific suggestion to create a means of speaking about the message of that goal to learners.

Awakening to Objects of Meaning in Science Learning Environments

Activities 4 to 8, which follow, provide an opportunity to consider a number of learning events and objects of meaning that may be used to speak significant messages about science in school settings. The purpose of the activities is to encourage discussion about these objects and to raise the discussion to the level of a critique of the signs and symbols that we all read in science learning settings. It is the constructive critique that we seek in these conversations as contrasted with a destructive criticism of efforts to create learning environments. A constructive critique challenges our values and goals and the approaches we use to accomplish them in an effort to awaken us to the kinds of messages we create in the classroom setting.

To stimulate discussion and to provide an example of the kind of comments that others have made, I provide excerpts from a discussion held by a small group of student teachers. These excerpts are designed to stimulate discussion in your own groups about possible messages embodied in the activities and ways that we set up learning environments, and to serve as an example of the kind of discussion that might take place within your own group.

Activity 4: Photograph of Students' Mealworm Container Display

The photograph in Figure 5.1 shows vials of mealworm larvae that have been placed on a shelf in a middle school classroom. Students have been working with the mealworms as part of a unit on insect development. This photograph was taken after students spent one session with the mealworms, making observations in science notebooks. Each pupil has placed his or her own mealworm in a vial labeled with his or her initials. Science class takes place on Tuesdays and Thursdays from 2:00 to 2:45 PM. Examine the photograph as you read the excerpts from the student teachers' small group discussion, and then answer the questions that follow.

Excerpts From the Student Teachers' Small Group Discussion: Linnea was the first to comment, "It seems as though one of the messages might be that science is active, ongoing, and messy. Because things are so disordered, though, it might suggest that it is awfully disorganized. The strongest lingering message that I recall from labs is the sterility of everything and the smell of formalde-

FIGURE 5.1 Students' meal-worm container display.

hyde. This display shows what learners are doing in a more friendly and inviting way. They come over to pick up the mealworms, and look at them, and hopefully talk about them. This would say to me that I, as a student, am doing science."

Marc pointed out that the labeling of the vials showed that there was concern that they be identified in a systematic way. He suggested that perhaps the date might be placed on the vials so that students could monitor and chart daily changes in their notebooks. Then Marc added a different view: "To me it says that it is okay to put living things in little bottles and poke them and prod away. I don't like that message, because it says that science can do anything it wants with animals and other living things without any consideration for their well-being. I don't like that being the message for students."

Shiraz pointed out that it was exciting to see live creatures in the classroom and that involving the students in discussions about what was happening in their development showed an interest in having students share their ideas with one another, much the way that science proceeds. Shiraz also pointed out that the display was not really a display at all, but that the vials with larvae seemed placed on the shelf as an afterthought—without care, that other things were on the shelf and were hastily pushed to the side. Shiraz suggested that more could be done to speak a message of care and organization by having a better space cleared away. He suggested that the bottles be labeled with individual students' names and dates and times to keep a better record of the development of the larvae.

Linnea noted that a list of students' questions from the small-group discussion could be placed near the mealworms. Doing this might help to emphasize the importance of the activity. Magnifying equipment could also be stored nearby so that students would be encouraged to make closer, careful observations.

Marc said that it was exciting to see pupils working with what he called real resources. "If I were a student in this classroom, I would be thrilled to think of science as a topic that could be studied not just from the textbook but from using real resources. There must be some ways that the teacher could help deliver the message that animals must always be treated with care. I think that that is one of the problems with a lot of science classes, and that is how the negative message that you can just kill and dissect animals whenever you want to sometimes gets across."

> What are your views on the kinds of messages about science and science learning that might be conveyed through the mealworm activity and display?

> How might you, in your role as teacher in the classroom, enhance and extend the quality of messages about science and science learning for students through this mealworm activity and the display of student vials?

Activity 5: Rituals of Interaction as Objects of Meaning

In school settings, participants often use and observe recognizable dialogue patterns and routines that learners experience as part of the culture of schooling. These patterns tell students that this is school and that there are rules of speaking and interacting that serve as cultural rules, letting students know that they may speak at certain times and in certain ways. These patterns or rituals of dialogue or actions can be analyzed as interaction structures that tell students not only how communication will proceed in classrooms but something about the ways that knowledge in a field is generated. Teachers may use signals and teach learners to interpret and use signals to send messages about how communication will take place. For example, teachers may begin a class by standing at the front of a room with a certain expression or hand signal indicating that the class is ready to begin. Or they may use certain interaction structures that serve as messages about how talk will take place during different subject matter discussions. Consider the very typical pattern of interaction in science class that we have all experienced. The teacher asks a question and looks for students to respond. Students who are interested in responding give a signal such as raising their hand. The teacher calls on a student, and the students put their hands down, and everyone listens to the respondent. Here is an example:

Ms. Lewis:	All right, we will move on now into some ideas about what it is about the structure that keeps the ball up. Who has an idea about how this works? Who knows? Hands up. (Several students raise hands. Teacher looks around.) Marcus.
Marcus:	I think that the way that the lower part of the structure is spread out wider makes it stronger at the bottom. Then we just build on that up to the point of breaking, um, we sort of need to stop then when things don't hold up any longer.
Ms. Lewis:	Good idea. Good response. You're on the right track. Does anyone else have an answer? (Several more students raise hands. Teacher looks around again.)

The sole reliance on this interaction structure speaks several messages about how learning takes place in the classroom and how knowledge is held in the field of science itself. The form of teacher asks a question, seeks response from students with hands raised, and student responds to question speaks messages about who has the answers in the classroom and who asks the questions, about who is permitted to ask questions and direct and organize inquiry in science.

What other kinds of messages are conveyed through the ways that interaction and communication settings are organized in school environments?

Describe a different pattern of classroom interaction that would send different messages to learners about how discussion in science might proceed. What will be the messages of science learning in the environments that you create in your classroom? What will you do to create these messages?

FIGURE 5.2   Small-group discussion.

Activity 6: Learning Groups

The groups shown in Figure 5.2 are in the first stages of a discussion of their plans for building the highest paper tower possible to support a golf ball.

> What messages about science might be conveyed to students working on such a problem in small groups such as this?

> What other sorts of groupings and seating arrangements are possible in the science classroom? List at least three. What messages about science might be conveyed in each setting you describe?

Activity 7: On School and Classroom Walls

The images on school and classroom walls are powerful sources of messages to students about science and science learning. Complete the following tasks as you consider the photographs shown in Figures 5.3 to 5.6.

Figure 5.3 is a display of athletic trophies located at a high school entrance. Figure 5.4 shows posters of students' research projects. Figure 5.5 shows the periodic table of the elements displayed on a wall in a seventh-grade physical science classroom. The periodic table is not a specific topic of study in the students' program. The aquarium shown in Figure 5.6 is located in a corner of an eighth-grade classroom surrounded by equipment boxes. The aquarium

FIGURE 5.3   School entrance trophy case.

FIGURE 5.4   Display of students' research projects.

FIGURE 5.5 Periodic table of the elements.

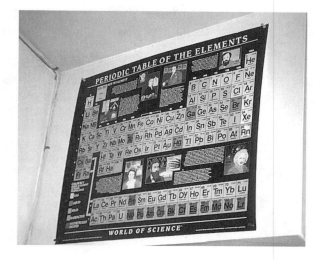

FIGURE 5.6 Hidden aquarium.

contains six goldfish (two varieties) and is not used in conjunction with a particular aspect of the stated curriculum.

Discuss the types of messages conveyed in each photograph about what science is, how it proceeds, and how accessible it is to students.

Refer to the list of goals you generated in Activity 1. How do the images assist or obstruct in sending the messages that you have identified?

Make suggestions as to how the messages of the display or image might be enhanced.

Activity 8: Conducting Semiotic Interpretive Studies

With a small group of peers, visit a university or school science classroom.

Select an example from each large category you developed in Activity 2. Interpret the types of messages that are available to you about science in an analysis of this classroom setting. Present a constructive critique to your peers of the messages and meanings available for science learners in this setting. In your critique, pay close attention to the particular needs of the population of students in that setting.

What will be the messages of science in the learning environments you will create in your classroom? What will you do to create these messages?

Resources to Consider

CHE 450G **Accident Procedures**. Department of Chemistry, University of Kentucky [On-line]. Available: http://www.chem.uky.edu/Courses/che450g/safety/

This Web site provides guidance to prevent laboratory accidents and answers questions about what to do if accidents happen. Accidents for which safety procedures are described include cuts, burns, toxic gas inhalation, chemicals splashed in the eyes, and laboratory fires. The site also includes a sample safety release form.

Fisher, D., Henderson, D., & Fraser, B. (1997, April). **Laboratory environments and student outcomes in senior high school biology**. *The American Biology Teacher, 59,* 214–219.

This article provides background information about research on science classroom environments and reports on one study of student perceptions of the laboratory classroom learning environment. The findings indicate that students' attitudes and achievement are affected by their perceptions of the classroom laboratory environment. The *Science Laboratory Environment Inventory* (SLEI) is present in its entirety in an appendix following the report.

Gallard, A., & Tippins, D. (1994). **Language diversity and science learning: The need for a critical system of meaning**. In McLeod, B. (Ed.), *Language and learning: Educating linguistically diverse students.* Albany, NY: State University of New York Press. (State University of New York Press, State University Plaza, Albany, NY 12246)

This chapter uses vignettes to illustrate some complex issues involved in developing learning environments suitable for students with a first language other than English.

Shapiro, B., & Kirby, D. (1998). **A semiotic reading of the messages of science learning in a school science learning environment**. *Journal of Science Teacher Education, 9,* 221–240.

Bonnie Shapiro and David Kirby discuss the variety of semiotic messages that students receive about the culture of science in their science classes. A significant feature of the article is a list of the types of messages in the science learning environment, including architectural messages, text and curriculum messages, social and behavioral messages, and messages associated with school and district policies.

References

Brown, T. L., & Lemay, H. E. (1990). *Chemistry: The central science*. Upper Saddle River, NJ: Prentice Hall.

Fraser, B. J. (1986). *Classroom environment*. London: Broom Helm.

Fraser, B. J. (1994). Research on classroom and school climate. In D. L. Gabel (Ed.), *Handbook of research on science teaching and learning* (pp. 493–541). New York: Macmillan.

Geriovich, J. A. (1992). OSHA's new chemical lab standard and its impact on school science laboratories. *Journal of Chemical Education, 69,* 643–644.

Hunsley, J. R. (1995). The chemical hygiene plan. *Journal of Chemical Education, 72,* 543–544.

Loughlin, C. E., & Suina, J. H. (1982). *The learning environment*. New York: Teachers College Press.

Mandt, D. K. (1993). Teaching the teachers lab safety. *Journal of Chemical Education, 70,* 59–61.

Moore, J. T. (1990). A course in laboratory and stockroom management. *Journal of Chemical Education, 67,* 166.

National Research Council (1996). National Science Education Standards. Washington, DC: National Academy Press.

Nelson, J. H., & Kemp, K. C. (1985). *Laboratory experiments for Brown and Lemay*. Upper Saddle River, NJ: Prentice Hall.

Shapiro, B. (1998). Reading the furniture: Broadening the notion of text in semiotic analysis. In K. Tobin & B. Fraser (Eds.), *International handbook of science education* (pp. 609–621). Dordrecht: Kluwer.

Shapiro, B., & Kirby, D. (1998). A semiotic reading of the messages of science learning in a school science learning culture. *Journal of Science Teacher Education, 9,* 221–240.

Sorum, C. H. (1963). *Laboratory manual of general chemistry*. Upper Saddle River, NJ: Prentice Hall.

Wheeler, C., Gallagher, J., McDonough, M., & Sookpokakit-Namfa, B. (1997). Improving school-community relations in Thailand. In W. Cummings & P. Altbach (Eds.), *The challenge of Eastern Asian education: Implications for America* (pp. 205–220). Albany: SUNY Press.

6

Learning in the Science Classroom

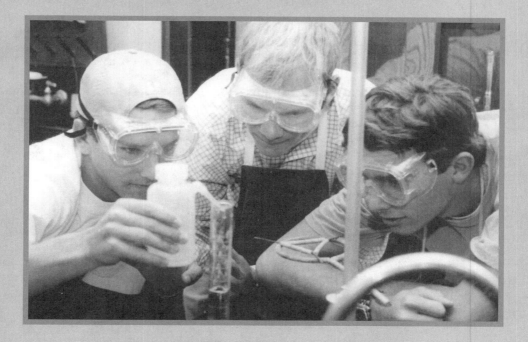

Our understanding of learning today is very different from just a few years ago. Rather than thinking of students as empty vessels waiting to be filled with science facts and formulas, we now view students as knowledge constructors who bring a wealth of experiences about the world and the universe to science classes. This prior knowledge plays a critical role in science learning and must be considered by the teacher when planning and engaging students in science learning experiences. Learning experiences that reveal to students their naive ideas or alternative conceptions and actively engage them with objects and events can stimulate the construction of new science understandings. Teachers must be mindful of the fact that students construct knowledge within a social context. Science understandings are negotiated through interactions with teachers and students and have meaning when situated within the learner's culture. Language and communication are important in students' negotiation of science understandings that are personally meaningful.

In a science classroom influenced by this constructivist view of learning, the teacher is called on to take on a new role. Rather than a giver of information, the teacher is a facilitator of student knowledge construction. Teachers must challenge students with learning experiences that make them think deeply about the world in which they live and the universe. Students' construction of meaningful science understandings can be aided by a number of conceptual tools, including concept maps and analogies. Concept maps aid science learning by helping students build relationships between ideas, while analogies are useful because they help students understand new science ideas by linking them to familiar ideas. Even the textbook has found a new role in the modern science classroom, as only one of a number of resources available to both teacher and students. To say that learning is the student's responsibility does not tell the whole the story of teaching and learning in a science classroom influenced by constructivism. Teachers are vital to students' success and face many challenges associated with providing appropriate learning opportunities for students and helping them construct meaningful science understandings.

The three cases in this chapter address several issues associated with teaching in ways that facilitate students' science learning. The first case focuses on student expectations for science learning. In this case, a biology teacher rethinks her own assumptions about science teaching and learning as she deals with students' frustrations associated with learning genetics concepts in nontraditional ways. The second case illustrates how a teacher's use of probing questions and analogical reasoning was successful in helping a middle school student construct meaningful understandings of several key concepts related to electric circuits. And the final case uses layers of commentary, a novel case-building approach, to highlight several challenges a physics teacher and his students faced when adapting their roles to meet the ideals of social constructivism.

■ ■ ■

Corn Kernels, Critical Thinking, and Classroom Control

Carolyn W. Keys and Melissa Dunavant

In this open case, Carolyn and Melissa describe a dilemma created when Melissa tried a problem-solving laboratory with a tenth-grade biology class. As a student teacher, Melissa wanted to provide her students with real-world science examples and allow them to use their own thinking skills. She expected that her students would make some important connections between genetics concepts and the real world as they determined the genotypic and phenotypic ratios for Indian corn. Much to Melissa's dismay, far from being excited by the lab, her students quickly became disengaged and off-task, and she was left trying to figure out what she did wrong. The case is followed by Melissa's reflections on the dilemma and a response to the case written by Carolyn, Melissa's methods course instructor and student teaching supervisor.

Melissa, a student teacher, was enjoying her Saturday afternoon browsing around in a local craft store with her friend and colleague Janice. She was selecting a few ears of brilliantly colored Indian corn to decorate her house for autumn, when she realized that the corn illustrated the concept of phenotype that she had been teaching in biology class over the last few weeks. "Hey, this corn shows a three-to-one phenotypic ratio," she said to Janice. "If I use this in class, the students will be able to see how dominant and recessive alleles are expressed in real life. They can see the phenotypic ratio and reason backward to the genotypic ratio. What a great 'aha' experience!" She bought several ears of corn and began thinking about her lab on the way home, excited that she had come up with a concrete idea for teaching that week.

After Melissa had shown the corn to her cooperating teacher to make sure it did express the genetic characteristics she thought it did, she wrote her lesson plan and prepared a worksheet to go with the lab activity. When she finished, she was very pleased with her product. The students were going to count the number of red and yellow kernels, infer the phenotype, and then from the phenotype infer the genotype. She included some thought-provoking questions on the lab worksheet that tied several important genetics concepts together. Melissa had also purchased some purple, pink, and white corn that showed incomplete dominance, so that students who quickly solved the complete dominance example could take on a second problem that was more challenging. This lab was going to be an opportunity for her students to do some thinking and apply what they had learned about dominant and recessive alleles, genotypes, and phenotypes. Melissa remembered from her methods class that it was important to have students engage in problem solving, not just follow cookbook labs by rote. She also agreed with her methods professor that, to understand biology, students need to see a relationship between abstract concepts and real organisms. She thought that using Indian corn would motivate her students and encourage them to make connections between genetic terms and their meanings. She also thought that the three-to-one phenotypic ratio illustrated by the yellow and red corn was so obvious that her students would jump on the problem and quickly arrive at solutions.

On Wednesday, Melissa started her first-period biology class by reviewing the basic concepts that the students had been using in their study of genetics. She then announced that the class was going to have the chance to discover the phenotype and genotype of Indian corn in their lab groups. She quickly went over what she expected them to do and explained that the red and yellow corn was "simple corn," while the purple, pink, and white corn was "challenge corn." She suggested that everyone try the "simple corn" before they took on the "challenge corn." With a smile, she passed out the laboratory worksheets and waited for the students to begin work.

The first 10 minutes seemed to go very smoothly. The students chose ears of corn, went back to their groups, and dutifully began counting the yellow and red kernels. Melissa circulated among the groups, making sure everyone was on task. Soon, she began to hear murmurs of discontent. Several students began making negative comments, and it was apparent she was meant to hear them. "What does she want us to do? I don't know what to do. Does she know what she wants us to do?" The talk began getting louder. Melissa went to over to help Samantha, Chris, and Holly. "I don't know what you're asking," Holly whined. As Melissa began to patiently explain how they should think about the ratio of their yellow to red corn kernels, she realized the class was really beginning to get noisy. She looked up. James, David, and Kevin were discussing the release of the newest science fiction film. Cassie and Jeremy were passing notes and giggling. Megan and Ryan were beginning to argue in loud voices about what the numbers of corn kernels meant. Melissa's heart began to beat a little faster. A bad feeling was rising in her stomach. She was afraid the class was getting out of control. Then Neil, who often disrupted the class, began picking the kernels out of the corn and throwing them at Michael. In a few moments, corn was whizzing around the room. Melissa felt herself blushing. Gathering her determination, she stopped the class, informed the students that corn throwing was not going to be tolerated, and led them through the analysis of their color frequencies and questions together as a class. She let the few students who had successfully completed the simple corn problem work on the challenge corn problem quietly in the back of the room.

After the last of the first-period students left the room, Melissa closed the door, walked to the back of the classroom where her university supervisor was seated, and slumped into a chair. Her planning period would be over in only 50 minutes, and she had to get it together for third period. "I thought that the phenotypic ratio was so obvious! Why didn't the students recognize the three-to-one ratio after all the Punnett Square problems we did in class? Why did they become frustrated so easily? I thought they would really enjoy the challenge of figuring out the corn problems. Especially the students who always do well and know all the answers. They seemed to be the most frustrated of all! Maybe asking students to apply concepts is too hard. Or, was it that I didn't prepare them emotionally for this lab? Should I try the lab again with third period?"

Questions for Reflection and Discussion

1. What would you do with Melissa's third-period class? What events of first period influenced your decision?

2. Do you agree with Melissa's initial idea that high school biology students should have opportunities to solve real-world problems and apply concepts? Why or why not? How important is application in biology class? Any science class?

3. Why do you think Melissa's students became frustrated so easily? Why do you think their behavior was a surprise to Melissa? How might their disruptive behavior be related to what Melissa was asking them to do?

4. When Melissa had to stop her class during the Indian corn lab and switch to all-class instruction, how did the students' roles in the class change? What would be the advantages and disadvantages of doing problem-solving activities as a large group?

5. What is Melissa asking with her question about preparing her students emotionally? How does past success in science and/or problem solving affect students' academic and social behavior? Can positive attitudes about problem solving be taught? Should they be taught? How would you go about teaching these attitudes?

■ ■ ■

Reflections on Student Real-World Problem Solving

Melissa Dunavant

I now realize that my students were frustrated during the genetics lab because they were not accustomed to using critical thinking to solve problems in their high school classes. My students were used to having the answers readily available in their textbooks or asking me to explain the answers to them. In particular, they had been taught that the procedures for biology labs were always listed step by step in their lab book. They never really had to think deeply about the meaning of a lab before their experience with the Indian corn. I now recognize they didn't understand that frustration was a good thing and that it is part of the scientific process. I wanted them to be frustrated, or challenged, but I didn't know I needed to prepare them for it emotionally.

As a veteran teacher, I continue to use many problem-solving labs and develop new ones each year. I begin the school year with activities that lay a foundation for a positive problem-solving attitude. I let my students know that, in my class, there is not always a right and a wrong answer. They're not going to be punished if they get something wrong. I also tell them that even if there is one correct answer, I'm more interested in the process of how they go about solving the problem. It's a process that we're looking for in science; knowledge doesn't switch on and off like a light-bulb. You might come up with several wrong answers before you hit the right one, and that is all part of the process. One of the first activities that I do with my students each year provides experiences that foster team building. In response to a simulated disaster scene, my students must decide which survival items to bring with them in a life raft. The activity illustrates to students that there can be more than one correct answer to a problem and that they must learn to come to consensus by justifying their reasoning in a small group. The second lab I do with my students involves no written laboratory instructions. I provide them with several unknown substances in small paper cups, such as vanilla-scented hand lotion and vanilla pudding, and invite them to use all of their senses, except taste, to identify the substances. This lab communicates to students that they need to determine some of their own lab procedures without relying on a set of written directions. While somewhat simple, these early activities teach the students that they need to rely on their own reasoning and that science involves observing, thinking, and discussing.

As the year progresses, I engage my students in several open-ended lab activities, such as discovering the double-helix structure of DNA and using cabbage juice indicator to develop their own pH scale for common household substances. Yes, I still do the Indian corn lab each fall when we study genetics, and I look forward to seeing how my students handle the experience.

Helping Students Become Problem Solvers Is Well Worth the Challenge

Carolyn W. Keys

As Melissa's methods professor and university supervisor for student teaching, I was very pleased that she had taken our discussions about student thinking in lab activities so seriously. I thought the lab she created for determining the genotypic and phenotypic ratio of Indian corn was an excellent example of the kind of activities we had talked about in methods class. When I arrived in her biology class on the day of the corn lab to observe and briefly looked over her lesson plan, I was eagerly anticipating the students' response. From my point of view, the lab was not as disastrous as Melissa described it, but I could see that the students were frustrated and did not know how to overcome uncertainty in problem solving. In conferencing with Melissa afterward, I tried to assure her that new kinds of lessons often do not work well the first time. I mentioned that students need to be explicitly told that they may not find the correct answer right away and to keep thinking about the problem. I urged her not to abandon her ideas about student scientific thinking and problem solving. As the weeks of student teaching went by, Melissa gained more and more confidence as a teacher. Far from abandoning her goals of generating student thinking, Melissa worked diligently to create meaningful laboratories, discussions, and assessments. By the end of the term, her persistence had paid off. The students knew what Melissa expected in terms of scientific thinking and took pride in being a member of the scientific community she had created.

The teaching of science as inquiry or problem solving is indeed challenging for experienced teachers as well as beginners. In problem solving, the procedures and even the problems themselves may be left open for students to determine, making many elements of the classroom unpredictable. However, as Melissa found, fostering students' learning in the processes of science is an important goal of science teaching. Problem solving teaches students to develop their own creativity, thinking skills, and communicative skills. In the long run, these skills may be more important than the learning of any particular science fact or concept.

Ms. Davis Sparks John's Understanding

Shawn M. Glynn

Ms. Davis, an experienced and dedicated teacher, had previously taught a lesson on electricity to her middle school students and assigned them follow-up readings in their textbook. One of her students, John, was having a particularly difficult time understanding several of the key concepts. Ms. Davis was not quite sure what to do but decided to use probing questions and analogical reasoning to help John inquire into the nature of electricity. In this closed case, authentic dialogue illustrates how Ms. Davis effectively used these two powerful instructional strategies to facilitate scientific inquiry. *Ms. Davis* and *John* are pseudonyms for individuals with whom Shawn has worked while investigating science teaching and learning. The case is followed by commentary from Nita A. Paris, a former high school science teacher and doctoral student in educational psychology.

Students bring many ideas to the science classroom, and some of these ideas can be used to help students construct new science knowledge. Teachers can help students link familiar ideas with unfamiliar ones by engaging students in science lessons that involve analogical reasoning. When students reason analogically, they use what they know about a familiar concept (analogue) to develop a better understanding of an unfamiliar concept (target). For example, students might compare the city or town they live in to the structure of a biological cell, with the mayor compared to the nucleus, the power companies to mitochondria, the bus system to the endoplasmic reticulum, and so on. An important part of using analogies is to help students realize that at some point the similarities between the analogue and the target end and, at that point, the analogy breaks down. When helping students reason analogically, teachers often use probing questions. These questions help students to clarify, justify, and extend their thinking (Montague, 1987). Analogical reasoning and probing questions are two powerful instructional strategies for helping students construct meaningful science understandings.

In the discussion that follows, a teacher, Ms. Davis, uses probing questions and analogical reasoning to promote a middle school student's inquiry into the nature of electricity. Having participated in a lesson on electricity with his classmates and completed the assigned textbook readings, John continues to have a difficult time understanding electric circuits. The dilemma that Ms. Davis faces is how to best help John inquire into the nature of electricity and develop an understanding of how electricity flows in an electric circuit. To do this, she must help John understand the concepts of resistance, conductor, and voltage and how wires, a battery, and a light bulb can be used to construct a circuit. It is clear to her that a one-on-one discussion is called for. Her goal in this discussion is to prompt John's inquiry and help him connect his relevant background knowledge to new concepts, thereby making the new concepts more meaningful. Her experience suggests to her that she can accomplish this by asking John probing questions that trigger his analogical reasoning about the concepts. She has had considerable success with these strategies in the past and hopes that they will prove beneficial in John's case. Ms. Davis describes analogies as inquiry tools.

JOHN:	I'm worried about the next science test, Ms. Davis.
MS. DAVIS:	Oh, what's giving you trouble, John?
JOHN:	The stuff on electricity and electric circuits in our last lesson.
MS. DAVIS:	Electricity concepts can be tough all right. Did you do the follow-up reading in your textbook?
JOHN:	I sure did. The reading is really hard. All the terms get me confused.
MS. DAVIS:	What were some of those confusing terms?
JOHN:	Well, I sort of know what a *circuit* is, but I'm not sure what *voltage* and *resistance* mean.
MS. DAVIS:	What were some of the other electricity terms or ideas that you read about?
JOHN:	Uh, I read about *wires,* and *batteries,* and *switches.*
MS. DAVIS:	Yes, these are important parts of an electric circuit. You seem to remember all the important ideas from your reading. Can you put these ideas together and explain to me how an electric circuit works?
JOHN:	Ah, no. That's the problem. I can't get a picture in my head of how this electricity stuff works.
MS. DAVIS:	Well, don't be discouraged, John. You've learned a lot of important bits and pieces from the text. Let me see if I can help you put these bits and pieces together, so you will understand how an electric circuit works. Perhaps an analogy might help. Do you recall when you and your classmates set up the aquarium in the classroom?
JOHN:	Sure!

MS. DAVIS: And do you remember me explaining how the water circulated in the aquarium?

JOHN: That was easy, not like this electricity stuff. When you explained how the water circulates, I could actually see the pump and filter.

MS. DAVIS: Right! Well, now I'm going to help you "see" how the electric circuit works by comparing it to water circulation in the aquarium. Look at the classroom aquarium while I describe again how the water flows through it in a circuit, or a connected path. A current of water is drawn through a pipe from the aquarium by a pump, which controls pressure. The water then flows through a filter, which slows the flow and catches impurities. Finally, the water returns to the aquarium through a pipe. Do you remember and understand that, John?

JOHN: Sure, Ms. Davis.

MS. DAVIS: Fine. Now think about this question. What might the water correspond to in an electric circuit? That is, what flows in the circuit?

JOHN: Electricity?

MS. DAVIS: Exactly! Very good. Now, the water is carried from the aquarium into the filter and back into the aquarium by means of plastic pipes. What do these pipes correspond to in an electric circuit?

JOHN: The metal wires?

MS. DAVIS: Right again. Now, in the aquarium, the pump provided the pressure to move the water through the tubes. In an electric circuit, what device provides the pressure to move the electricity through the circuit?

JOHN: How about a battery?

MS. DAVIS: Yes, indeed, a battery, or a generator. Now, for a tougher question. Like a pump, the battery produces a sort of electrical pressure. What's the correct name for this electrical pressure?

JOHN: I bet it's voltage.

MS. DAVIS: And I bet you're right! Now here's a really tough question. We stuffed cotton in the aquarium filter to clean the water. This also had the effect of reducing the amount of water that flowed through the pipes in a given period of time. Likewise, in an electric circuit, the use of some poorly conducting metals in wires can reduce the amount of electricity that flows in a given period of time. In an electric circuit, what do you call this reduction in flow?

JOHN: Resistance!

MS. DAVIS: Correct, John, I think you've got it. To sum up, let's list here on the board some of the features of our aquarium water circuit that correspond to those in an electric circuit:

> water—electricity
> flowing water—electric current
> pipes—wires
> pump—battery

pressure—voltage
filter—poor conductor
reduced flow—resistance

MS. DAVIS: Now, John, keeping these features in mind, explain to me how an
electric circuit works.

JOHN: OK, I'll give it a try. An electric circuit is an unbroken wire path
through which electricity can flow. For the electricity to flow, there
must be a source of voltage, such as a battery. How much electricity will flow through a circuit in a given period of time depends on
how much resistance there is in the material that makes up the
wire. So how's that? I guess I've got this circuit business down pat.

MS. DAVIS: Very impressive, but we're not done yet. I still have a few tricky
questions.

JOHN: OK, Ms. Davis, give me your best shot.

MS. DAVIS: Look at this diagram of an electric circuit; it's similar to the one in
your textbook [Figure 6.1]. The circuit contains a charged battery
and a lit lightbulb. What would happen to the electricity flowing
through the circuit if you cut the wire and pulled the ends apart?
Would you get a different result if you cut the wire before or after
the lightbulb?

FIGURE 6.1   A charged battery
and a lit lightbulb.

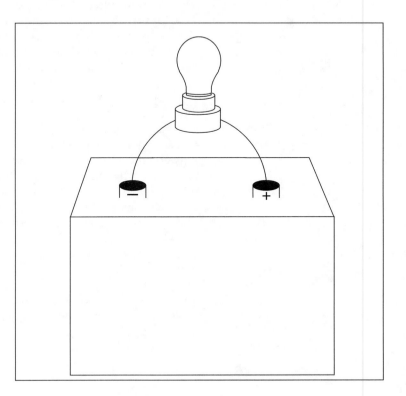

JOHN: Those are tricky questions, for sure. Hmm, let me use the aquarium water circuit analogy. If I cut the pipe returning water to the tank, the water would continue to flow but probably spill out on the floor. On the other hand, if I cut the pipe taking water from the tank just above the water line, then the water would stop flowing. Now, I'll apply this analogy to your circuit. If I cut the wire before the bulb, then electricity would flow but spill out of the wire. If I cut behind the bulb, then electricity would stop flowing. Am I right?

MS. DAVIS: No, you are not, although your reasoning is good. When you cut or break an electric circuit at any point in the circuit, the electricity stops flowing everywhere in the circuit. That's the function of an electrical switch, by the way; it interrupts the circuit, stopping the flow of electricity.

JOHN: But why wasn't I right, Ms. Davis? I used the analogy.

MS. DAVIS: Because, John, no analogy is perfect. Analogies help us to understand some aspects of a new concept, but at some point every analogy breaks down.

JOHN: If analogies can lead us to wrong conclusions sometimes, then I think we shouldn't use them at all.

MS. DAVIS: That, John, would be like throwing the baby out with the bath water, if you'll forgive me using another analogy. Analogies can be a big help to me when I explain new concepts and to you when you try to understand them. The trick is to use analogies carefully, keeping in mind their limitations and the wrong ideas that can arise when an analogy is carried too far. Used carefully, analogies can help you a lot, John, just as they've helped many of the famous scientists we've spoken about.

JOHN: Which scientists?

MS. DAVIS: Oh, astronomers such as Johannes Kepler, who drew an analogy between the movements of the planets and the working of a clock. And physical scientists such as Joseph Priestly, who suggested the law of electrical force by drawing an analogy from the law of gravitational force.

JOHN: Oh, yes, I remember their names. They used analogies, huh?

MS. DAVIS: Certainly. Analogies are important inquiry tools. They can help us to make the jump between old ideas we already understand and new ideas we're trying to learn.

JOHN: Is science the only area where I can use analogies?

MS. DAVIS: You can use analogies in all your subjects, John. They are powerful tools for inquiry and understanding. But do keep in mind their limitations.

JOHN: I will, Ms. Davis. And thanks a lot. I'm not worried about the test anymore.

Questions for Reflection and Discussion

1. Create a different analogy than the one used by Ms. Davis to help John learn about an electric circuit. Have a classmate analyze the extent to which your analogy might help clarify and enhance a student's understanding of an electric circuit.

2. Choose a science topic that you are familiar with but that is difficult for students to understand. What probing questions might you ask to trigger students' analogical reasoning about concepts central to the topic?

3. What are some learning strategies, besides probing questions and analogical reasoning, that science teachers can use to promote the process of inquiry in students and help them to think critically and meaningfully about key scientific concepts?

■ ■ ■

Analogies Are Never Perfect, But Darn Useful

Nita A. Paris

Analogies can be powerful science teaching tools. Students who are provided with analogies learn science concepts in more meaningful ways when compared to students who are taught without analogies (Brown, 1992). However, as indicated by John's response to Ms. Davis's question, "What would happen to the electricity flowing through the circuit if you cut the wire and pulled the ends apart?" misconceptions can and do occur.

Analogical reasoning in young learners is more likely to occur when their knowledge is coherent, rather than fragmented (Goswami, 1992). Conversely, when students' knowledge about the analogy is incomplete and inaccurate, they are likely to develop misconceptions (Wood, Woloshyn, & Willoughby, 1995). As we see with John, students may lack coherent scientific knowledge. John's answer, "If I cut the wire before the bulb, then electricity would flow but spill out of the wire," indicates that he has not yet come to understand an important difference between electricity and water. That is, water is composed of molecules, and electricity is the result of interaction of electrical charges. Although John learned bits and pieces about electricity from Ms. Davis' lessons and his reading, his knowledge is still incomplete and fragmented.

Furthermore, as this case shows, and as many teachers have experienced, analogies are never perfect. The important difference between the basic nature of water and electricity is an example of where the analogy breaks down. As a result of this imperfect fit, misunderstandings may develop.

How could Ms. Davis help John understand the difficult concept of electric circuits without contributing to his misunderstandings? She could steer his thinking by asking probing questions and by giving hints as he engages in analogical reasoning and by presenting analogies in a systematic way. The Teaching-With-Analogies (TWA) model (Glynn, Duit, & Thiele, 1995) provides guidance for using analogies to help students learn difficult science concepts. The operations in the TWA Model are

- Introduce the target concept (unfamiliar)
- Review the analogue concept (familiar)
- Identify the relevant features of the target and analogue
- Map similarities
- Indicate where the analogy breaks down
- Draw conclusions

In her discussion with John, Ms. Davis completed all of the operations of the TWA model with the exception of one. She initially failed to indicate where the analogy between the water flow in the aquarium and the electrical flow in the circuit breaks down. Perhaps Ms. Davis assumed that John could figure this out by himself. John's misconception became apparent with his answer to Ms. Davis's tricky question. Pointing out where the analogy breaks down delineates the limits of the analogue concept and highlights the characteristics of the target concept. When teaching with analogies, teachers should carry out each of the operations of the TWA model if they hope to minimize the possibility of misconceptions such as occurred with John.

Analogical reasoning is an important inquiry tool that, when used in conjunction with probing questions, can help students link together and make sense of important science concepts. By using a systematic approach to teaching with analogies, science teachers can facilitate student learning of science as inquiry.

Social Constructivism: A Referent for Thinking About Teaching or a Way to Teach?

Kenneth Tobin

Morrell, who was in his second year of teaching science, used constructivism as a method for increasing student autonomy and emphasizing problem solving for his grade-11 physics class. Through his discussions with Ken, a science education researcher, Morrell began to see the power of using constructivism as a referent rather than a method for teaching. This case includes a vignette and associated discussion as an illustration of the power of using social constructivism as a way of thinking about the teaching and learning of science. As author of the case, Ken introduces Morrell's views on using constructivism both before and after the lesson captured in the vignette along with his own postlesson response. Morrell's pre- and postlesson discussions are presented in his own voice.

■ Morrell's Prelesson Views

One of the interventions that I employed in my physics classes was to assign students the task of designing complex-order problems of the kind they encountered in the physics examination. I knew the great value of this process from firsthand experience, in that the process of designing complex application-type questions for examinations was a higher order cognitive process and causes one to deliberate intently on the many domains of the topic. I reasoned that this thinking process was highly beneficial toward the construction of the students' own knowledge about the topic of force and motion and, further, how this knowledge relates to other bodies of knowledge. In the process of developing these questions, students are in a sense forced to consider how one domain of physics relates to other domains. One of the

125

very strong advantages of this process is that, as students focus on these relationships, alternative frameworks may become evident and cause cognitive dissonance, which will hopefully lead students to reassess their knowledge in light of the constructs that do not fit well into their existing cognitive frameworks.

A problem-solving task was given to the students at the end of a unit on force and motion as part of some revision and consolidation activities. Given that there were six groups in the class, the process of designing problems and sharing solutions with the rest of the class was time-consuming. The number of available lessons in a school term was few in light of the amount of curriculum I was required to cover. In addition, the pressure of meeting the examination schedule was an ever-present concern. I estimated that the question-designing process would take about a lesson and a half, and the sharing process about three lessons. In effect, this was a week's worth of activity, a fact that caused me some underlying tension, given the aforementioned pressures on time that constrained me in the environment in which I worked.

Students initially had some difficulty in the process of designing a complex application question. For almost all of them, this was the first time they had been asked to actually design a question as opposed to answer a question. I moved from group to group and offered very general, nonspecific assistance in terms of encouraging students to blend a variety of concepts in their questions and avoid one-dimensional-type problems. The process of sharing the developed problems took the form of one or two members from each group taking control of the classroom environment and presenting a written form of the problem to the rest of the class. I permitted students to ask the presenters questions of clarification, and then I allocated time, usually about 10 minutes, for the class to attempt to solve the problem. During this time, I either attempted to solve the problem myself or observed other students, individually or in their working groups, solving the problem. Following this period, the presenting student elicited a solution from the other students. I encouraged the presenters to adopt my role and attempt to probe and question students for answers rather than just present the solution.

Ken Tobin's Notes on the Class Problem

The Prisoner and the Guillotine
A man sentenced to the guillotine has decided to pass the time working out the physics behind the process. It takes a minimum velocity of 9.5 ms^{-1} to cut off a person's head. The mass of the blade is 5 kg. What is the required height of the guillotine? What is the force required to cut off a person's head?

Calculation of the height from which the blade had to be dropped to reach the minimum speed was a routine matter for most students. Not quite as straightforward was the calculation of the force with which the blade impacted the criminal's neck. One student, Brian, demonstrated his group's solution to the problem. The force of impact of the blade on the neck was reasoned to be equivalent to the gravitational force on the blade. Morrell readily accepted the solution as correct ("Which is of course the same as we get if we use F = ma. That's great! Thanks Brian!").

The solution seemed counterintuitive to me. The following comments taken from a transcript of the lesson show the essence of my concern.

TOBIN: Intuitively, it seems wrong, because the force would be greater if you drop it from 10 meters than if you drop it from 2 cm, or than if you don't drop it at all. So if I'm the person who is to be beheaded and I get a choice, I'll say, "Don't raise that so high, just give me the 2-cm drop."

I was the only person in the class to raise a question about the viability of the solution. Morrell defended Brian's answer ("It's the same amount of force if you drop it from 1 meter as a 100 meters, according to F = ma.") before making the following concession:

MORRELL: Yeah. There is something not quite right about that. I have thought the problem out once before. Not this problem but a similar one, and I can't for the life of me remember the reasoning for it. But I will.

There was no effort on the part of Morrell, Brian, or the other students to consider what physics they knew that might lead to an alternative solution. Throughout the short interchange, Brian remained at the front of the room and endeavored to counter my suggestions and defend the viability of his group's solution. ("In this problem . . . we assume that the body has no resistance. There isn't any friction.") However, when the lesson concluded, there were no further attempts to resolve the contradiction that was present for just a short time. The matter of the force required to sever the head of the man was no longer an issue. The next lesson dealt with new content, and there were no subsequent conversations about the task or its solution.

Questions for Reflection and Discussion

1. How can co-teaching lead to the evolution of learning environments that are consistent with social constructivism?

2. From a social constructivist perspective, what teaching strategies are most likely to enhance the learning of science?

3. How can equity issues be incorporated into a social constructivist perspective on the learning of science?

4. What strategies might Morrell have used to emphasize the significance of knowledge being personally and socially viable?

5. Morrell seems to equate teaching in a constructivist mode with student-centered learning. What are the advantages and disadvantages of thinking in this way? How can constructivism be used to improve the quality of teacher-centered activities?

6. How might Morrell use social constructivism to address his concerns about insufficient time, the need to cover more subject matter, and the need to prepare students for tests?

7. In what ways might Morrell's valuing of constructivism and autonomy for students have benefited his students? In addition to the learning of physics, are there probable benefits for life out of school from participating in activities like the prisoner and the guillotine?

8. How do Brian's opportunities to learn physics in the prisoner and the guillotine problem compare to those of students in his group and the class? What could Brian and/or Morrell do to increase the learning of all students?

■ ■ ■

Perspectives on the Cutting Edge of Learning

Kenneth Tobin

It is preferable to consider social constructivism as a way to think about knowing and learning rather than as a method of teaching and learning. Constructivism, as described by Glasersfeld and his colleagues (e.g., Glasersfeld, 1995; Staver, 1998; Tobin, 1993), assumes that all knowledge is constructed by cognizing beings and does not exist independently of knowers. A social constructivist perspective assumes knowing and learning to involve interactions described in terms of recursive interrelationships between individual, social, and cultural components. Making sense of experience in terms of what already is known is the essence of a constructivist perspective on learning.

This perspective serves as a reminder that learning is a responsibility of individuals, who experience the events and phenomena of a sociocultural universe in which interactions involve participants and the cultural resources of a community. For knowledge to be accepted as true (or viable), it has to be compatible with other viable knowledge, survive tests to disconfirm its applicability, and enable those who apply the knowledge to meet their goals. Since the focus in this case is on individual actors in social contexts, it makes sense to describe interactions in terms of sets of behaviors, associated goals, beliefs about what is appropriate, and the contexts in which the interactions occur. Even though individuals construct knowledge, all knowing is socially embedded because, although it is possible for individuals to isolate themselves from other cognizing beings, it is never possible to be insulated from sociocultural institutions such as language.

A referent—which consists of a set of theoretical ideas taking the form of verbal propositions, narratives, and images of practice—can be used while reflecting on action and/or inaction to make sense of what is happening and to identify ways to improve the quality of teaching and learning. Many theoretical frameworks, such as constructivism, can be used as referents to maximize learning by adapting and enacting the roles of teachers and students and interactions among them.

Learning by doing in the presence of others can involve the construction of knowledge that is accessible and representable by language (i.e., related to a referent in a conscious way) and other tacit knowledge that is inaccessible to language and exists only in action. Bourdieu (1992) used the term *habitus* to describe an unspoken fabric that shapes what happens in a community so that some practices feel right and are sustained without explicit awareness and others feel alien and are not supported. Without the conscious awareness or intent of anyone in a community, interactions can constrain unsupported actions in ways that catalyze adaptations and promote an evolution of knowledge in action.

For example, when teachers and students are pursuing incompatible goals, teachers can make microadjustments to facilitate the attainment of shared goals (i.e., to improve the quality of teaching and learning). Accordingly, participation in a community can be a source of learning without a conscious awareness that learning actually is taking place. In this way, conventions and customary ways of participating in a community are honed by participating with those who know and can do (i.e., by interacting with teachers). Learning can be explicit when someone who knows corrects others whose practices do not conform to the acceptable norms of a community, or, as is often the case, self-corrections can occur, with or without conscious intent, to facilitate individuals' meeting their goals.

An epistemology of practice implies that knowledge exists in action, as a form that is different from any description of it. After the event (i.e., out of the action setting), it is not possible to reflect on knowledge in action, by speaking or writing about it, since any reconstruction involving language is necessarily an incomplete representation of what happened. For example, while teaching, reflection in action cannot address all components of knowledge in action, because much of what occurs is not authentically described by language. To improve teaching by doing, or to learn in ways that lead to improvement, it is necessary to teach, particularly by co-teaching with others who are familiar with the communities in which one wants to teach (e.g., urban schools, advanced chemistry).

Two criteria must be met if a teacher wants to improve teaching through the use of constructivism as a referent. First, a teacher must reflect carefully on the roles of teachers, students, and other stakeholders in relation to constructivism. By so doing, a teacher can plan activities using constructivism as a referent to create new teacher and student roles, metaphors, and images of practice. Second, the teacher must enact the curriculum in ways that allow all stakeholders to participate and to construct an adaptive set of roles that are mutually supportive and culturally appropriate. As the teacher enacts the curriculum in the ways envisioned in the planning process, teachers, students, and other stakeholders can fine-tune their roles by participating as newly crafted roles are enacted. Teaching facilitates the creation of evolving sets of knowledge in action to include tacit aspects of teaching that extend beyond what can be spoken and written and the initial descriptions of roles.

Morrell used constructivism as a referent and particularly highlighted the need for students to have autonomy to pursue goals that would reflect what they knew of physics, their interests, and their needs to review and relearn in order to be successful in the activity. He arranged them in groups so that they could teach and learn from one another and employ whatever resources they needed to make sense of the physics problem they were constructing and solving. The students were able to work at their own pace and collaborate with whom they wished. The element of competition between groups made the activity game-like in some respects, and students looked to make their problems more difficult for others to solve through the use of a variety of tactics that gave them insights into ways in which physics can be applied to the universe. As the problems were formulated and solved in an iterative process, there was no doubt that all students engaged in physics in a way that was impressive. The activity provided a context for deep engagement in the conceptual aspects of physics and application of formulae in ways that had the potential to extend beyond "plug and chug" physics.

Even though Morrell was able to transfer control to students for decisions about what to do, how to do it, and when to undertake tasks, the microculture of the physics classroom constrained the actions of students in significant ways. The students' own ways of making sense were set aside in favor of the semantics of physics. It was not customary in this class to ask for evidence to support the viability of a particular solution, and it was not common to challenge solutions to assigned tasks. Accordingly, when I challenged Brian's solution to the guillotine problem on the grounds of common sense, the challenge was not taken seriously and was not pursued as an opportunity to learn physics. If my warrant had been based on one of the theorems of physics, it may have been dealt with differently. For example, if I had asserted that Brian's solution did not take account of the total energy of the blade, only the potential energy, then the claim may have been taken seriously, because the competing claims were both from the physics domain.

This issue is significant because many students feel intimidated in bringing forward challenges when the basis for their challenge is their everyday commonsense knowledge. Morrell had not promoted the custom of justifying solutions, actively seeking alternatives, and selecting from the alternatives the most parsimonious of the viable solutions. Furthermore, and of importance from a constructivist perspective, students were not encouraged to speak up when claims made no sense to them. Perhaps they did not see their own knowledge as a foundation for making sense of physics and developing the discursive practices of a community populated by those who know physics.

While the potential for engaging in deep thinking about physics was possible, it was clear when the class as a whole tackled the guillotine problem that the main engagement concerned application of formulae that fit the data given in the problem. Other forces (e.g., relatively little time remaining in the semester, a need to administer a test, a significant amount of subject matter still to be covered) constrained the interactions within the classroom community to an extent that the greatest concern seemed to be to get finished and move on to a new activity.

■ Morrell's Postlesson Views: Critique of the Prisoner and the Guillotine

The activity was a little more time-consuming than I had anticipated. On average, the class was getting through only about one and a half questions per lesson. I was tense about how much time remained before the students must sit their examination for this unit of physics. Brian's group was one of the last to present its question. In my mind, I was well over the time period I had allocated for this activity. I did not actually solve Brian's guillotine problem myself but was probably involved in observation of other students. The solutions of students who created the problem were not heavily scrutinized at this stage of the activity but were all too easily accepted by me and, as a result, were accepted on faith by all other students in the class. The cues I enacted in accepting Brian's solution, ending discussion, and moving on to another segment of the lesson, were completely sufficient for the students to fully accept the solution based on a warrant that I had accepted it. With hindsight, the amount of power that I held as a teacher in that context was indeed astonishing.

After reflecting on this intervention, I regard it as quite beneficial for the students. Many of the questions and solutions were very imaginative and did for the most part correctly and successfully blend many of the domains of the topic together, partially at least, in accordance with my constructivist aims. There was regrettably a lack of open discussion about the interrelationship of the various domains of the topic, which would have been undoubtedly beneficial. This activity would have presented, in my view, greater learning value if I were not constrained by the ever-present contextual time pressures in my work environment.

The biggest overriding factor that I've seen is the time limitation: We've got x amount of time to do y amount of stuff. These sorts of activities, where you're getting students to design their own experiments, are time-consuming. . . . I mean, we are working within a time limit. There is a lot of work to be developed in that sort of curriculum. Even the textbooks are currently designed around the format of our syllabus. It is pretty jam-packed—you can't afford to rest on your laurels. There is a lot of information to get through, and the course is based on information. You can't afford to vary too much from the approved program. There is some point that you have to cut and say, "We have to go on."

Core concepts are developed in class along with the more refined detail and implications. I am getting the kids to actively sit there and think about core concepts and the implications they have. How do they fit in? That activity I am making them do fits well into the learning process. There is great value in the process of sitting down and having to think about physics, not doing a problem, not solving a mathematical problem or solution, but just to sit there and think about where particular ideas really fit in. If students can link physics with other domains of their cognitive framework, in a meaningful way, then they won't have isolated concepts.

Teaching in a constructivist mode requires discipline. It's very easy to fall into that teacher-centered model. It's easier to teach that way. You can get up there and start giving out information, or you can sit down and think how to present this information such that it does fall into that constructivist mode. How can I give information that relates to those kids' cognitive frameworks as they already exist as they come into my classroom? That's very hard, and it is something I'm attempting to do. If I were to do my own self-assessment and say how well I am doing, I would say that I wouldn't be a star performer. But I am making progress.

Conscious and Unconscious Teaching

At a conscious level, Morrell taught in ways that were consistent with constructivism. He emphasized autonomy for students, chances to interact with peers, opportunities to work at their own pace, and to pursue areas germane to their own interests. Each of these strategies made sense from a constructivist perspective, and as Morrell monitored what was happening in the classroom, he was able to fine-tune the learning environments of students.

Morrell also was somewhat anxious about the time-consuming nature of the activity sequence. At a level that was beyond his consciousness, he undertook his roles in ways that moved the activities toward a conclusion. After he had read some of my interpretive comments, Morrell linked his actions to the need within this school to prepare students for examinations in a timely manner and also to cover the requisite subject matter of the course. Many of his actions that were designed to hasten the conclusion to the activity were not deliberative during the enactment of the curriculum. It was only afterward, when his attention was drawn to these actions, that he identified a probable rationale for what had happened. At the time of enacting the curriculum, these forces were beyond language and were part of the habitus. Of course, there is much more to the habitus of Morrell's physics class, and it is likely that his explanations of what happened in the class are only the tip of an iceberg. An important implication of this likelihood is that reflection on action—assisted with field notes, analytic memoranda, and videotapes—can assist in the creation of cognitive objects around which rich conversations can revolve, leading to the emergence of catalysts for change. However, even the richest of stimuli will not elicit everything that occurs and might be considered in a quest for educational improvement. An essential tool in learning about science teaching and learning is to engage in teaching activities. By participating with others in a community of learners, teachers can experience the habitus and construct tacit knowledge in action as well as those parts of a knowledge spectrum that are accessible to description, objectification, and adaptation through the aegis of language.

Resources to Consider

Baker, D., & Pilburn, M. (1997). *Constructing science in middle and secondary school classrooms.* Needham Heights, MA: Allyn & Bacon. (Allyn & Bacon, Needham Heights, MA 02194)

This textbook presents a wealth of information about recent advances in science teaching and learning. The authors, Dale Baker and Michael Pilburn, answer the question

What is constructivism? and then discuss the nature of the constructivist student and the constructivist classroom. The theme of teaching for conceptual change is highlighted in most of the book's 15 chapters.

Kovalik, S., & Olsen, K. (1998, March/April). **The physiology of learning—Just what does go on in there?** *Schools in the Middle, 7,* 32–37.

Susan Kovalik and Karen Olsen explain why teachers should view learning as a "body-mind" activity rather than brain function alone. They point out that learning occurs through body–mind processing of sensory input and emphasize the importance of the amount and kind of sensory input provided in classrooms. The authors describe six levels of sensory input to consider when planning for instruction.

Ruef, K. (1992). *The Private Eye: Looking/thinking by analogy.* Seattle, WA: The Private Eye Project. (The Private Eye Project, 7701 31st Avenue NW, Seattle, WA 98117)

This book models many strategies for helping students develop analogical reasoning in science through interdisciplinary connections. Kerry Ruef illustrates the use of a jeweler's loop as a tool for helping students construct analogies.

Tobin, K. (Ed.). (1993). *The practice of constructivism in science education.* Mahwah, NJ: Lawrence Erlbaum Associates. (Lawrence Erlbaum Associates, 10 Industrial Avenue, Mahwah, NJ 07430)

The chapters in this book, edited by Ken Tobin, illustrate different perspectives on constructivism and its relationship to the teaching and learning of science and mathematics.

Venville, G., & Treagust, D. (1997, May). **Analogies in biology education: A contentious issue.** *The American Biology Teacher, 59,* 282–287.

Grady Venville and David Treagust discuss the integral role of analogies in the history of biology and in modern biology teaching and learning. They explain that analogies are useful in biology teaching for their motivational value and because they can help students construct new knowledge but can lead to learning misconceptions when students are not familiar with the analogy. A particularly informative part of the article is the discussion of Glynn's Teaching-With-Analogies Model and the FAR (Focus, Action, Reflection) Guide developed by Treagust and his colleagues.

References

Bourdieu, P. (1992). *Language and symbolic power.* Cambridge, MA: Harvard University Press.

Brown, D. E. (1992). Using examples and analogies to remediate misconceptions in physics: Factors influencing conceptual change. *Journal of Research in Science Teaching, 29,* 17–34.

Glasersfeld, E. V. (1995). *Radical constructivism: A way of knowing and learning.* Washington, DC: Falmer Press.

Glynn, S. M., Duit, R., & Thiele, R. (1995). Teaching science with analogies: A strategy for constructing knowledge. In S. M. Glynn & R. Duit (Eds.), *Learning science in schools: Research reforming practice* (pp. 247–273). Mahwah, NJ: Erlbaum.

Goswami, U. (1992). *Analogical reasoning in children*. East Sussex, UK: Erlbaum.

Montague, E. J. (1987). *Fundamentals of secondary classroom instruction*. Upper Saddle River, NJ: Merrill/Prentice Hall.

Staver, J. R. (1998). Constructivism: Sound theory for explicating practice of science and science teaching. *Journal of Research in Science Teaching, 35,* 501–520.

Tobin, K. (Ed.). (1993). *The practice of constructivism in science education*. Hillsdale, NJ: Erlbaum.

Wood, E., Woloshyn, V. E., & Willoughby, T. (1995). *Cognitive strategy instruction for middle and high schools*. Cambridge, MA: Brookline Books.

7

Learning in the Laboratory and Informal Settings

L aboratory work, field work, and informal learning experiences are central to science teaching and learning. They provide students with opportunities to investigate firsthand the world in which we live. When engaged in laboratory work, students practice scientific skills, learn concepts and principles, and may develop a greater appreciation for the work of scientists. The laboratory may be used to clarify what students have read about in textbooks or heard during lectures but is better used to engage students in inquiry and problem-solving experiences that lead to the develop of meaningful understandings. Work begun in the laboratory may be extended to include excursions to field and natural settings, as well as informal venues such as museums. For many students, outdoor science excursions are some of their most memorable school experiences. Field trips to wildlife preserves, state or national parks, power-generating plants, and seashores allow personal investigation of phenomena, organisms, and events not possible within the walls of the classroom. Along with the pedagogical benefits of laboratory and field work come some potential concerns. Teachers must consider student safety, necessary materials and equipment, and other logistics essential to the development of meaningful science learning in informal settings. To be sure, laboratory and field work must be purposeful and well planned, but even then the intended learning outcomes many not always be achieved. For laboratory and field work to be successful, teachers must truly believe in the value of these instructional approaches and develop the competence and confidence needed to make them worthwhile learning experiences for students.

The three cases featured in this chapter illuminate dilemmas associated with laboratory and field work. The first case describes a chemistry teacher's endeavor to engage his students in an inductive laboratory on gas pressure when they are not ready for this type of learning experience. A former middle school teacher addresses the benefits and costs associated with taking students on an overnight environmental education field trip in the second case. And in the final case, a teacher discusses her attempt to use constructivism to guide her laboratory instruction and the difficulties it caused for her and her students. Both the first and third cases make use of the layered commentary approach to case writing, which provides for the inclusion of multiple perspectives regarding the dilemmas highlighted in the cases.

■ ■ ■

A Pressure-Packed Problem

Steven Fleming

This open case describes a teacher's attempt to introduce the concept of gas pressure to a group of high school chemistry students. Steve uses an inductive approach to introduce the concept of gas pressure to his students and then attempts to lead them in a postlaboratory discussion of their findings. The students' responses to Steve's questions about gas pressure tell him that something has gone wrong, and he is left contemplating why they didn't learn what he hoped they would from the laboratory. The case is followed by Steve's reflections on the laboratory experience and commentaries by Gene Chiappetta, a university science educator, and Rachel Williamson, a veteran teacher and doctoral student in science education.

I have taught high school chemistry for 7 years. Early in my teaching, I realized that the average level of prior school science knowledge possessed by most students is low, especially in the physical sciences. Further, the lecture and problem solving that accompanied the traditional chemistry course that I had taken in high school would most likely not succeed with today's students. The traditional chemistry course utilizes a great deal of mathematics to solve word problems, which could potentially pose difficulties for many students. Additionally, this type of course contains too much abstract subject matter. I have learned that high school students require many opportunities to observe chemical systems and to manipulate laboratory equipment to gain some familiarity with chemical phenomena, as represented in school science. Therefore, the use of many laboratory activities has become standard practice in my chemistry courses.

Among the fundamental concepts of chemistry are the behaviors and properties of gases. Recognizing the need for laboratory instruction, I planned a set of introductory activities in which the students worked in groups of three, rotating among several lab stations. Each station was designed to engage the students in a short inquiry activity related to some aspect of pressure and gases. The students began their investigations at the start of the laboratory period. As I watched their progress and monitored the lab, I noticed that most of the students were following the instructions at each station and trying their best to perform the task at hand. As the period progressed, the students moved from station to station and many seemed to be enjoying the activities. After about 30 minutes, all of the students had visited each station and were ready to return to their seats. I then moved into position to conduct a postlaboratory discussion of their results, calling on students to put forth correct ideas about pressure and gases. I will never forget what happened next.

I began the discussion with the first lab station, which consisted of two shoes, one of which was a high-heeled woman's dress shoe and the other a large flat sandal. The students were to compare the amount of force that would be exerted on them if someone stepped on their toe wearing either of those shoes. I asked Maria to explain what she had observed as her group passed this station. She said, "I wouldn't wear none of them shoes, 'cause those ain't cool." I was shocked and tried to refocus her on the topic at hand. She sat and stared blankly at me as if my face had suddenly vanished. One student wanted to know how much the person who was wearing those shoes weighed, and another wanted to know if the person had one dress shoe and one sandal on at the same time. I was amazed. How could they not see the connection between these shoes and the amount of force exerted on a given area?

After regaining my composure, I thought this must be too difficult an example to start with and moved on to explain the next station. The next station consisted of three equal-sized transparent containers, each containing a different number of equal-sized colored wooden balls. The colored balls represented molecules of a gas. I called on Freddy to explain which container he thought might have the greatest number of gas molecules colliding with the container. Freddy said, "I think it will be the one with the least number of little balls because they will have more room to move around faster in the can." I asked the class if they thought he was correct, and again, the room was quiet. I wondered what was happening. How could they not be drawing valid conclusions about gas pressure from these stations? This pattern continued as I moved from station to station, with only sporadic interludes of conceptual connections being made. What was going wrong?

Questions for Reflection and Discussion

1. Why did Steve's students not respond to his postlab questions or respond with incorrect answers?

2. What strategies can high school science teachers use to build critical knowledge to better prepare their students for laboratory work?

3. How can a laboratory approach be used effectively when working with students who have unique background experiences outside the teacher's realm of experience?

4. What are some strategies teachers can use to guide students in making valid connections between classroom discussions and laboratory experiences during postlaboratory instruction?

5. In using an inductive approach, Steve first engaged his students in what he thought were appropriate investigations and then during the discussion found that they had not learned what he thought they should have. If you were in Steve's place, what modifications would you make to the lesson for the next period's class? Would you stick with the inductive approach?

■ ■ ■

Reflections on My Pressure-Packed Problem

Steven Fleming

From the start of the postlab discussion, I could tell that the students were having difficulty. They couldn't make the connections between the investigations they did in the lab and the concepts I hoped they would come to understand. I believe they didn't make the connections I hoped they would because the investigations didn't make sense to them. The investigations I prepared for the students made sense to me, but that is because I could see how they were related to the concepts. Even though my students attend the same high school I did and live in the same community I did when growing up, our backgrounds are different. My Dad's work in the chemical industry and the things I did as a kid brought me in touch with gases and ideas about pressure, and my own learning in chemistry classes helped me better understand my experiences with gases. With the changes that have taken place in Houston since I was in high school, my students' experiences with gases and pressure are sure to be very different from mine.

In retrospect, I should have prepared differently. One thing that I could have done is to talk with my students before the lab to find out about their experiences with gases and pressure. Knowing about their experiences would have enabled me to modify the investigations or design new ones for use in the laboratory. In addition, I could have planned my postlab discussion to be more interactive, with students asking each other about what they did while visiting each station and what understandings they constructed from the investigations in which they were engaged. I could also have asked probing questions to help my students focus on the major concepts I was trying to teach. As a result of my experiences with this lesson, I now realize that I must put more effort into helping students make connections between what they do in the lab and the science concepts I hope they will learn. I have come to view my role as a guide. I want to be able to guide my students to make appropriate connections between the understandings and experiences they bring to science class and scientific explanations for the phenomena we study.

Build Conceptual Knowledge Before Laboratory Work

Eugene L. Chiappetta

Steve, I am happy to learn that you are using the multiple lab station approach with some of your chemistry classes. When you provide students with firsthand experiences and many examples of an abstract concept, you are on your way to building an effective curriculum. However, please do not become too disappointed with the results. There are several things to consider about your students and ways to modify your instruction that may help your students construct meaningful understandings from the laboratory experiences.

You and I have talked about how different the students are today from when you attended high school in the very same building where you are now teaching. If you are correct in your assessment of what students know when they enter your classroom, then in your mind, pressure should be a familiar concept to them. I would say this may be true for many of your students. You have understood a great deal about pressure since the time you were a boy pumping up bicycle tires and basketballs, jumping up and down on the basketball court, and listening to your father talk about the pressurized gas containers that he maintained at the chemical company where he worked. I agree that most of the students in your chemistry classes do not have your background of experiences and understanding of pressure, or many other science concepts. They may have quite different firsthand experiences with pressure, and as a consequence, these students do not perceive the world around them as you view it. Although each of your lab stations has concrete objects and simple directions, the students are not altogether clear about what they are looking for and how this relates to the unit of study.

I bet if you give more thought to your students' prior knowledge, you would surely identify some ways to precede the lab station exercises with more instruction. Doing this will provide your students with a conceptual base to assist them in learning about gas pressure and making sense out of what they experience in lab. Consider spending more time providing prelaboratory instruction before you involve students in inductive laboratory experiences. Build a conceptual framework for students and even some specific knowledge to facilitate learning in the laboratory and the construction of knowledge.

Last, I recommend that you modify your thinking about the postlaboratory discussion. Take a longer view of this instructional aspect of science teaching, realizing that many students may still have a fragmented notion of pressure, even after many firsthand examples of the concept. Remember, one time through a lab does not ensure understanding an idea. During the postlaboratory discussion, call on many students to assess their answers to the questions pertaining to a particular lab station. Ask certain students to return to a lab station and to demonstrate their understanding of the principle under discussion. Further, in the next class period, conduct a review of the lab, again calling on students to demonstrate their understanding of gas pressure. In addition, devise a new example of gas pressure to challenge their understanding. This situation will serve as another opportunity for you to examine students' comprehension and alternative conceptions of the content.

■ ■ ■

Active Engagement Doesn't Always Equal Learning

Rachel Williamson

Steve, I found many positive aspects about the lab experience you designed to facilitate students' understanding of gas pressure. First, I commend the inductive approach that you used and your efforts to meet the students where they are. So many times, we science teachers fall into the trap of teaching the material instead of the student; your case points out the importance of placing the learner first. Second, your use of an inductive approach that allows students to build conceptual understanding from interacting with materials is certainly appropriate. I know from experience the time and effort required to plan and set up this type of learning experience for our students, but I believe it can lead to effective and permanent learning. Finally, I support your use of postlab discussion sessions to facilitate understanding of the concepts and procedures addressed in the activities and to bring closure to the lesson.

The experience described in your case highlights a problem I have also encountered when doing laboratory activities. That is that students can be engaged in an activity, well behaved, and seemingly focused on the procedures, yet still not have a clear understanding of how the lab relates to the subject material discussed in class or to real-world situations. I agree with Eugene, you should not become disenchanted with your laboratory approach. Neither I nor anyone else I have ever read can offer a definitive answer on how to teach so that all students will learn.

Let me share with you some suggestions for modifying your laboratory activities that may enable your students to realize more effective learning. In addition to the students' low level of formal science knowledge, I would suggest that they have had few opportunities to engage in laboratory work and therefore do not really know how to utilize laboratory procedures in ways that maximize conceptual understanding. I have found that students often come to my classes with such poor laboratory skills that they are unable to learn from laboratory activities. In this regard, more prelab explanation of the concepts and demonstration of the procedures, as well as discussion of what *might* be observed during the lab, may help your students develop confidence in their abilities. A second suggestion that may help guide and develop students' laboratory skills would be to include a reflective activity sheet for students to fill out during various phases of the laboratory activities. This activity sheet could include questions that help them focus on details that are important for understanding lab procedures, the concepts addressed in the lab, and the real-world applications of the concepts. In addition, these activity sheets could be used to guide postlab discussions. A final suggestion concerns the postlab session. During this time, I would focus more directly on assessing and facilitating student understanding in the following ways: (1) Call on many students to answer questions concerning lab procedures, findings, and implications, and (2) ask lab partners to confer with each other about a question and reach a group consensus before offering an answer.

I applaud you for the use of an inductive laboratory approach and for the concern you have for your students' learning. I encourage you to continue to use this type of laboratory learning experience with your students.

■ ■ ■

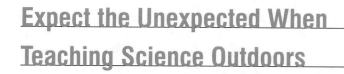
Expect the Unexpected When Teaching Science Outdoors

Michael Kamen

As a young middle school science teacher, Michael jumped at the opportunity to work collaboratively with a naturalist to provide his students an overnight environmental education experience. He knew his students would benefit from firsthand experience with their local natural history and was excited about the many opportunities for social and academic growth. At the same time, his eyes were opened to costs he had not previously considered, ranging from schedule disruptions to liability and safety issues. Michael was left wondering how to balance these and other costs with the benefits of teaching in an outdoor setting. In this closed case, Michael explores the complex issues surrounding the use of the outdoor learning environment for science instruction. The case is followed by commentary from Teresa Coker, an environmental educator.

During my 10 years teaching, I had many opportunities to take students on overnight environmental education field trips. While I believe that such trips are valuable educational experiences, I have often pondered how to balance benefits versus costs. Trips require a great deal of planning, and they disrupt schedules and increase liability. Teaching in an outdoor setting provides students with many opportunities to learn but also exposes them to risks and teachers to liabilities beyond those normally existing in a classroom.

One of my first experiences with an overnight environmental education field trip was when I was teaching middle school science at a school on Long Island, New York. This school had a contract with a local nature center to provide one of their naturalists for an ongoing environmental education program, including a 3-day trip to the east end of Long Island. The itinerary included beach ecology, dune ecology, a tour of a lighthouse, a beach night sit, cooking activities, a star-gazing activity, and an exploration of local Native American culture.

The school administrators were very supportive of the program and field trip. I had the advantage of working with our assigned naturalist, Peter, who not only knew the area where we were headed and had a variety of activities to offer but also came into my classes with preparation lessons and follow-up activities. The experiences he planned for the trip were tied into the concepts and topics from the school's 3-year environmental program.

Peter provided the tents and made arrangements for our camping site. He had contacts with state, county, and local resources. Local experts would join our group for periods of time, increasing supervision and adding knowledge and unique perspectives. Peter arranged for us to visit a museum, and he set up a lighthouse tour with the Coast Guard. He also arranged for us to retreat to a church recreation room if the weather became a problem. Everything was so well planned and running so smoothly I was unprepared to confront, for the first time, the issue of liability.

With much excitement we were preparing to load the bus, when I was handed an envelope by Colin, an energetic sixth grader with an affinity for precarious situations. As I opened the envelope, assuming it was Colin's medical consent form, I found a note explaining that, because of their religious beliefs, his parents did not give permission for Colin to receive medical treatment of any kind in any situation.

Having to make a quick decision, I decided to let Colin be included, thinking he would really benefit from the trip. He had always been a bit of a social outsider, and I hoped that sharing this adventure would bring him a little closer to his classmates. As the trip progressed, I remember being keenly aware of Colin running mindlessly across a road, nearly hanging from the rail atop the lighthouse, balancing (barely) atop a concrete wall at the remains of a World War II bunker, falling into a thorn bush, and generally seeming to flirt with disaster at every opportunity. While I undoubtedly exaggerated the risk in my mind, I realized that if Colin did require urgent medical care I would have made sure he received it—even if it meant violating his parents' wishes. I am forever grateful that I was not faced with this choice and will always remember the relief I felt as he was warmly greeted by his parents on his return.

Another incident on that trip made me realize the risks that arise from bringing students to a less-controlled environment. Peter had included a beach night sit on the agenda of activities. A night sit is a time for students to sit alone in the dark and experience the sounds, feeling, and sights at night in a natural environment. Students often reflect on this as a highlight of their outdoor experience. On this cool autumn evening, Peter and I spaced the students out on the beach facing the ocean at about 100-yard intervals. They were given instructions not to move or talk. Comfortably dressed in layers and wearing wool hats, two of the girls were settled in and beginning to enjoy the sounds of the waves breaking on the beach and looking at the stars above when they slowly became aware of something or someone moving behind them. The shuffling in the sand became louder, and they could make out the shadow of a man watching them from behind and slowly working his way closer. Determined to follow our previous instructions, the girls foolishly stayed in their places as the man crept slowly closer from behind. They were scared but stayed quietly in their spots. Eventually Peter, who was patrolling the length of the night sit from behind, saw and approached the stranger. As he headed toward him, the stranger turned and approached Peter. The stranger pointed directly at the dim figures of the girls sitting on the dark cold beach wrapped in winter coats with pointed wool hats, and excitedly whispered, "Seals!"

While becoming aware of the risks, my eyes were opened to the rich learning opportunities of taking students outdoors. They saw how sand dunes actually move and were amazed at fences and trees nearly covered. They saw the beauty of the beach at night while learning about the interdependency of all living things. The entire class became fascinated with Colin's bird journal. He had been recording every species of birds that he saw and soon had everyone in the class looking for and identifying birds. The students learned more about bird species than we could ever have taught them in a traditional classroom setting. The experience also promoted social growth, as some of the less academically successful students excelled at the tasks and activities on the trip.

At last we returned to school and to our classroom curriculum, where I realized that my lesson plans had no real connections to our recently completed trip. While I knew that the trip was worthwhile, I wondered how long-lasting the benefits would be and what I could do in the future to more fully exploit such opportunities for their educational potential.

I am still struggling with these issues. While the benefits of taking students into the field may seem illusive, I believe they are significant. Students often recall field trips long after they have forgotten many other academic experiences. I am grateful to have had Peter as a model to demonstrate how careful planning and vigilance can decrease, although not eliminate, the risks. I see outdoor learning experiences as a balancing act as I try to weigh safety and curriculum issues against maintaining excitement and allowing spontaneity that can lead to unforeseen growth and learning.

Questions for Reflection and Discussion

1. What are your personal limits to the kind of liability you are willing to expose yourself to for your students?

2. What are the legal issues surrounding medical treatment and the need for medical release forms when taking students away from school?

3. What resources are available at the local, district, and state levels for planning and implementing outdoor learning experiences?

4. How can you measure the benefits for your students from an outdoor educational experience such as the one described in this case?

5. What can a teacher do to maximize the learning from an outdoor learning experience before, during, and after the trip?

6. What issues may arise with your colleagues when you plan an extended field trip?

7. Under what conditions would you consider telling parents or guardians that you would prefer that their child not go on an extended outdoor field trip?

8. What are some benefits of collaborating with a person like Peter who is very knowledgeable of the outdoor area you plan to visit with your students? How might you identify and make contact with such a person?

■ ■ ■

Balancing the Benefits and Costs of Outdoor Learning

Teresa S. Coker

As an environmental educator, I believe that the benefits of overnight environmental education field trips greatly outweigh their costs and that one should work to minimize costs. In his case, Michael discusses some of the benefits such as the promotion of social growth and the development of long-lasting memories. I would like to add to this list.

For me, it was on an overnight environmental education field trip that I first saw how all the sciences worked together to explain the world. In school, science is subdivided into separate fields of study. In the outdoors, the disparate pieces of knowledge from the separate fields of science naturally intermingle in most discussions. I appreciate science so much more now that I have experienced it holistically. The field trip altered permanently my view and understanding of science.

But, I agree with Michael that there are costs with which to contend when leaving the school building. Liability should be a concern but not a deterrent. The outdoors should not be viewed as a chaotic learning environment. Strive to manage this unique learning environment by working closely with knowledgeable outdoor education staff to plan not only academics but safety as well. True, one will never be able to anticipate every situation, such as the person approaching the girls on the beach, but life in school can be just as unpredictable. Visit the field trip site in advance to experience as many of the activities the students will engage in as possible. As a teacher who knows the students well, you will be in a better position to anticipate their actions and reactions if you have experienced and participated in the planned activities before the trip. Also, work to prepare the students. For instance, take them right outside the school building for an activity before the trip. This will provide opportunities for you to assess how the students respond in this type of educational setting and allow you to make explicit to the students your expectations for them in this unique learning environment. The more they know about what to expect and what is expected of them, the more successful the whole experience will be.

To help maximize your benefits, include pre- and post-trip activities in the classroom related to the field trip. Plan specific learning objectives for the trip, and make sure students know what the objectives are and how they will be held accountable. And most importantly, take time to smell the flowers and enjoy learning. Your attitude and actions will speak volumes.

Finally, realize that just as it took time to learn how to effectively teach and manage a classroom, it will take time to learn how to maximize the benefits and minimize the costs for overnight environmental education field trips. But I truly believe the effort will be rewarded in the educational and social benefits reaped by the students.

Shining the Light on
Constructivistic Activities

Jill Bailer

Jill is an experienced middle school teacher who stays abreast of trends in science education and is participating in the current science education reform. For her, constructivism is a new idea regarding how to approach teaching. In this case, which includes layers of commentary, Jill describes her attempt to incorporate constructivism into her laboratory instruction and the problems it caused for her and her students. Commentaries on the case are provided by Eugene Chiappetta, a university science educator, and Andrew Kemp, a graduate student in science education and former physics teacher.

I have taught middle school science for the past 8 years. Recently, I realized the need to update my science content and pedagogy and returned to a local university to begin a master's degree program in curriculum and instruction. Science teaching appears to have undergone a major shift in thinking since I graduated from undergraduate school. For example, *constructivism* is a term used frequently during discussions about teaching and learning. This idea is one that I have had to wrestle with lately. Some literature suggests that constructivism is a theory to explain how we learn, while other literature suggests that it should be used to guide planning and teaching. It has always been my practice to try new ideas in the classroom, and this apparently new way to approach science teaching intrigued me, in spite of some doubts. Further, I wondered if I understood constructivism well enough to implement the idea into my instruction. Could I write a constructivist-based lesson? What would it look like? How would the students respond to this new way of doing things in our class? Will the students really have a better understanding of a science concept?

Eighth-grade physical science is a difficult course for most middle school students. The content requires an understanding of algebraic concepts along with pretty sophisticated science understandings. In my first year to teach this subject (my expertise lies in the life sciences), I searched for new methods to help students understand abstract science concepts. In my readings to prepare a research paper, I found a series of lessons on the properties of light that were purported to be written in a constructivistic format. I decided to implement these lessons. The materials were gathered, and we were ready for a new adventure. I introduced the lessons by saying,

> Today we are going to try something new. I am not going to tell you what you should be learning. I want you to construct your own ideas about this subject. Be sure to read all the directions on the lab before you begin. The materials you will need are in the labeled boxes, and you can collect them when needed. You and your lab partners should work together as a group to complete the tasks.

Some of the students began to read the directions, some went to gather the materials needed for the first lesson, and others began to talk. As students settled into their work, I walked around the room answering questions about the setup. "Yes, you do need two wires to connect the battery and the lightbulb. There is some electrical tape in the box at the front of the classroom; maybe taping the wires to the battery will help. If the light is not bright enough, tape two batteries together end to end." The room lights were turned off, and the experimenting began. Miniature lightbulbs flashed on and off, wires were loosened and reattached, and predictions were made and tested. Students discussed the answers to the questions within their group and began to construct their own knowledge and make sense out of what they had seen and experienced.

Over the next week, we continued with three other lessons in this manner. The students followed written directions, collected materials, and conducted the experiments. Unfortunately, they experienced some minor problems with directions that were vague and materials that were unfamiliar. Comments and questions began to arise from the students, "I don't understand what I'm supposed to see with this activity," or "I didn't understand yesterday's lesson, and now she wants me to use it to understand today's lesson. Why are we doing this? It doesn't make any sense." My response was to encourage them to keep trying, fully believing that they would eventually understand the concepts under study.

At the end of the series of lessons, there were some thinking problems to complete, and I felt these would be a great way of testing the students' understanding of light. The students worked very hard on the quiz, and my sense was that we had gotten off to a great start toward comprehending the concept of light. Imagine my reaction when only two of the students demonstrated some sense of what we had studied during the entire week, and their understanding was limited at best. No one had grasped many of the very basic principles of light. Constructivist-based lessons are supposed to be a way to allow students to construct their own knowledge, but these students had constructed erroneous knowledge and had not made sense out of what they observed. Where did we go wrong? Was it me, the instruction, the students, or a combination of all three? Or perhaps my view of constructivist teaching was too narrow. Could other instructional strategies have been used to complement this lesson?

Needless to say, I was extremely disappointed by my first attempt at constructivist teaching. As I began this adventure, the saying "Be a guide on the side, not a sage on the stage" kept ringing in my ears. As the students struggled through the lessons, I felt that I was being that guide on the side, but it seemed that the type of guidance that I was providing was not enough. Reexamination of the entire process leads me to believe that some vital parts are missing in my understanding of constructivism.

Questions for Reflection and Discussion

1. What strategies are critical to implementing a constructivist-based physical science laboratory experience for middle school students? secondary students?

2. How could you take a more traditional laboratory exercise that you have conducted often and make it more constructivistic?

3. What are some of the traditional instructional strategies that have been used by science teachers that can be modified so that they are more effective in helping students to construct fundamental science understandings?

4. Constructivism is sometimes described as an epistemology rather than a teaching method. What is epistemology? How is an epistemology, like constructivism, related to science teaching and learning?

5. What are some of the basic tenets of constructivism? What does it mean to teach science in ways that are consistent with constructivist tenets?

■ ■ ■

Constructivist Teaching Is Like Building a Jigsaw Puzzle

Eugene L. Chiappetta

I am delighted to find you attempting to infuse new educational ideas into your classroom. You cannot be faulted for trying to use constructivism to guide your teaching. Unfortunately, many teachers are confusing hands-on activities and discovery learning with teaching guided by constructivism. Real-life and firsthand experiences do not equate to learning or understanding the subject under study. Nevertheless, it is very compelling to believe that if you give students a problem to work on and the equipment to figure it out, the intended learning will result. You may be disappointed, as you have come to realize.

The construction of knowledge requires more guidance and perhaps more direct instruction than you may have been led to believe. When teaching students about light, you must spend some time setting the stage and providing some background before you involve them in laboratory work. Begin by determining what the students know about light. This can be accomplished in many ways. A demonstration on light can provide a concrete way to get students' attention and to assess their knowledge. It can also place them in the position to state what they believe about light and to put forth alternative conceptions that they hold. A carefully planned discussion can also serve the same purpose. At some point, a short lecture or demonstration may provide students with some insights and meaning for the topic.

With some background and discussion, the students will be better prepared to form new knowledge and modify what they already know about light. Now, perhaps the students can undertake a hands-on activity that permits them to observe, first-hand, properties and behavior of light in the laboratory setting. Further, many other types of instructional activities will benefit students, such as reading, writing, viewing videos, and discussing. It is important to keep in mind that you must be sensitive to what students are thinking and feeling. Are the students finding the instruction meaningful? Are they changing their conceptions about important aspects of light? Are you providing information that organizes their thinking and directs their learning? Are you using the laboratory to let students construct understandings about phenomena that can readily be constructed and using other strategies to formulate ideas that cannot be constructed in the laboratory?

Jill, you might think of constructivist teaching as similar to assembling a jigsaw puzzle. Would you ask students to fit the pieces of a puzzle together if they had no idea about the picture that was supposed to result? Probably not. This is why I stress the need to provide students with an *orientation* as to what it is about light that they are going to study. What properties are you going to address with these middle school adolescents? You should place key terms on the board, and ask the students to tell you what they understand about these properties and other related phenomena. Provide plenty of time for students to write down their thoughts in their science notebooks. The process of *eliciting* students' beliefs and ideas at this point in the instruction is critical to the constructivist-based approach. The key is to arrange the instruction so that it begins with *what students know and believe* and, from this point on, provide carefully designed experiences to challenge or confirm students' conceptions of light. In addition to laboratory sessions, many other types of instruction are necessary to facilitate the construction of knowledge. When you feel the students have had enough instruction, then help each student check his or her understanding of light, and compare and contrast their views with what they recorded at the beginning of the unit.

Constructivism: A Guiding Light

Andrew C. Kemp

Rather than view Jill as the teacher, for the moment, let us look at her as a learner. She realized that her *prior knowledge* of pedagogy was not working for all her students. She therefore *constructed* some new knowledge of constructivism. She attempted to *understand* constructivism and to *apply* it. By *reflecting* on her experiences, she recognized that she obtained results different from those she expected. She now recognizes that her knowledge and understanding were incomplete, and she promises to take steps so that her next attempt to apply the tenets of constructivism in the classroom will lead to more satisfactory results. In effect, Jill has experienced the five basic elements of the constructivist approach to learning. If we really teach as we are taught, then Jill is in a sound position to become the "guide on the side" that constructivists advocate.

The guide on the side metaphor is powerful if applied correctly. Some teachers, like Jill initially, confuse teaching based on constructivism with an indirect style of teaching. But a guide does not hide the intended destination from the travelers. Instead, a guide tells the travelers where they are headed. In addition, a guide should also take into account where the travelers are now and where they are able and willing to go. Perhaps one or more of these elements was missing from Jill's first experience in applying the tenets of constructivism.

As Eugene points out, *it is crucial to find out what students already know*, that is, where they are now. To find out what the students already know about a topic, the teacher may simply ask them or use less direct techniques such as group brainstorming, concept mapping, and discrepant event demonstrations. The students, as well as the teacher, can benefit from understanding their current knowledge structures, because these structures shape perceptions and bring meaning to the learning situation.

Once the students' relevant conceptions have been identified, the teacher and students can together decide where they are able to go next. The teacher and students can decide how to learn the designated knowledge and how to put it to use. In between the *construction* and *application* of knowledge, students must come to *understand* what they have learned. To assist in understanding, teachers can provide students with exploratory experiences and opportunities to express what they now think in relation to what they believed previously. Coming to an understanding usually requires more than advancing linearly along a preplanned path, such as a set sequence of lab activities. Between the beginning and end of a unit, the teacher-guide must be prepared to follow many paths—branching, winding, and full of unexpected encounters. A critical component of coming to understand is the desire to understand. The students must be willing to go where you wish to guide them. Otherwise, some will get lost along the way and may never catch up. Students will not be motivated to learn if they do not see any personal relevance in the science content or skills you try to teach them. A hands-on approach to teaching can help students to appreciate science as a fun class, but it does not necessarily translate science into a subject they use outside of class. The teacher can assist students by using real-life examples and by letting students pursue related topics of their own devising.

A vital and often overlooked tenet of constructivism is for the students to *reflect* on their knowledge. They have to take a look at themselves, to look back at where they were and where they are now. Journal writing, role playing, and long-term science projects can all assist students in this reflection.

Above all, it is important to remember this: Students *always* construct their own knowledge. *This fact is true regardless of the way they are taught.* What we want is not just for learners to construct their own knowledge but for students to construct *more* and *better* knowledge for themselves. This distinction is subtle but crucial, and recognizing it will help any teacher apply the theory of constructivism more effectively.

Resources to Consider

Chiappetta, E., Koballa, T., & Collette, A. (1998). **Laboratory and field work**. In *Science instruction in the middle and secondary schools* (pp. 182–207). Upper Saddle River, NJ: Merrill/Prentice Hall.

In this chapter, the authors describe the purpose of science laboratory work and discuss five types of laboratory approaches that science teachers may consider using: science process skill laboratory, deductive or verification lab, inductive laboratory, technical skill laboratory, and problem-solving laboratory. Also included in the chapter are laboratory teaching tips and suggestions for leading pre- and postlaboratory discussions and field trips.

Landis, C. (1996, September). *Teaching science in the field*. Columbus, OH: ERIC Clearinghouse for Science, Mathematics and Environmental Education. (ERIC Digest No. SE 058 899)(ERIC Clearinghouse for Science, Mathematics and Environmental Education, 1929 Kenny Road, Columbus, OH 43210) Also on-line, available: http://www.ericse.org/digests/dse96-7.html

Encouragement for engaging students in science learning experiences in the out-of-doors can be found in this summary report prepared by Carol Landis. In addition to offering suggestions to ensure that outdoor learning experiences are successful, the discussion provides information about subject integration, overcoming gender bias, and utilizing the urban environment. Over 40 references are included along with several Internet sites.

Pierce, W. (1998, January). **Linking learning to labs**. *Science Scope, 21,* 17–19.

Middle school teacher Wendy Pierce shares a five-step protocol that she developed to help students make connections between laboratory experiences and the science concepts she wants them to learn. The steps of the protocol are reflective writing, action, dialogue notes, direct teaching, and journal writing. The protocol is consistent with conceptual change theory and provides a routine for students to follow in addition to allowing for direct encounters with science materials. A sample lesson plan that uses the protocol is included with the article.

Rita, R. (1998, May). **Integrated constructivism**. *The Science Teacher, 65,* 24–27.

How can laboratories be modified to incorporate constructivist ideas? Ronald Rita describes how he did it in this article. He tells about three labs—one on gas laws, a second one dealing with soap dish microbiology, and a third about shell chemistry—in which his students designed their own experiments. Rita points out that, because students are not used to the expectations associated with constructivist-based learning, a transition period is needed before they feel comfortable with the approach.

Yeager, R. (1995). **Constructivism and the learning of science.** In S. Glynn & R. Duit (Eds.), *Learning science in the schools: Research reforming practice* (pp. 35–58). Mahwah, NJ: Earlbaum.

Robert Yeager discusses constructivism as way of thinking about science teaching and learning in this easy-to-read chapter. He touches on the influence of cognitive scientists in developing constructivism as guiding ideas in science education, the dependence of language and communication on learners' construction of understanding, and how the tenets of constructivism might be implemented in science classrooms. The chapter includes nine examples of constructivist teaching practices observed by Yeager and several colleagues in Iowa science classrooms.

8

Controversial Issues
in the Science Classroom

Science by its very nature is value laden and thus involves controversy. On the television news and in newspapers, we hear about the controversies surrounding cloning, waste disposal, the origin of life, and use of natural resources. Because these topics and so many others evoke emotional responses, science teachers intentionally focus their instruction around them to provide students with opportunities to carefully consider real-world problems. Students are extremely motivated to discuss these topics in science class, particularly when they touch on issues of personal, family, or community relevance. Decisions of what topics to address and how to introduce them to students can be complex ones for science teachers. Controversy in science classes may also arise from unintended learning outcomes. In the course of normal instruction, a teacher may engage students in activities or give information that can have unanticipated consequences. For example, the mention of the commercial use of the base indicator phenolphthalein as a laxative may result in a student testing its effect in a sports team's water cooler. Regardless of the science subject, teachers need to stay alert to controversy. Topics that are too emotionally charged or are above the students' comprehension level should be avoided. And, of course, some controversies arise without warning. Science teachers, especially those new to teaching, should seek the advice of school administrators and colleagues about the inclusion of controversial topics in their curriculum and how to respond to unexpected controversies. Above all, science teachers must act as reflective professionals and consider the benefits and potential harms associated with introducing controversial topics into their science instruction.

The four cases in this chapter represent just a sample of the many controversies that science teachers may face. In the first case, a first-year teacher finds that preserving the habitat of the spotted owl is an issue too hotly contested in one Oregon logging town for students to debate. The second case tells of how students' offended reactions to a video documentary (*A Brief History of Time,* 1997) of physicist Stephen Hawking caused a physics teacher to question the open-mindedness of people in her small, rural community. In the third case, a middle school teacher explains how he responded to students who felt the need to interject the biblical story of creation into a discussion of biological evolution and how it affected his teaching. And the final case highlights a biology teacher's response to a student who discovers during a class assignment that her parents may not be her biological parents.

I Like Spotted Owl Almost
as Much as Fried Chicken!

Norman G. Lederman

Should old-growth forests be logged for their valuable timber, or should logging be stopped to preserve the habitat of the spotted owl? As a first-year biology teacher and newcomer to a small Oregon town, Sandy Blair (a composite of several teachers with whom Norman has worked) attempts to make science instruction relevant to her students' everyday lives by having them debate this question. As Norman explains in this open case, Sandy's efforts to use this emotionally charged issue to teach about the environment and ecology raise more controversy than she had expected, and she is left wondering whether the decision to hold the debate is a wise one. A response by three veteran teachers, Stephanie Cannon, Sajin Chun, and Pam Kitchens, follows the case.

Before entering the field of teaching, Sandy Blair considered a career as a researcher in a medical laboratory. Following the completion of her master's degree in vertebrate physiology, she participated in an internship in a medical laboratory. It was during this internship that Sandy became a bit concerned about the prospect of spending the rest of her life as a bench scientist. She enjoyed people and was not sure she would find fulfillment in a career with what she perceived as limited interpersonal opportunities. One of Sandy's friends suggested she might enjoy teaching, and, after further reflection, she took the plunge and entered a teacher education program at a large Midwestern university. This was not a popular choice with Sandy's parents. They were very proud of the prospect of their daughter becoming a famous scientist. Sandy's parents had always wanted her to become a medical doctor, but a Ph.D. was an acceptable alternative. Now their daughter was not only turning down her chance to be a medical doctor, but she had also decided to enter a field with little status or economic reward.

However, the disappointment felt by her parents was not enough to deter her from her newfound career goals, and she successfully completed the teacher education program. During the program, Sandy was placed in a rural setting with an extremely creative mentor teacher. She thrived in an environment where limited resources necessitated the use of creativity. Furthermore, she appreciated the freedom from bureaucratic hassles afforded by the relatively informal administration of a rural school district. As a consequence of her highly rewarding preservice internship experience, Sandy set out to find a position as a biology teacher in a rural school. How else could you explain how the daughter of a wealthy Chicago physician found herself as a first-year biology teacher in rural Philomath, Oregon?

Philomath is a city of approximately 10,000. The school district enrolls 1,750 students and has one high school. The high school includes grades 9 to 12, and there are a total of 555 students. There are three science teachers, two of whom teach biology classes. Philomath is known as a logging community; this means that most people are employed in ways that are somehow linked to the logging industry of Oregon. The adult community can accurately be described as blue-collar. The population of Philomath has been increasing in the past few years because a wealthy logging industry executive has provided an endowment that will pay full college tuition expenses for 4 years to all students who graduate from high school. Consequently, education-oriented individuals see some merit in moving to Philomath. Nevertheless, the stress on education in Philomath cannot be described as especially strong.

Most of the students in Sandy's 10th-grade biology class are fulfilling science graduation requirements. Students need 2 years of science to graduate, and biology usually constitutes the second year. Few students take chemistry or physics. In general, the science department attempts to provide science instruction that is motivational and active. Most important, there is a consistent and concerted effort to provide a relevant context for all science concepts. Most of the students who graduate from Philomath High School will not be attending college, so the science faculty wants to offer a curriculum that meets the needs of students who will likely not take any additional science beyond high school.

The principal of the high school is very supportive of his staff and is particularly interested in having science and mathematics curricula of the highest possible quality. It is not uncommon for the principal to walk in and out of classrooms on a daily basis. These visits are not threatening to teachers as the atmosphere is strongly supportive and the visits are motivated more by curiosity than an intent to evaluate.

The students and teachers have just returned from Christmas vacation and are ready to tackle the January/February doldrums in which holidays are few and far between. It is also the rainy season in Oregon, which means few days of sunshine or dry weather will appear for several months. Sandy is beginning the portion of her course that places a strong emphasis on the environment and ecology. During the fall semester, students develop foundational knowledge in biology; the spring semester is more capstone by design, as synthesis and application of knowledge developed during the fall are the norm.

There is currently a heated debate in Oregon about the logging of old-growth forests. These forests contain valuable timber that can reap high profits in the logging industry, and logging companies have been running short of places that provide a productive yield. On the other hand, old-growth forests are the primary habitat for spotted owls, and the once abundant population of this species has decreased, perhaps by excessive logging, to a level that has placed it on the endangered species list. Sandy sees this very timely issue as a wonderful hook to capture students' attention while learning basic principles of ecology. What could be more relevant?

Although she is an inexperienced teacher, Sandy is well aware of the possible problems that can result from the discussion of controversial issues in her science classroom. Still, she wants to capture the energy of students' emotions and redirect it to facilitate the learning of biology. She knows there are strong feelings within the community about the spotted owl controversy. The community is not necessarily against discussions of controversial topics in school, but on this particular topic, emotions run high.

Most important to Sandy is to be sure to structure instruction in such a way that she cannot be accused of attempting to indoctrinate her students into one position or the other. She decides to organize her instructional unit around a debate, and thinks she can use the debate as motivation to have students learn a lot about ecology. The general organization of her unit begins with students' becoming aware of the controversy surrounding the population of spotted owls and efforts to continue logging old-growth forests. She then asks students to take an informal stand on the issue through an oral discussion and written assignment. Sandy then places students on debate teams, being careful to ensure that at least half the students are on the side of the debate opposite to their actual beliefs. She had learned about this structured controversy debate approach in her science methods course. In theory, students having to publicly argue a position opposite their true beliefs will be motivated to be much more thorough in their research of the position they must defend. In short, the debate technique is supposed to avoid having students just focus on the perspective they had before the debate.

The unit Sandy has planned will last for about 4 weeks, and it involves students in required laboratory activities and readings, student-designed investigations, and student-designed library research. Again, the primary motivation is preparation for a class debate on whether to continue logging old-growth forests. The students all appear to be excited about the debate. Naturally, some would prefer to debate a side different from what they have been assigned. Nevertheless, Sandy appears to have captured their attention, as the students certainly do not mind focusing on a topic they talk about outside of school and in their homes each day around the dinner table.

The students have been actively engaged in preparing for the debate for over 2 weeks. Sandy is extremely encouraged by the students' enthusiasm on independent assignments as well as their unusually high attentiveness during formal class meetings. On several occasions, the students have attempted to find out where Sandy stands on the debate, but she is careful not to let them know. The students are quite ingenious and may be gathering more information on her beliefs than she realizes:

JOHNNY:	So, Ms. Blair, do you think we should save the spotted owl?
SANDY:	That's for you to decide.
BOB:	Where did you grow up?
SANDY:	Chicago.
SALLY:	What did your father and mother do?
SANDY:	Didn't I already tell you my dad was a doctor and my mother had her hands full raising me and my sister?
PETER:	That's right, don't you ever pay attention, Bob?

These types of interactions are not uncommon in Sandy's class. The students like her and are naturally interested in some personal aspects of her life. With respect to the upcoming debate, the students are well aware that Sandy's parents were not from a blue-collar background and lived in rather comfortable surroundings. They are also very aware that Sandy is a biology teacher and most likely holds the same views as those scientists interviewed on the nightly news and in the newspapers. Many of Sandy's students have been discussing the upcoming debate with their parents, and their parents have been asking rather pointed questions about Sandy's background and beliefs.

It is now several days before the debate, and Sandy decides that she should have a class discussion about the rules to be followed during the debate. After all, she does not want the debate to turn into a shouting match. She really wants the students to focus on the scientific aspects of the controversy and how science, technology, and society are intimately related in such controversies. Following is a segment of Sandy's predebate discussion with her class.

SANDY:	I think we need to be clear about the ground rules for the debate. I know you all have strong feelings and you have prepared well, but we need to make sure things are orderly and that everyone who wants to talk has a chance.
	First, each team will have a chance to make some introductory comments. You will have one member of your team do this, and he or she will have no more than 5 minutes. After each team has made its introductory remarks, we will move into a rebuttal stage where each team will have 3 to 5 minutes to respond to the comments made by one of the other teams. We will keep rotating among teams until there are about 15 minutes left in the class period. Then each team will have 2 minutes to make some final comments.
	I know I don't need to say this, but remember your arguments should be based on the scientific knowledge you have learned related to the controversy. Remember, the purpose of this is to use what you have learned in science to help you make a decision.
BARB:	How will you decide who wins the debate?
SANDY:	There won't be a single winner. You all can win if you make sure that your arguments can be supported by the scientific facts.
RICK:	So how will we be graded? Won't the winners get higher grades?

SANDY: I told you, there won't be any winners and losers. You just need to defend your team's position with the facts.

Before much time has passed, the students' discussion shifts from the rules of the debate to personal and family values. Many students in the class come from families in which the primary source of income is the logging industry, while others have parents who are either professionals or earn income from industries unrelated to logging. Consequently, the money provided by the logging industry is significant for the daily survival of some students' families, while other students have the luxury of being able to have an active concern for the environment and the survival of an endangered species. The discussion quickly turns to arguments about whose concerns should be given priority and whether certain individuals' beliefs and values should supersede those of others. The discussion quickly deteriorates into students from various teams arguing with each other about the stupidity of the other team's position. Sandy tries to redirect the discussion to little avail. The students obviously have a strong emotional stake in the controversy that goes well beyond Sandy's instructional intent.

The next day Sandy receives a message from the principal. He would like to talk with her about the upcoming debate. He has received angry phone calls from numerous parents concerning her intent. Those parents against the laws prohibiting the logging of old-growth forests are very concerned that Sandy is trying to convince their sons and daughters that saving the spotted owl is the most important priority. Several of these parents have lost their jobs because of the laws protecting the spotted owl's habitat. Those parents who happen to favor protection of the spotted owl are concerned that ideas other than science are being discussed in science class. They would rather only biology be included in the biology course curriculum. Several of the parents are so concerned that they ask permission to attend the debate. The principal wants to know Sandy's response to these claims, and he wants her to provide her reasons for having the debate.

Later that day, several students from the debate team against protection of the spotted owl's habitat are seen wearing buttons that say, "I Like Spotted Owl Almost as Much as Fried Chicken." It is not clear whether the buttons are meant to be humorous or the expression of sincere sentiment. The student body appears to be divided on how to interpret the intent of the buttons.

It is now Wednesday, and the debate is scheduled for Friday. Tensions are high, and many concerns are swirling around the heads of faculty, students, and the administration.

Questions for Reflection and Discussion

1. What does Sandy think the students will learn by having this debate? Do you think the debate should take place as planned?

2. Should all students be required to participate in the debate? Should certain students be prohibited from participating? Should concerned parents be allowed to observe the debate?

3. What does Sandy believe about the spotted owl controversy, and won't this affect how she grades students?

4. Some people in communities in Oregon and other Northwestern states believe that the spotted owl controversy is not science and should not be debated by students in science class. Do you agree or disagree? What are your reasons?

5. What should be done about those students not enrolled in Sandy's biology class who have expressed their concerns about the spotted owl controversy?

6. Are the problems Sandy faces her fault, or was the reaction unavoidable? What school rules or policies might have helped Sandy avoid the problems or deal with them effectively?

7. For some of Sandy's students and their parents, the spotted owl controversy is an either–or issue of survival: the survival of a species or their families' economic survival. What points of agreement and compromise could Sandy and/or her students introduce to encourage dialogue about issues regarding the spotted owl controversy rather than debate? What are key differences between debate and dialogue?

■ ■ ■

Why Not Consider Dialogue Instead of Debate?

Stephanie L. Cannon, Sajin Chun, and Pamela J. Kitchens

In Sandy's case, the spotted owl controversy has inflamed an already divided community. As students make ready for the debate, the tension between those who have the luxury of being concerned for the environment versus those whose survival is based on logging the old-growth forests has spilled over into the school. The emotional intensity associated with the issue has led to a distrust of Sandy and is threatening to undermine her relationships with students and their parents.

Four questions seem to be at the heart of the dilemma facing Sandy: (1) Should science instruction deal with issues that are emotionally charged? (2) Is debate the most appropriate instructional strategy to use when dealing with controversial issues? (3) Should concerned parents be permitted to attend the debate? (4) How should Sandy's principal and colleagues respond to her dilemma?

First, Sandy's use of a relevant and timely issue to motivate her students is an excellent idea, but perhaps she should have chosen an issue less emotionally charged. Those students whose parents have strong feelings about the issue will likely have difficulty presenting unbiased arguments during the debate. Instead of achieving her intention of having students explore the spotted owl issue from multiple perspectives, preparation for the debate seems to have further polarized Sandy's students and attracted undue community attention. We feel that Sandy could have achieved her instructional goals by choosing another issue that would have been less emotionally charged for the community. Such issues as logging the rain forest or overfishing the oceans would have allowed Sandy to teach about the environment and ecology and provided her students with opportunities to make science-related decisions.

Second, since the community is already experiencing economic winners and losers, it makes no sense for students to rehash the issue in a class debate where winners and losers are again identified. As an alternative to debate, Sandy could have chosen to engage her students in dialogue about the spotted owl controversy. When engaged in dialogue, students strive for greater understanding of the controversy. The focus is on seeking agreement rather than finding flaws and differences. Dialogue does not focus blame or identify winners and losers but contributes to a heightened concern for different perspectives regarding a controversial issue. The desired outcome of dialogue is the realization of a negotiated solution to which all parties contribute.

An extension to student dialogue could involve bringing together experts that represent different stakeholders to share their views on the controversy. Experts— including ecologists, Sierra Club members, loggers, and sawmill operators—could work with the students to identify possible solutions. The involvement of these experts could help to alleviate the uneasiness felt by a number of Sandy's students and their parents.

Whether the spotted owl controversy is addressed via debate or dialogue, we believe that parents should not be allowed to attend the class. Their presence will only serve as a distraction for students and most likely add to the emotional intensity of the class. If dialogue is used to address the controversy, possible solutions could be presented as posters. The posters could be displayed at a local shopping mall, and parents could be invited to study them. After reading the posters, parents and other members of the community may become more informed about the controversy and more tolerant of different views.

Finally, Sandy deserves the support of her principal and colleagues in dealing with this dilemma. Ideally, Sandy would be assigned a mentor who could advise her about potential problems and help her resolve problems when they arise. In this instance, we believe that Sandy would have benefited greatly from the insights a veteran teacher could provide, particularly one who is a longtime resident of Philomath and is knowledgeable of community beliefs and values. The mentor may have viewed the spotted owl controversy as too volatile for classroom debate and suggested another topic or dialogue as an alternative to debate.

Feeling Sorry for Stephen

Kimberly L. Harmelink

This open case describes the negative reactions that Kimberly received after showing the video *A Brief History of Time* (1997) to her physics students for the past 3 years. The video is a documentary of the physicist Stephen Hawking and discusses black holes and the big bang theory. The ideas portrayed in the video were contradictory to the religious beliefs of Kimberly's physics students. In this ongoing dilemma, Kimberly cannot decide whether to continue showing the video. A response by astronomer Harry Shipman, who uses the work of Stephen Hawking (1988) in his own teaching, follows the case.

I have wanted to teach ever since I was a little girl. I remember sitting my younger brother and sisters down in our basement and forcing them to play school with me. Of course, I was always the teacher in this pretend game! I also remember always liking science, chemistry in particular. I actually won first place in the school science fair in the seventh grade. That was a big thrill for me. I used to read my Dad's old college chemistry books, too. There was something about mixing chemicals and wearing a white lab coat that excited me. I can remember writing about wanting to be a teacher in my English journal in the 11th grade. When it came time to enter college, I spent a few years as a prepharmacy major. My father is a pharmacist, and I admire him greatly. Eventually, however, my true nature prevailed, and I ended up graduating with an undergraduate degree in science education. Straight out of college, I was offered a teaching position in a small, rural high school. I was hired to teach physics, physical science, and chemistry.

This school is very small, indeed. Its enrollment is around 300 for grades 9 through 12. The community in which the school is located is very tight-knit. Everyone knows everyone else. There is a lot of pride in this community. It is part of a city school system, and years back, when outsiders tried to merge this system with a larger county one, the entire town protested. The students actually organized a walk out. Religion is very important to this community. Most of the citizens, if not all, attend church regularly and hold definite beliefs about God and the beginnings of our universe. I did not realize how strong and mature these beliefs were until I began showing this one particular video to my physics class.

The video was *A Brief History of Time* (1997), the documentary of Stephen Hawking, the physicist. I first saw this movie with my husband during our dating years. We actually saw it on one of our very first dates. I was just blown away by the movie. The questions that Dr. Hawking asked were so thought provoking. His theories on black holes were particularly interesting to me. When I began teaching science, I felt that my physics students should be exposed to this movie. None of them had even heard of Stephen Hawking, and this bothered me. He is, after all, one of the most famous physicists of our time. My intentions for showing the movie were not to challenge the religious beliefs of my students. I simply wanted them to be aware of this one particular scientist and his accomplishments. I also just wanted them to think a little.

The students who wind up in my physics classes are very intelligent. They are high achievers and place a lot of importance on making the grade. They are always the cream of the crop in our school. They work so hard, I often worry about them getting enough free time. They are usually pretty witty but polite at the same time. I never expected the comments they gave me after viewing *A Brief History of Time*. They included the following:

- "I only think Stephen Hawking gets so much attention because he is in a wheelchair."
- "Stephen Hawking does nothing but ask a bunch of questions. He does not bother to answer any of them."
- "Stephen Hawking asks too many questions. He does not have the right to do that. The mysteries of the universe are for God to know, not man."
- "Stephen Hawking is just wrong. There was no such thing as the big bang. The Bible says that God created Adam and Eve and that began the history of man. It is as simple as that."
- "It is obvious that Stephen Hawking is not a religious man. If he would just read the Bible, he would understand the origin of the universe."
- "I just don't like Stephen Hawking. He is weird. The things he says are too far out there."

I would not be telling the truth if I said these comments did not bother me. I have shown this video for the past 3 years, and while the students in my physics classes have changed, the comments to this video have not. I am concerned that showing this video has been a mistake. My physics students seem to be quite offended by the fact that Stephen Hawking asks the questions that he does. For me, however, questioning and contemplating the design of our universe are what science is all about. It makes me sad, but showing this video to my physics students seems to be a waste of time. I do not know if I will show it again next school year.

Questions for Reflection and Discussion

1. Should Kimberly show this video to her physics classes again next year? Why or why not?

2. What does Kimberly believe about Stephen Hawking and his work? How does this affect her expectations for students' reactions to the video?

3. What learning goals might Kimberly have had for her students related to the Hawking video? How might Kimberly's choice of learning goals have influenced her students' reactions to the video?

4. Kimberly does not say how she introduced the video to her physics classes. How could a teacher introduce the video so that students focus on the enormity of the questions asked by Hawking with an open mind?

5. How might reactions to the video differ among students attending a large suburban high school? An inner-city high school? What factors might be responsible for reactions that differ from those of Kimberly's students?

6. Obtain a copy of the video *A Brief History of Time* (1997), and view it. What pieces of the video would you consider showing to high school (or middle school) students during science class? Give reasons for your choices.

■ ■ ■

Stephen Hawking, Cosmology, and God in High School

Harry L. Shipman

Kimberly's dilemma presents us with a most interesting case. Its richness stems from the many ways that a teacher could use the Hawking video in the classroom. Does she want her students to appreciate Hawking's scientific talents? His struggle to overcome his disability? The deep questions that cosmologists ask? His use of the word *God* in a scientific discussion? Because Kimberly doesn't state specific goals in the case, it can stimulate a variety of thoughtful conversations among a group of teachers who read and reflect on it. I could follow a variety of different paths in my reaction to the case but will focus on one: Hawking's comments about religion. These insensitive comments may be one source of the strong negative reaction from some of Kimberly's students.

It has recently become fashionable for science writers to use the word *God* in science popularizations. Hawking is no exception. The video includes two famous one-liners. In one, he asserts that "God not only plays dice but throws them where they cannot be seen." Hawking also claims more extravagantly that the discovery of a unified theory of the laws of nature "would be the ultimate triumph of human reason—for then we would know the mind of God." This closing sentence of *A Brief History of Time* (the book; 1988) appears elsewhere in Hawking's work, including the video.

But making flip comments about God is not the same thing as seriously addressing the issue of science and religion. Hawking's brief sentences are a bit like Monty Python jokes: meaningful and maybe even funny if you understand the context, and potentially offensive if you don't. I don't know Kimberly's students, but my students who are conservative Christians find Hawking's one-liners offensive. For what it's worth, I also dislike the one-liners, for different reasons. I'm an astronomer, not a conservative Christian; I understand the jokes, but see them as trivializing a deep issue.

By showing the entire video, including the one-liners, Kimberly brought the issue of religion into her classroom. Should she plan to show Hawking's heroism and omit the religion, she can present selected portions of the video. It's easy to edit with VCRs; I do it at home—telling my students, of course, that they are seeing edited material. I'd never burn 90 minutes of class time with the Hawking video, or with any video for that matter.

I'm not sure that we are doing a service to our students, though, by ducking the issue of science and religion. I now think it's a mistake to simply tell the big bang story in an astronomy class—even if you include the evidence, which shows that it is science—and ignore the religious connections. Science educators David Jackson, Liz Doster, Lee Meadows, and Teresa Wood (1995) have shown that the way we teach sensitive scientific issues like cosmology and evolution leaves some students with the mistaken impression that you can believe in the big bang, or you can believe in God, but you can't believe in both at the same time.

Fortunately, the voices of some theistic scientists like John Polkinghorne (1994), Owen Gingerich (1994), Nobel Laureate Charles Townes (1995), and others like the philosopher Ian Barbour (1997) are beginning to be heard. A believer in God can certainly accept the big bang. Some scientists go further. Our contemporary picture of cosmic evolution provides a very natural place for a Supreme Being, a Creator. Biological evolution is a bit more subtle, but the National Association of Biology Teachers has specifically excluded the terms *impersonal* and *unsupervised* from their definition of what evolution is. How much of this discussion should enter the classroom and how much should be reserved for individual teacher–student conversations depends on the teacher, the students, and the school environment. I do introduce this material in classes in a state university with no difficulty. I appreciate that the situation might be different if I taught in a school like Kimberly's.

Sensitive issues deserve a sensitive treatment. Hawking's one-liners are not a sensitive treatment of the dialogue between science and religion. If I were Kimberly, I'd show excerpts from the video, if I used it at all.

■ ■ ■

Religion or Science: Revisiting the Scopes Trial in Seventh Grade

Joseph Conti and P. Elizabeth Pate

This closed case portrays the tension a middle school science teacher experiences when faced with two competing referents: valuing student opinion and input into the lesson; and at the same time, wanting students to examine a value-laden issue objectively. This case describes how Joe chose debate as a means by which middle school students research and discuss the topic of evolution. It shares his dilemma of figuring out how this experience affected him as a teacher and how it might have affected the students. The case is followed by Joe's reflections on the experience and how he now teaches evolution and is then followed by a response written by Lawrence Scharmann, a science educator who has written extensively about teaching evolution in school.

I was first a biologist, then a teacher. Bachelor's and master's degrees in biology and wildlife ecology, respectively, gave me a strong background in the science areas. I also worked in laboratories for over 6 years and published a number of scientific articles. Switching careers, I felt teaching would be a challenge and a great way for me to share my experiences and knowledge of science. Although I intended to teach high school biology, I began teaching in a middle school, where I have been teaching for the last 12 years. My teaching has allowed me to share my experiences. But what a challenge teaching science is in the middle school, especially when the topic of evolution is studied. I struggle with helping my students learn about the scientific tenets of evolution while acknowledging their own personal opinions on the issue. Sometimes it is especially hard because my students are struggling with their own identity and trying to figure out what they believe and what they don't believe.

A familiar topic in most middle schoolers' life science (or biology) texts is how organisms have changed, or evolved, over time. In a recent guidebook intended for teachers, parents, school administrators, and policy makers, the National Academy of Sciences has reinforced the teaching of evolution:

> There is no debate within the scientific community over whether evolution has occurred, and there is no evidence that evolution has not occurred. ("Panel Affirms Importance of Evolution Classes," April 10, 1998)

According to the newspaper article, teaching evolution still causes trouble in schools, even though more than 70 years have passed since the John Scopes case and a later Supreme Court ruling on the matter. John Scopes was convicted of violating a Tennessee law against teaching evolution, and over 10 years ago, the Supreme Court ruled that public schools cannot teach that God created the universe. But when considering the emotional, moral, and intellectual development of students at the middle school age, the topic of evolution is often approached cautiously by many teachers. This is especially true when the material goes directly against the religious views of many students and families.

Despite fears around teaching this subject in a small, rural middle school in Northeast Georgia, all basically went well. Until a few years ago.

That year, one of my seventh-grade classes included a large number of extremely bright students who were very outspoken. Needless to say, the discussion around Darwin and evolutionary theory was lively! I let everyone express their own views, and encouraged the students to value each other's opinions. However, the discussion began to get out of hand when two of the students began a light argument.

Frank mumbled, "That's NOT what the Bible says! Evolution is just a theory. The Bible tells me what to believe."

"But, it's good science! It is a theory, but there is evidence that supports it. What about evidence from fossils or evidence from genetics? Besides, if God didn't want us to question and wonder and seek knowledge, He wouldn't have given us the mental capacity to think!" retorted Jimmy.

I thought fast because I wanted to capitalize on this heated discussion. I wanted to see if the students could engage in scientific debate. I wanted to value their opinions and input, but at the same time I wanted them to examine this value-laden issue objectively.

After discussion with my colleague Elizabeth about issues related to student input and developmental needs of middle school students, I decided to challenge Jimmy and Frank, along with any others who wanted, to take sides and debate. I established guidelines with one limitation in mind: that religion was not to be an issue in the debate. In other words, evolution had to be debated on its own merits. There would be two sides: proevolution and antievolution.

Frank and Jimmy immediately rose to the challenge, and several others from the classroom took sides. We decided that each group would have 1 week to conduct research and collect evidence that would support their position.

The debate started out great. Both sides were ready to defend their positions. We began by tossing a coin to see who would present first. The debaters had done their homework. The antievolution side started the discussion by presenting a variety of theories about evolution. They then pointed out what was wrong or incomplete about each theory. The proevolution side countered with evidence that supported each theory. Each group was truly trying to argue their case objectively.

However, after about 13 minutes of lively discussion, the proevolution side had made several good counterattacks that the antievolutionists could not respond to. There was an eerie period of silence from this group, followed by a response that went something like, "Yeah, well in the Bible, it says that. . . . "

I immediately called, "Time out!" The debate was halted, and everyone was reminded of the limitations: Evolution had to be debated on its own merits. The debate continued until once more it heated up so intensely that the antievolutionists again brought up the Bible. At this point, I felt that as rules were again being violated the debate should be ended. There was some rumbling from the debaters and some continued discussion as the students went back to their seats.

Even though I was the one who called an end to the debate because we just couldn't seem to get away from personal opinions and beliefs on the topic, I felt a sense of loss. The students were sharp; they were charged with emotions; and they were doing a great job at presenting their sides. There was tension in the air, but that tension wasn't all negative. These kids were truly impassioned about what they were saying. It was great to see them so excited about an intellectual and controversial topic. I felt compelled to halt the debate because the rules were broken. Yet I wanted to continue because it was affording students the opportunity to wrestle with their own views, sort fact from religion, and analyze their own beliefs.

This was the first and last time I tried a science-based only debate on the topic of evolution. I chose this activity—debate on the science behind evolution—in spite of the fact that I could have been stepping on hazardous ground, as students and parents may have been upset that religious input was stifled. Certainly, I did not want to re-create the Tennessee Scopes Trials in this Georgia community!

Questions for Reflection and Discussion

1. Can or should teachers illustrate for students ways in which the biblical story of creation and the theory of evolution are different, yet complementary, ways of answering questions about the origins of life? If so, what examples or methods can be used that are sensitive to students' beliefs or changing beliefs?

2. How can a debate, such as the one Joe described, be handled so that lively discussion can occur about evolution without exposing the value-laden beliefs of the students?

3. What kinds of evidence illustrate proevolution and antievolution?

4. How can curriculum be organized around value-laden topics in science that is sympathetic to the emotional, moral, and intellectual development of students at the middle school age? At the high school age?

5. How do we reconcile that, in cases such as these, on the one hand we seek to value student input and, on the other hand, stifle student thoughts and beliefs?

■ ■ ■

Joe's Reflections on Debating Evolution

Joseph Conti

Several years later, on analyzing what occurred in the classroom, I had these thoughts:

When I first started teaching, I wanted my students to know everything that I knew and appreciated about science, and this included the theory of evolution. Because this theory seemed so believable to me, I somehow wanted students to see its logic as well. After all, I thought, if I could at least acknowledge this theory as possibly being true, why couldn't they? I was a Catholic by birth, had grown up in a Catholic household, attended Catholic schools from first through twelfth grades, and graduated from a Catholic-based university, where I learned about evolution theory from a priest. I had hoped my classroom debate would have at least enlightened students to evolution's possibility. Maybe it did, but it appeared to me that in the minds of at least some students, walls were erected that could not be overcome by science. This was a fact I would have to learn to accept.

I have since come to realize that it was not my place to sequester religious beliefs, and I may have inadvertently done this by not letting those particular students have their say. Maybe I shouldn't have stopped the debate. On the other hand, I also understand and accept the prohibition of religious discussions in the public school classroom as mandated by law. Therefore, I probably will never attempt a formal debate on such a controversial issue in a public school classroom again.

I continue to teach evolution theory and how it relates to genetics in my science classes as it occurs in the school text. In recent years I have had students continue to challenge this theory individually in class, and I accept their opposition to it. I tell students that evolution theory is just that, a theory, that can never be proven but that enough science evidence exists for it to be at least believable. I leave the option of belief up to the students without giving them my own opinion (since younger students are so impressionable). Also, if opposition to it brings up any dialogue of a religious nature, I tell students we are not allowed to discuss this or any other topic in religious terms. We could discuss opposition to evolution on scientific grounds as some scientists do.

My presentation of evolution theory is not intended to challenge student's religious beliefs but simply to challenge their thinking about how life could have changed over time. If they find the theory to conflict with their religious beliefs, I suggest to them that they discuss the issue with their parents and clergy. It has taken some years for me as a teacher to feel comfortable with the approach I have just described with regard to the teaching of evolution. You might say I have undergone a sort of evolution myself.

■ ■ ■

Teaching Evolution: Debate Versus Discussion

Lawrence C. Scharmann

> The teacher of biology has an opportunity—and an obligation—to point out some of the practical implications of Darwinian theory for human conduct. A thoughtful biologist cannot fail to find (in Shakespeare's words) "tongues in trees, books in the running brooks, sermons in stones. . . . " If he is interested in people as well as in things—and a teacher should be, even if a researcher is not—he will want to help students hear the sermon. (Hardin, 1973, p. 15)

I urge biology teachers not to try to convince a student to believe in evolution. Echoing the sentiments expressed so eloquently by Garrett Hardin, it is far more important to have students realize that although they may find aspects of evolution questionable, we virtually all accept the practical implications and beneficial consequences of evolutionary thinking (e.g., antibiotics, herbicides, etc.). Evolution, like any theory, is an extraordinarily powerful explanation that can be used as a tool to solve problems; it doesn't need to be true, it just needs to work as a problem-solving heuristic.

The most difficult dilemma for teachers is to convince students that in providing a theory as a new tool, we are not making a return of any other tool (e.g., religious beliefs) a condition for accepting the new one. But is it possible for secondary science teachers to provide explicit instruction on evolution in such a psychologically responsible manner? The answer to this question depends greatly on each individual teacher's willingness to adopt instructional strategies that are far more student centered than most secondary science teachers are accustomed to using (Duschl & Gitomer, 1991; Scharmann, 1993).

This shift in instructional approach is especially crucial in relation to the teaching of evolution. Why? Because when students have difficulty with a topic they perceive to be controversial, they may simply not be ready to adopt a position on evolution that is consistent with the one held by a practicing biologist (or biology teacher). Rather than pushing students too far too soon (teaching evolution as fact, accept it or not), ignoring their need to struggle with a healthy intellectual and/or emotional challenge (by sidestepping the topic), or attempting to meet their intellectual needs by using a teacher-directed comparison of competing theories (i.e., evolution vs. creation science), teachers need to find more responsible, holistic, and persuasive alternatives (Nelson, 1986; Scharmann, 1993). Indeed, teachers need to provide students with opportunities to get part of the way there with reference to understanding the tools of science (i.e., theories) the way that a biologist does.

If I had given this advice to the teacher in the case, he might claim that in choosing to use a debate format he was involving students in research, making learning participatory for his students, and providing them an intellectually challenging vehicle for examining a crucial scientific issue. While all this is true and the appearance of student centeredness is certainly present, the use of a debate as the primary instructional vehicle is nonetheless a suspect decision. Debates are usually structured to obtain a group reward; in other words, because there exists an element of competition (proevolution vs. antievolution), there can typically be only one winner. When applied to controversial issues, debates tend to exaggerate differences and exacerbate tensions.

The logic used by the teacher to include students in their own learning was excellent, but rather than giving up and returning to traditional teacher-centered instruction, I suggest modifying the debate into an organized small-group peer discussion; a discussion that employs student–student interactions followed by student–teacher exchanges (maybe even a lecture or two) and a final reflection activity.

Good small-group discussions differ from debates in that participants are not trying to convince one another concerning who is right or wrong. The result of such a discussion, which employs sound cooperative learning practices, aims at assisting each individual to participate in group decision making without necessarily agreeing with the final group consensus. When applied to controversial issues, small-group peer discussions permit each group of four to five students to determine their rules of discussion without the threat that their views might not agree with that of their teacher or other peer discussion groups. The culminating reflection activity permits individuals to reconstruct personal viewpoints independently and obtain an individual reward. In addition, reflections might simply be a personal journal entry read only by the teacher (not shared with fellow classmates or even parents); it is this reflection, however, that enhances an individual student's chances of getting part of the way there in thinking through a more informed personal view of evolution.

Getting part of the way there can provide students with a place to stand between what many students might initially perceive as competing dichotomies (e.g., proevolution vs. antievolution; Christianity vs. atheism). This place to stand is analogous to a reference made by Duschl and Gitomer (1991), in summarizing conceptual change teaching strategies, as "positioning the learner for the next step." Positioning students to take that next step is pivotal if we hope to promote a more adequate understanding of the nature of science and why biologists consider evolution theory as their most powerful contemporary tool. If we fail to provide this place to stand, at best we risk students' memorizing what they think we, as teachers, want to hear. At worst, we risk alienating their future study in the biological sciences.

Broken Blood Lines

Ava L. Bozeman

As a student teacher, Ava looked to Mickey Daniels, a 20-year veteran biology teacher, for guidance and support. One day during their prep period, Mickey told Ava about a genetics lesson on determining the probability of human offspring blood types and how the lesson led a student to discover that the man and woman she grew up with as her parents were really not her biological parents. In this closed case, Ava describes how Mickey dealt with this most uncomfortable dilemma. A response to the case is provided by John Penick, a science educator and coeditor of *Biology: A Community Context* (Leonard & Penick, 1998).

I met Mickey while I was student teaching and was impressed by her teaching skills and with her relationship with her students. After 20 years of excellence in teaching science, Mickey was well deserving of her recent nomination for district Teacher of the Year. Often during our planning time, I asked Mickey about different classroom situations and how she would handle them. She answered all of my questions with the same confidence she exhibited in her teaching. During one of our discussions, she told me about an incident that occurred about 10 years ago when she was teaching at a different school.

At the time, Mickey was teaching in a small high school in a neighboring county. The student population of this particular school was ethnically diverse, but the majority of the students were African American. Mickey told me that she enjoyed teaching there because of the diverse population and her good rapport with the students and their parents.

Near the end of a genetics unit, Mickey taught a lesson on different blood types. It did not involve students typing their own blood but made use of available family information to strengthen the students' understandings about independent assortment and probability. She also intended for the lesson to serve as another way to illustrate how to use a Punnett square.

Mickey began the lesson with an introduction of the different blood types. She explained that blood type O is considered to be the universal donor and that people who are type O can receive only type O blood. She went on to discuss blood types A, B, and AB in turn. Mickey then showed the students an example similar to the one in Figure 8.1, which illustrates two people with two different blood types and the possible blood types of their offspring.

After showing this example, Mickey gave the students an activity to complete as homework. The activity sheet had a space for recording the student's blood type and the blood types of his or her parents. The students were to use the Punnett square to determine the possible blood types of their parents' offspring.

The next day Linda, a bright and well-mannered student, came to Mickey before class for help in using the Punnett square. Linda said that she did not believe she was using it correctly, because her blood type was not among those possible for her parents' offspring. She showed Mickey her completed activity sheet, and it revealed that Linda's mother's blood type was A and her father's was AB. Linda was blood type O.

"Linda, are sure that you have the correct blood types for your parents?" Mickey asked.

"Yes, I found them on their medical charts in their bedroom."

"Are you sure that you are blood type O?"

"Yes," Linda replied.

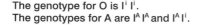

Mother has blood type "O" and Father has blood type "A."

The genotype for O is $I^i I^i$.
The genotypes for A are $I^A I^A$ and $I^A I^i$.

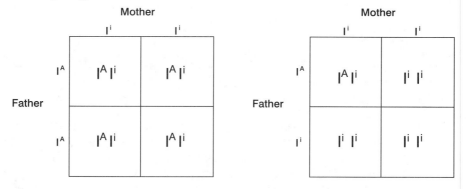

Offspring of these parents can have blood types A or O.

FIGURE 8.1   Mickey's Punnett square example.

Mickey was sure that if Linda's information was correct Linda could not be her parents' offspring, but she was less sure about what to do next. Should she tell Linda to go home and talk to her parents or tell Linda that she may be adopted? Mickey decided to tell Linda that the Punnett square results are probabilities and not definite. Linda accepted Mickey's answer and went to her desk for the start of class. That night, Mickey called Linda's parents and explained what had happened. It turned out that Linda had been adopted, and her parents had not found the right time to tell her. They told Mickey that they would tell Linda immediately but suggested that she stop doing this activity with her classes. Mickey followed their advice and never did the blood type activity again.

Questions for Reflection and Discussion

1. Should Mickey have used this activity with her classes? Explain your reasons.

2. What guidance should a teacher give students about accessing personal information, even from family members?

3. How could the activity be modified so a teacher would not encounter Mickey's dilemma?

4. Was Mickey correct in telling Linda that "the Punnett square results are probabilities and not definite"? How would you have responded to Linda's question about the Punnett square results?

5. How might parents or guardians be informed about class assignments in order to avoid a dilemma such as that encountered by Mickey?

6. How should a teacher deal with sensitive information that a student discovers about his or her family through a class assignment?

■ ■ ■

Real Science May Lead to Unexpected Outcomes

John E. Penick

In our teaching today, we encourage teachers to think of their students as they plan lessons and carry them out. We further exhort teachers to design lessons so that students are learning in context and have a need to know and learn the information presented. By doing so, we feel that the students will find the lessons and knowledge relevant and be motivated to learn. Here is an example of a situation where the teacher did, indeed, make the lesson relevant to the student involved. The learning, however, went well beyond what the teacher had imagined.

The issue here is not just about one student learning in an awkward manner that she was adopted; rather, it is about teaching, learning, becoming more aware of our surroundings and ourselves, and growing up. Of course, the student and family in this case are impacted, perhaps even negatively, but one should not blame the teacher for this any more than we should blame the math teacher when a student learns enough to calculate that less than nine months elapsed between the time of her parents' marriage and her own birth.

Genetics, by definition, is looking at causes and consequences, not just of genes, chromosomes, and genotypes but of phenotypes as well. Good teachers sincerely hope that their students will ask new and insightful questions and come to new understandings and see possible consequences as a result of their teaching. It's always awkward when young people begin to ask questions about sensitive subjects. We also know that the awkward questions get more difficult as the student gets older. But, at some point they need answering, usually sooner rather than later.

As the parents noted in this case, they "had not found the right time to tell her." Don't blame the teacher here; she did not tell the student. Instead, she prepared the student with knowledge and skills that the student applied. Once equipped with such learning, the teacher is not responsible for when the learner chooses to use it. Sometimes you can look for the right time, and sometimes the right time finds you, often when you least expect it. While this does not make it any less embarrassing or inconvenient, it does provide a teachable moment for all. The issue will rarely go away in any other fashion.

It's easy to understand why the teacher felt upset and would choose not to do this lesson again. But, if all teachers quit teaching anything that students could use to find out what their parents did not want them to know, we would have to close schools, and very quickly. If ignorance is our goal, then this is a fine plan. Instead, we must assume that all of our students are becoming adults and need to be well educated to deal with and place value on adult problems and issues, including potentially unpleasant outcomes.

Eliminating this lesson from her curriculum sounds very much like the response of someone who does not have a clear rationale for teaching the lesson and who has not thought through the possible consequences of students doing the assignment. How differently the teacher (and students, perhaps) might have responded had she looked at the possible outcomes, brainstorming with students to identify those with potentially deleterious effects, thus indirectly warning students about what could be found. Few would be surprised if the student in question didn't already have some questions about her own origins, based on physical characteristics, comments by others that she didn't much resemble the others in the family, or strangely missing pieces of history.

If teachers quit teaching particular aspects of their subject because a parent complains, we can easily look forward to a curriculum where little beyond rote facts can be taught. And many of even those facts might also be gone or distorted as the Flat Earth Society members join forces with those who are firmly convinced that no one has walked on the moon and the videos we have all seen were filmed in the

Nevada desert or on a film stage. A free society implies a free educational system, where truth, no matter how painful, is the expectation in our classrooms.

I encourage the teacher to teach this lesson in future years but to prepare students for real outcomes. Tell the students that "In our class we do real science; as is the nature of science, we don't always know the outcome before we begin. When we find new information, we must then analyze, seek alternative explanations, and test our ideas. Science does not provide the value of new ideas; we, ourselves, must determine that. Sometimes we will find things we can't believe. Go on, be skeptical, but never stop questioning and investigating. That is the way of science."

Resources to Consider

A brief history of time [Video]. (1997). (Available from Paramount Productions, Hollywood, CA)

This 84-minute videocassette is based on Stephen Hawking's book of the same name that was first published in 1988. The video does an excellent job of revealing aspects of Hawking's genius, the struggles he faces as a sufferer of motor neuron disease, and his ability to convey very complex scientific ideas in a way that most people can understand. Points in the video are considered offensive by some viewers because of Hawking's sometimes flippant references to religion and God in his discussion of the origin and workings of the universe.

Goldfarb, T. (1997). *Taking sides: Clashing views on controversial environmental issues*. Guilford, CT: Dushkin/McGraw-Hill.

This book examines 18 controversial environmental issues in terms of the contrasting perspectives of leaders in the field. Author Theodore Goldfarb highlights issues associated with the disposal of wastes, the environment and technology, philosophical and political issues associated with the environment, and issues pertaining to the environment and the future.

McCann, W. (1997, May). *Teaching about societal issues in science classrooms*. Columbus, OH: ERIC Clearinghouse for Science, Mathematics, and Environmental Education. (ERIC Digest No. SE 060 622) (ERIC Clearinghouse for Science, Mathematics, and Environmental Education, 1929 Kenny Road, Columbus, OH 43210) Also on-line, available: http://www.ericse.org/digests/dse97-1.html

In this condensed, four-page publication, Wendy McCann presents a wealth of information about science-related societal issues, including a rationale for addressing them in science classrooms and suggestions for implementation. Also included are lists of Internet and print resources on different aspects of science-technology-society.

National Academy of Science. (1998). *Teaching about evolution and the nature of science*. Washington, DC: National Academy Press. (National Academy Press, 2101 Constitution Avenue, NW, Box 285, Washington, DC 20055. 800-642-6242) Also on-line, available: www.nap.edu/readingroom/books/evolution98

This seven-chapter work includes discussions of scientists' views of evolution, how evolution explains the diversity and similarity of life on earth, and the nature of science as a means to understand the natural world in which we live. It also contains several activities for teaching about evolution and the nature of science and guidance for selecting appropriate instructional materials. Answering the questions about evolution frequently asked by students and parents should be easier after reading this book.

Science, technology and society (STS) [On-line]. School of Library and Information Studies, University of Alberta. Available: http://www.ualberta.ca/~slis/guides/scitech/kmc.html

This Web site is an excellent resource for science teachers interested in incorporating STS into their classes. Links from the main site include the history of science, the philosophy of science, and computers in society. Unique aspects of the site are a list of STS newsgroups and listservs and a section that provides titles and abstracts of recently published STS-related books called "Food for STS Thought in Print."

Stahl, R., & Stahl, N. (1995). *Society and science: Decision-making episodes for exploring society, science and technology*. Menlo Park, CA: Addison-Wesley.

This book, authored by Robert and Nancy Stahl, is a wonderful resource for strategies that are useful in addressing STS topics in the secondary science classroom. The book includes structured decision-making episodes that can be used with middle school and high school students.

References

A brief history of time [Video]. (1997). (Available from Paramount Productions, Hollywood, CA)

Barbour, I. (1997). *Religion and science: Historical and contemporary issues*. San Francisco: Harper.

Duschl, R. A., & Gitomer, D. H. (1991). Epistemological perspectives on conceptual change: Implications for educational practice. *Journal of Research in Science Teaching, 28,* 839–858.

Gingerich, O. (1994). Dare a scientist believe in design? In J. M. Templeton (Ed.), *Evidence of purpose: Scientists discover the creator*. New York: Continuum Publishers.

Hardin, G. (1973). Ambivalent aspects of evolution. *American Biology Teacher, 35,* 15.

Hawking, S. W. (1988). *A brief history of time.* New York: Bantam Books.

Jackson, D. F., Doster, E. C., Meadows, L., & Wood, T. (1995). Hearts and minds in the science classroom: The education of a confirmed evolutionist. *Journal of Research in Science Teaching, 32,* 585–612.

Leonard, W., & Penick, J. (Eds.). (1998). *Biology: A community context.* Cincinnati, OH: South-Western Educational Publishing.

Nelson, C. E. (1986). Creation, evolution, or both? A multiple model approach. In R. W. Hanson (Ed.), *Science and creation: Geological, theological, and educational perspectives* (pp. 128–159). New York: Macmillan.

Panel affirms importance of evolution classes. (1998, April 10). *The Athens Banner-Herald*, p. 8A.

Polkinghorne, J. (1994). *The faith of a physicist*. Princeton, NJ: Princeton University Press.

Scharmann, L. C. (1993). Teaching evolution: Designing successful instruction. *American Biology Teacher, 55,* 481–486.

Townes, C. (1995). *Making waves*. Woodbury, NY: American Institute of Physics.

9

The Role of Technology in
Science Teaching and Learning

Since the advent of microcomputers in the 1970s, the number of computers in science classrooms has steadily increased. Today, few science classrooms are without them, and they are put to a variety of uses. Teachers use them to prepare lessons, check attendance, and record student grades, but their most important use by far has been in the role of instruction. The microcomputer can function as an instructional tutor to help students learn science concepts and skills through tutorials or simulations; and when coupled with other electronic technologies, such as CD-ROM players and sensors, the microcomputer can be used to collect and analyze laboratory data or engage learners in hypermedia-based adventures.

Recent advances in telecommunications have further enriched the science learning environment. From their own classrooms, students are now able to communicate with others around the world via e-mail and, when using the World Wide Web, to access information never before obtainable.

In a broader sense, technology is much more than the electronic products associated with our computer age. It encompasses the ideas humans use to solve problems and extend our capabilities as well as the artifacts and tools associated with mental activity (*Resources for Technology Education*, 1998; Veal, Jackson, Finnegan, Tippins, & Crockett, 1995). The process of problem solving that leads to extended human capabilities is called *design under constraint* (National Science Foundation, 1992) because it involves clarifying and finding solutions to problems that have many correct answers. This type of problem solving is often associated with the Science-Technology-Society-Environment (STSE) movement because the problems investigated are often linked to issues of social or environmental concern. Having students design an egg container that when dropped from some height above the ground will keep the egg from breaking is one example of a design technology problem investigated in science classes. Lessons like this are most frequently used for their motivational value and to help students understand the application of scientific concepts and principles within a simulated or real-world context. Whether using computers and other electronic devices or the associated thought processes, science teachers face many challenges as they incorporate technology in their classes.

The three cases included in this chapter highlight dilemmas associated with science teachers and students using computer technologies or engaging in design technology experiences. The first case reveals the challenges that one teacher faced when her ninth-grade students used the World Wide Web to gather information to answer their own questions about weather phenomena and forecasting. The second case describes a middle school teacher's initial experience using a design technology project to help her students learn about Newton's Third Law. An important dilemma in the case centers on the teacher's decisions about the cooperative grouping needed to facilitate the design technology lesson. The third case details a teacher's decision-making processes as she plans for the infusion of microcomputer-based activities into her middle school science class. The case focuses on the challenges associated with using different tasks and classroom arrangements to help previously low-achieving students learn science.

■ ■ ■

Does World Wide Web Surfing
Guarantee Learning?*

Joseph L. Hoffman

This open case describes a teacher's first effort to have students utilize the World Wide Web for a research project in a ninth-grade physical science classroom. Mary, a pseudonym for the teacher of the class, encouraged her students to develop questions pertaining to weather that had personal meaning and were broad enough to sustain them in a week-long information-seeking task. Using the World Wide Web, students gathered information about the topic, developed solutions to their questions, and prepared written reports to represent their new understandings. During the course of the investigation, Mary realized that her students experienced significant difficulty when using on-line resources for inquiry-based activities. This difficulty was attributed to students (1) having problems using search engines; (2) often changing their research questions to match available resources; (3) not assessing the credibility of resources; and (4) not taking the time to synthesize information they found on the World Wide Web. Commentary about the case is provided by Joseph Hoffman, the case author; Joseph Krajcik; and Elliot Soloway. All are science and technology educators with expertise in the student use of technological tools like the World Wide Web for long-term investigations.

*The case is based on synthesis of early research from the *Middle Years Digital Library Project* (1998) of teachers and students engaged in similar activities on the World Wide Web. This work was supported by the NSF/ARP/NASA Digital Library Initiative; by a grant from the NSF NIE Initiative for the University of Michigan Digital Library Project (RED-9554205); and by the University of Michigan.

Mary has been teaching mathematics and physical science for 10 years at Kennedy High School and is characterized by her colleagues as a dedicated educator who consistently achieves outstanding results with her students through the use of a wide range of instructional methods. One of these methods includes engaging students in research with print-based resources to foster in-depth construction of knowledge. In addition, her students have consistently used desktop publishing software to develop high-quality reports and other representations of their new understandings. The recent construction of a computer lab with 15 net-worked multimedia machines has allowed Mary to take greater advantage of technology, and she is one of the first teachers to consider using its World Wide Web connectivity for classroom work. Like the majority of her students, Mary has some experience with the use of the World Wide Web and has used it to obtain specific information of interest. Although Mary has mentioned the benefits of a diverse range of information available on the Web to her students, she has not required them to use it as a resource for a long-term assignment.

The ninth-grade science curriculum at Kennedy High School includes a 6-week unit on weather phenomena and forecasting, culminating with a 1-week project involving student library research on a specific weather topic. Mary modifies the project to utilize the computer lab and its connection to the World Wide Web as a method for students to obtain information rather than incorporating traditional print-based resources from the school media center.

Mary defines a set of tasks for her students: (1) Develop a broad question that has personal interest to you and your partner. (2) Locate information using an on-line search engine on the World Wide Web. (3) Gather specific information related to your question. (4) Develop a three-page report with both text and pictures explaining the solution or answer to your question. In addition to presenting these tasks, Mary clarifies that research questions should be able to sustain student work through an entire week. She remarks to her students,

> As you think about your research question, be sure to keep in mind that it should be a topic that will keep you busy all week. It shouldn't be a question that has a simple one-sentence or one-paragraph answer. You need to choose a question that will make you dig deep for the answer, and your report should show how hard you worked.

Mary is also concerned that some students may have varying levels of expertise in using computers and the World Wide Web. To ensure that student groups will succeed when locating information, Mary chooses pairs containing at least one student with prior experience with Web browsers and on-line search engines.

Mary is initially impressed with both the depth and open-ended nature of questions students develop for their research: How can I protect my family in case of a tornado? Why are tornadoes more unpredictable than hurricanes? What effect will global warming have on the weather where I live? In addition to students' questions, Mary is pleased with how adept some pairs are at using a search engine to enter specific search terms (i.e., tornado, global warming, hurricanes) and browse through various sites and pages on the World Wide Web. She comments to one group, "That looks like a nice site for learning about waterspouts; you two must be experts at using search engines."

However, 3 of the 15 groups experience difficulty using search engines, and Mary devotes a significant amount of time to coaching the students. She is encouraged by the end of the first on-line session when these students are able to use a search engine to perform simple searches and obtain information from the Web. Mary concludes the first session early to discuss students' progress. Many students mention they enjoyed surfing on the Web and browsing through weather-related sites but were frustrated by the lack of specific information about their questions. A number of comments included, "We saw some great tornado pictures but couldn't find stuff about protecting yourself." "There was a lot of information on hurricanes. . . . The information we needed was probably hiding in there somewhere." "I found a ton of really neat stuff on winter storms but nothing about my question." However, Mary is hopeful for the next session. She remarks, "I can see a lot of you were frustrated because you couldn't locate any information on your topic. Don't worry, we have a few more days in the computer lab, and I'm sure you will be able to find your answer tomorrow."

Mary continually monitors the progress of students during subsequent on-line sessions. She observes students continue to be eager to return to the lab and spend the entire hour using the Web to locate information on their topics. Mary is encouraged at the effort students put forth on this project and is pleased with the lack of discipline problems occasionally experienced in her classroom.

Toward the end of the week, Mary comments to her students, "This week is going by very fast, and I can see all of you are working very hard, but I just wanted to remind you that papers are due 2 days from now." This raises the excitement level of students, and they appear to work more feverishly at typing their papers, copying images from the Web, and inserting them into their documents. During the last 2 days of the project, Mary increases her level of scrutiny of student progress. She asks a number of groups, "How is your research going so far? Are you getting close to putting your paper together?" Although a number of groups appear to be making good progress, some student comments include "Our question was about creating a lightning-proof house, and we couldn't find that anywhere on the Web." " We wanted to research the effect of global warming on the trees in our neighborhood, but we haven't found it yet." "This is dumb. We've been looking every day and found cool stuff on tornadoes, but nothing about our question." Other student pairs decide to change their original questions to better correspond with the information they have found. Despite these setbacks, all students completed the assignment and turned in colorful, four-page reports.

Mary's assessment of the reports revealed a number of important insights. A number of students took advantage of the many forms of information on the World Wide Web by including in-depth explanations and colorful pictures on their topic. However, Mary observed many students had a tendency to accept Web-based information at face value without regard to the credibility of its source or accuracy. In addition, she noticed an inclination for students to include large sections of information in their reports that were clearly above their level of understanding. To further understand how students use the Web and the process they used to create their reports, Mary talks with two representative students, pseudonyms Nicole and Frances. Mary recalls that this student pair progressed well through the project and always seemed to be on-task as she circulated through the lab.

Mary asks the students, "Tell me about the question you picked for your research." This prompts a response from Frances: "We started with a neat question: Why do we have a lot of tornadoes in Michigan?" Interested in the reason they chose this particular topic, Mary asks them to explain how they decided on the question. Nicole answers, "We thought it would be a good question to ask because we have a lot of tornado warnings during the summer, and we learned about them in science." Mary notices a discrepancy and inquires, "This isn't the question you used for your report; why did you change your topic?" Nicole replies, "We tried to find answers for our question on the Web, but nobody had it. We spent 2 days looking, but we couldn't find it." Frances adds, "We did find a lot of good stuff on weather and tornadoes but nothing on Michigan tornadoes!" Nicole adds, "Since we couldn't find the answer and we were running out of time, we switched to how do tornadoes start."

Mary continues her discussion with Nicole and Frances: "How did you two spend your time on the Web?"

Frances responds, "We used the search engine a lot to enter search words, but only a few of the summaries looked good enough to visit the site. Some looked good but didn't have stuff on our question."

Nicole adds, "We saw a bunch of good tornado pictures that we included in our report, but nobody had the answer to our question. We changed our question to something we could find the answer to."

Frances interrupts, "On the last day we found a cool site about a kid that survived a tornado, but it blew up his house. He explained how tornadoes form and how dangerous they are. He had some cool pictures of what was left of his house."

Based on this conversation, Mary begins to understand how Frances and Nicole may have interpreted incorrect information from a source that lacked credibility.

Mary is also interested in how much time Nicole and Frances spent reading and evaluating the pages they found during their search. During further discussions, Mary determined students rarely paused to read the majority of information on the pages. In addition, some information and images they included in their report were almost word-for-word from the site they mentioned. On reflection, Mary is concerned with the quality of these reports compared to projects students have completed in the past with print-based materials from the library.

Mary expresses her concerns to a close colleague. "I thought my students would have a fairly easy time using the Web for this research project, but I was wrong. We used resources from the media center last year, and students did a great job. Although everyone says the Web has more information, my students seemed to have a lot of difficulty finding resources and using them." She continues, "I've seen it all during the past week: Some students couldn't find good sites, some changed their question to match information they found, students rarely stopped to read pages in-depth, and when they did they believed everything. And I even had some students copy pictures and text and paste it right on their report!" Mary makes this suggestion to her colleague, "If you are going to use the Web in your class, I would come up with some good strategies for helping students learn how to take advantage of it. I know I'll rethink my plan for next time!"

Questions for Reflection and Discussion

1. What are some problems encountered by Mary and her students in using the World Wide Web to research questions about weather? What advice would you give to Mary to address these problems?

2. Are the problems encountered by Mary's class unique to Web-based inquiry? How can dilemmas and lessons from this case be applied to student research with traditional print-based materials?

3. How can teachers effectively incorporate on-line resources into their classrooms and at the same time prepare students for research activities?

4. What unique characteristics does the World Wide Web possess that can enhance research activities in secondary science classrooms?

5. A number of proponents claim the World Wide Web is an ideal medium for learning. What recommendations should be made to teachers who are considering its adoption into the classroom?

■ ■ ■

Using the World Wide Web to Support Student Inquiry

Joseph L. Hoffman, Joseph Krajcik, and Elliot Soloway

This case represents a synthesis of early observations from students engaged in inquiry-based, information-seeking activities on the World Wide Web as part of the University of Michigan Digital Library (UMDL) and Middle Years Digital Library (MYDL) projects (University of Michigan, 1998). Hundreds of hours of baseline data from early projects and on-line sessions provided a basis for the design of a set of Web-based learning materials and pedagogical supports for leading on-line investigations in astronomy, geology, physical ecology, and weather. Thousands of students now use these sites as an integral part of their investigations where they can post research questions, obtain small collections of age-appropriate materials, search for additional information, and share and critique sites that are of interest. In addition, the MYDL pedagogical model provides a framework to scaffold students at all phases of their investigation.

The World Wide Web offers a unique and unprecedented resource through which teachers can facilitate student inquiry. As espoused by the National Science

Education Standards (National Research Council, 1996) inquiry driven by questions generated from student experience should be the central strategy for teaching science. The World Wide Web can provide teachers with excellent resources and tools to support students in pursuing solutions and background information to questions they find meaningful and important. The World Wide Web makes it possible for students to have access to a wide range of current and archived scientific information and data. Moreover, the information students access on the Web can be in various formats (graphic, video, text, sound). These various ways of representing information and data make it possible for students to learn in new ways. The Web also makes it possible for students to contribute their own ideas to a growing body of information shared by students. Such sharing of one's own information and ideas can increase student motivation. Although the Web offers unique possibilities, we do need to learn how to make use of this tool for teaching and learning. Just giving students access to the Web will not promote learning.

Although the World Wide Web makes it possible for learners to access information to support inquiry for questions of value, students will not engage in inquiry activities unless supported by teachers who promote such practices. Students need support in asking questions that will be of value to explore. Students also need support in learning how to find, evaluate, and synthesize information. Unfortunately, many teachers are not prepared and do not have experience in supporting such practices. Helping learners make sense of information related to an open-ended question is challenging, yet it is the type of learning strategy that is necessary for students to succeed in the world in which they live. Although the Web holds promise, teachers and researchers must struggle to learn how to make use of this tool. Following, we make a number of additional observations drawn from Mary's first attempt at engaging students in on-line inquiry. These include both a number of positive aspects and associated challenges. We follow the challenges with suggestions to help teachers support students in making use of the Web and its resources.

As the case illustrates, Mary's students experienced a high degree of motivation during the early stages of their on-line inquiry as they began searching for resources on the World Wide Web. This motivation might be attributed to the nature of their questioning. Research indicates that students who are encouraged to develop open-ended, personally meaningful questions are more likely to engage in long-term investigations (Marx, Blumenfeld, Krajcik, & Soloway, 1997). This is evident in the type of question Frances and Nicole posed at the beginning of their research: "Why do we have a lot of tornadoes in Michigan?" This question is both meaningful and open-ended, as they may have experienced a number of tornado warnings during the summer, and the answer or solution varies both in depth and complexity. In addition to their questions, the loosely structured nature of the World Wide Web may have contributed to the motivation of Mary's students.

Marchionini (1988) describes how environments like the Web offer learners unusually high levels of control, allowing them to "move easily among vast quantities of information according to plan or serendipity . . . or create their own paths through the information" (p. 8). Mary's casual observation of her students supports this notion as she noted that students enjoyed surfing on the Web and browsing through various sites. Her students seemed eager to use the World Wide Web to locate information on their question.

A second positive aspect of using the World Wide Web for inquiry activities was noted by Mary as she described the in-depth explanations and colorful pictures a number of students included in their final reports. The World Wide Web fosters students' constructing robust products by providing rich and various representations of resources in a variety of formats (i.e., text, images, sound, and video). Where traditional print-based resources are often limited by the quantity and type of information they can provide, on-line resources can offer extensive coverage of topics from a diverse range of perspectives. Access to rich and diverse representations of information can help students develop deep understanding of the content. For instance, one document might explain a concept using text and digital photographs. The same students might search the Web to find additional information. A new document might present a slightly different explanation with different illustrations and different data. By analyzing and synthesizing the information from these various resources and putting together various representations, the student can create understanding.

In contrast to the positive aspects of engaging learners in on-line inquiry, the case also illustrates a number of challenges. The first challenge is supporting students' searching for information. This challenge is illustrated by Mary's experience with 3 of her 15 groups that required additional support before they were able to use an on-line search engine to locate information. It is unknown if these student pairs had additional difficulties with other aspects of using the search engine or taking advantage of the information they found during later stages of their research.

Our work with the MYDL project suggests learners require a substantial amount of support as they attempt to take advantage of technological tools in on-line environments. Wallace et al. (1998) describe how students experience difficulty using on-line search engines as they can often return too many hits or contain sites that are useless or irrelevant. In addition, learners may not have appropriate background knowledge about their question to enable them to enter appropriate terms into search engines. However, we should not be discouraged by this finding. Using new tools (a hammer, car, or the Web) always requires start-up efforts. However, the time devoted to helping learners use the World Wide Web won't be worth it unless they use the tools a number of times throughout the school year to support their inquiry. We won't invest the time it takes to drive a car only to drive it once; similarly, we shouldn't invest time to help students use the World Wide Web unless we plan to let them use it multiple times.

Fortunately, teachers can support learners in a number of ways while using search engines on the World Wide Web: (1) Include short orientation sessions where the teacher can model appropriate search techniques and discuss how to select useful resources. (2) Allow students in class to express and demonstrate how they searched for a topic, and allow others to comment on their techniques. (3) Provide sufficient background information experiences (i.e., discussions, readings, experiments, activities) to enable learners to make wise choices of terms for use in on-line search engines.

A second challenge illustrated in this case is the difficulty students experienced in locating resources pertaining to their questions. Mary heard a number of students express frustration with not being able to find specific information or the answer to their questions. Her students attributed this difficulty to "maybe it's hiding in the Web, and we have not found it yet." Specifically, Frances and Nicole commented on the frustration experienced during their research: "We tried to find answers for our question on the Web, but nobody had it. . . . We spent 2 days looking, but we couldn't find it." Unfortunately, this frustration caused a number of students, including Frances and Nicole, to abandon their original questions and opt for more feasible (but less open-ended) questions.

Our work has shown that many students have naive conceptions regarding the type of resources available on the World Wide Web. Many learners believe the Web contains an infinite amount of resources and can provide answers to any question regardless of its scope or complexity. However, this is far from the truth. Whereas the World Wide Web does provide extensive resources on a vast number of topics, it is loosely configured with no central organizational structure (in contrast to a traditional library indexing system). In addition, on-line search engines simply retrieve resources but do not sort appropriate sites for the age of the users or intention of their query. Students also fail to realize the Web may not be the best source of information for all questions. Other resources can provide more appropriate information for students: encyclopedias, periodicals, professional journals, interviews, or experimental investigations. Complicating this further is a common behavior of students searching for a single, correct answer to a question, similar to other traditional school tasks.

Because students do not have well-developed information-seeking skills, teachers need to support students in learning these skills. Teachers can use a variety of techniques to help learners improve these information-seeking activities: (1) Preview World Wide Web sites, and develop small collections of age- and topic-appropriate resources for use by students.* (2) Discuss the complicated nature of research, and stress the need for multiple sources for determining a solution or answer. (3) Present a variety of resources available on the World Wide Web and its limitations. (4) Encourage students to maintain a focus on their original open-ended questions and avoid modifying or changing them to suit the resources.

A final challenge, and perhaps the most critical in research activities, concerns the lack of time students invest in analyzing and synthesizing the resources they find on-line. As the case illustrates, Mary was troubled when she observed that students did not thoroughly synthesize information and simply accepted it at face value without regard to the credibility of its source or accuracy. For example, Frances and Nicole treated a site written by a nonscientist as factual and as a result included erroneous details in their report. Also, Mary observed that Frances and Nicole included

---

*A major effort of the University of Michigan Digital Library (UMDL) project is the development, testing, and implementation of Java-based interface to the Digital Library called Artemis. The Digital Library is populated with an extensive set of age-appropriate collections for middle and high school physical science students. See Wallace et al. (1998) for a full description of the Artemis and the Digital Library.

some information that they copied directly from the site. On second reflection, these results should not surprise us. Students typically find information from only one source: their textbook. Moreover, rather than synthesizing information from textbooks, learners often look for short answers to questions found at the back of the chapter. Synthesizing and evaluating information from a variety of sources requires new learning strategies.

A number of insights can be extracted from these observations. One issue relates to the use of the World Wide Web as an information source. The Web differs greatly from other resources, as its contents are largely unchecked for accuracy or reliability. Unfortunately, novice learners have difficulty discerning the quality of sources or may simply not invest the time to evaluate resources. Learning how to evaluate resources is an important skill that learners need to acquire. A second issue is the lack of time learners invest in synthesizing the information they encounter on the World Wide Web. This problem is not necessarily unique to digital environments but may be complicated by the nature of its loosely structured environment; students can simply select other resources if the information is not easily understood. This could lead to the habit of continually searching for the ideal resource and not expending the required effort to make sense of more complicated information.

Once again, teachers can use a number of strategies to support students in evaluation and synthesis of on-line resources:

1. Provide contradicting articles from the World Wide Web for learners to evaluate.
2. Model and discuss appropriate evaluation and synthesis skills.
3. Encourage learners to share resources and content summaries with peers.
4. Require multiple information sources for student final reports.

A number of the episodes described here can be traced to the initial definition of the task by the teacher: develop a broad question, gather information on your question, and develop a report. Unfortunately, Mary loosely defined the task for students, given their previous successful experience with a number of projects using print-based materials. As a result, the majority of students did not produce the type of research or report Mary had expected.

Similar occurrences have been documented in the MYDL project in a study of science students' use of the World Wide Web for inquiry-based activities. To assist in defining a more specific task, the project has made the inquiry process visible to students (see Figure 9.1) and developed scaffolded supports for teachers to incorporate as part of a complete on-line investigation. These components include the following:

1. Ask questions that are significant and have real-world purpose and meaning.
2. Plan the investigation by developing steps to help structure work during the investigation.
3. Search the World Wide Web with on-line search engines or using MYDL-approved sites.

FIGURE 9.1   Middle Years Digital Library (MYDL) investigation wheel.

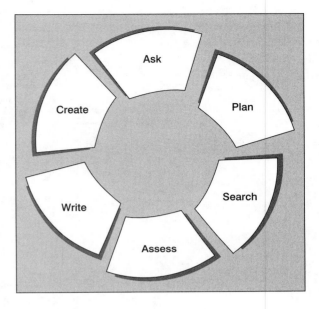

4. Assess the quality of information to determine if it makes sense, is interesting, and is trustworthy.

5. Write and reflect on the information.

6. Create rich representations of new understandings through the synthesis of information.

Although this process is not unique to on-line environments, it provides a necessary framework to support and scaffold students during each phase of an investigation.

Using the World Wide Web to support student inquiry holds tremendous potential. Access to an unprecedented breadth of information and data can provide students with the opportunity to ask and find solutions to worthwhile and meaningful questions. However, the Web by itself cannot support learners in the inquiry process. To make use of the World Wide Web, students need to use powerful learning strategies to locate, evaluate, and synthesize information. Students will not learn these strategies on their own unless supported by the teacher. The Web can be a powerful tool, but like any tool, we must learn how to use it effectively. As we have described, a number of teaching strategies do exist to support students using the World Wide Web as a powerful learning tool.

Learning About Newton's
Third Law Through Linguine

Sharon E. Nichols and Glenda Bell

In this closed case, Sherry and Glenda describe a teacher's initial experience using a design technology project to teach science. Marilyn, a pseudonym for a 13-year veteran with whom Sherry and Glenda have both worked, teaches science at a culturally diverse middle school in a large urban setting. She teaches five 90-minute science classes daily, each involving inclusion students, with the exception of one gifted and talented class. The case provides a glimpse into Marilyn's seventh-grade classroom as she engaged her students in a structure-building activity to learn about Newton's Third Law. Issues related to design technology and cooperative learning are reflected as these adolescent learners undertake the task of designing a linguine book holder. The case is followed by commentary from Marion J. "Dee" French, a university science educator and former middle school teacher, and Robert Wicklein, a technology educator with expertise in design technology.

While attending a summer science institute, Marilyn participated in an activity featuring a technology design approach to science teaching. The approach was novel to Marilyn, as she had no prior experience in the area of technology design. The objective of the activity was to use four pieces of copy paper and 1 foot of tape to build a tower. Using only the materials given, they were challenged to see who could build the tallest tower that could withstand 30 seconds of wind blown from a fan. In a period of 20 minutes, Marilyn worked quickly with her two partners to build a tall, but somewhat swaying structure.

As she waited for their tower to be tested, Marilyn began to conjure up images of her seventh graders becoming involved in a similar experience. She considered that structure building would be an ideal way to teach her unit on Newton's Laws through problem solving. Not only that, but the group work approach would reinforce cooperative learning. Marilyn thought about the challenges of making a stand-alone tower out of the four pieces of copy paper and 1-foot strip of masking tape. It had been quite difficult for the teachers to construct a workable structure, and many towers gave way due to the flimsy materials. She looked on as her group's tower, like several others, blew over after several seconds of being subjected to the fan's wind. While it had been humorous to laugh at the many unsuccessful tower designs, Marilyn thought this could be disastrous to the sensitive feelings of her students. She would need to find materials that would be more likely to produce a stable structure. After some thought, Marilyn envisioned a different structure building task altogether—her students would build a linguine book holder. The linguine would be an inexpensive resource, and better yet, the firmer noodles would be easier for students to manipulate.

The following October, Marilyn prepared to teach Newton's Laws to her students using her adapted technology design plans. Marilyn had mixed emotions as she anticipated the fun of the structure building coupled with images of linguine flying across the classroom. Would her students engage in the activity and successfully build the linguine-based structure? To explore students' experiences associated with Newton's Laws, Marilyn spent a day discussing objects and motion and places where students have seen or felt forces at work. The second day, Marilyn introduced the structure-building activity. She explained that the task was to construct a structure that could hold the science book. Her directions were concise:

> You are to work in a groups of 2 or 3. Each group will receive 15 pieces of linguine and 1 yard of masking tape. You may break the linguine. Remember—scientists do not put science equipment or materials in their mouths, so likewise do not put the linguine in your mouth. Handle it with care.

Marilyn gave one final reminder, "This is not a competition. Everyone *will* help each other to succeed!"

Marilyn watched as students organized themselves and began to negotiate how they would accomplish the task.

Typical of adolescents, girls selected to work with girls, and boys worked with boys. Alejandro, Patrick, and Jermaine were quick to form their group. Patrick volunteered to gather the necessary materials from the supply table at the front of the room. The boys readily exchanged opinions about how to make their linguine book holder. Alejandro quickly became the idea guy of the group. His suggestion to build a log cabin type design seemed like a good one. Jermaine decided he could work to break the linguine into equal log pieces, and, upon the approval of his mates, he began this task. Patrick decided he could be the log holder and work with Alejandro as the log taper. Marilyn noticed that the boys, like many others, looked around as they worked, checking to see the strategies and progress of other classmates. There were as many variations in design as there were groups!

Shyla sat alone at one end of a table. Past experiences involving Shyla in group work had proved to be unsuccessful—both for Shyla as well as her group mates. Marilyn knew that the lack of success experienced by Shyla was due to her unique learning needs and not because of her gender. Shyla was a slow worker, she spoke hesitantly, and was easily frustrated; there was mutual understanding between Shyla, her classmates, and Marilyn that she best participated by working alone. Marilyn observed with concern as Shyla refrained from getting involved in the building activity. Shyla rested her head on the table for nearly 5 minutes, looking over her crossed arms, skeptically watching the work of others. Marilyn brought over the linguine and tape and encouraged Shyla saying, "You can do this Shyla! I *know* you can do this!" Shyla sat up and began to build a book holder. The first attempted design fell apart, as did her second, third, and fourth arrangements. A table group nearby laughed, pointing at Shyla's heap of noodles. Shyla shot a sharp glance at the group, gave a frustrated growl, and then proceeded to make a fifth attempt. The 30-minute time limit had elapsed, and Marilyn announced that it was time to stop work and prepare to test their designs.

Marilyn wondered if many of the structures would work. How would these young people feel if their structure falls apart in front of the class? What kinds of experiences did students have negotiating their roles in the groups? Did everyone feel valued in their group? Would they ultimately internalize the science concepts associated with Newton's Third Law?

The moment for testing the linguine structures had arrived. Students stood by their designs and watched as Marilyn went to each group and placed a science book on top of the various linguine structures. There were oohs, ahhs, and laughter as the linguine structures either collapsed or stayed intact under the weight of the text. Alejandro, Patrick, and Jermaine were thrilled when their log cabin design easily maintained its sturdy form. Other designs also survived, including ones having a four-tripod base, a large triangle, and a Star of David-shaped structure. Shyla's design, however, did not fare so well. Her arrangement of three vertically intersecting strands of linguine collapsed quickly under the book. Likewise, a group featuring a pole design and another with a flower blossom were somewhat disappointed at the quick demise of their structures.

Marilyn shared a few observations with the group. She pointed out that while scientists sometimes come up with great model ideas, they don't always work out. The group then compared their various designs to analyze why some worked better then others. Marilyn listened carefully and noted students' comments such as: "Things are pushing up." "There's a force on this side and against that side." "Gravity pulls it down." Marilyn revisited these ideas and terms in the days that followed. Given that one of Marilyn's major beliefs is that *all* students should experience successful learning in her class, she declared that the activity was not yet over. They still had 15 minutes of class time left, and some structures needed to be fixed. Those whose structures had passed the test were to work with others to adapt a workable design.

Marilyn watched as Shyla picked up her three-strand design and began to add appendages to reinforce one side of her structure. Jo and Janelle gave Shyla brief words of encouragement and then quietly looked on as Shyla resumed working with the linguine. After a few minutes, Shyla called Marilyn over to retest the structure. Several groups watched as Shyla's structure strained and leaned to the right but finally remained intact with the book on top. Her classmates cheered and congratulated her. Proudly, Shyla placed her "Leaning Tower of Pisa" alongside other group structures on the side counter. It did not take long for others to successfully redesign their structures and pass the test.

At the end of sixth period, Marilyn looked at the countertops filled with a vast array of odd-looking linguine structures. The floor was not covered with linguine, as she had previously imagined might happen. She felt confident that an important beginning had been made toward helping her students internalize Newton's Third Law. Everyone—including Shyla, her most challenging special education student, as well as the gifted and talented students of her fifth-period class—had participated in the activity and persisted to accomplish the task. Marilyn felt her belief reinforced that problem solving involving hands-on experiences is an excellent way to engage *all* students in science learning. She was anxious to find more design technology activities, as she was sure this would fit well with the upcoming human body unit.

Questions for Reflection and Discussion

1. How does learning about Newton's Laws using a technology design approach compare with more traditional use of physical science problems posed in science textbooks?

2. Marilyn indicated students were to work in groups; however, this criterion was not upheld for Shyla. Should she have required that Shyla be involved in a group? If so, who should be responsible to ensure Shyla's involvement in a group?

3. Are inclusionary classrooms or cooperative learning strategies necessarily beneficial to all students? Why or why not?

4. Was the competitive aspect of the activity essential for motivating students' participation in the technology design activity? Explain your response.

5. How would you evaluate student learning taking place in the technology design activity?

Marilyn's Decisions About Using Cooperative Learning

M. Jenice "Dee" Goldston

This case looks at teacher decision making centered on the use of a cooperative learning approach. The teacher's intent was to help students learn about Newton's Third Law by engaging them in a design technology experience. Teacher decisions that emerged as the case unfolds highlight an expanding view of inclusion, one that provides all students with an opportunity to experience some of the benefits of cooperative group work.

Marilyn's decision to have students tackle the design project suggests that she is a risk taker, having experienced a similar activity only once before. It also suggests that she knows well the capabilities of her students and what kinds of challenges motivate them to learn. Her decision to use cooperative learning groups also provides considerable insight into her beliefs about how adolescents learn. Marilyn would likely agree that cooperative group activities provide students with learning experiences that allow them to construct shared meanings related to forces and motion. These constructed meanings are affected by learners' cultural backgrounds, values, and experiences. She might also feel that, while cooperative learning does not eliminate competition, it does direct competition away from individuals and toward groups, and as a result makes new learning experiences less threatening.

Given what we can infer about Marilyn's beliefs about learning, an unexpected twist to the case was her decision to allow Shyla not to participate as a member of a group. Marilyn stated that by mutual understanding in the class, Shyla was allowed to work alone and other classmates would leave her alone. While there may be very good reasons for Shyla's isolation, the unfortunate aspect of Marilyn's decision was that Shyla did not participate as an active member of the learning community and was deprived of opportunities to learn the skills of collaboration and teamwork considered essential in today's job market. Working alone on the design activity likely centered classmates' attention directly on Shyla, which perhaps strengthened her feelings of failure and embarrassment when her linguine book holder fell apart under the weight of the science book.

Marilyn's decision near the end of the lesson to have successful team members assist less successful teams represented a turning point in Shyla's learning. When Jo and Janelle came forward to help her rebuilt her design, Shyla experienced some of the benefits of cooperative group learning, including the opportunity to share her ideas with others, receive assistance, and have her work valued. Unfortunately, Shyla's experience with Jo and Janelle does not seem to be one planned for by Marilyn. Marilyn could have used her knowledge of her students to carefully select one or two students who could have worked successfully with Shyla throughout the lesson. She could have monitored Shyla's group closely and encouraged positive interactions among group members. Marilyn also could have had students work in pairs. Pairing tends not to require the complexity of personal skills needed to interact with many diverse individuals in a larger group. Marilyn could have used pairing students for collaborative learning as a stepping stone for all her students, including Shyla, to later work in larger groups. Also, Marilyn might have considered engaging her students in activities to help them develop respect for the ideas of others and the recognition that each student has something important to contribute to the work of the class. This may have fostered a tone of acceptance among the students, making it easier for everyone to work together as a team.

Marilyn's knowledge of her students and the series of decisions she made during the lesson helped her move closer to the ideals often associated with cooperative learning: positive interdependence, face-to-face interaction, and individual accountability. But additional reflection about Shyla and the opportunities she missed by not working in a group may encourage Marilyn to try different ways to involve Shyla and other students like her in cooperative learning experiences in the future.

■　■　■

Design Technology and Science: The Perfect Partners

Robert C. Wicklein

The successful application of cooperative learning environments is common practice in most technology education programs. Therefore, it is no surprise that this approach was equally successful within Marilyn's science class. The teaming efforts of students to work together to solve problems is essential for the preparation of an informed citizenry and has been advocated by governmental and business leaders for many years (Secretary's Commission on Achieving Necessary Skills, 1992). Additionally, the use of appropriate competitive events within the learning structure has equally been a motivator for students of all ages. Furthermore, the use of manipulatives further strengthened the learning event by allowing students to be engaged with more than one domain of learning (e.g., cognitive, psychomotor, and eventually affective). All of these factors played into a seemingly very successful learning event for Marilyn and her students.

Two observations concerning this instructional approach are worth noting. First, although the linguini structure may be motivating and helpful in getting students to internalize Newton's Third Law, it also creates an ambiance in the learning environment that may be less than desired. Students may find it difficult to distinguish between the reality of the linguini structure and the scientific understandings that Marilyn was intending to have her students develop. Often, students need authentic examples based in reality to understand an abstract concept such as Newton's Third Law. Without the realness associated with the learning activity, students may become caught up with the emotion of the assignment without developing the scientific understandings that was the original instructional intent. Marilyn had her students do a form of analysis after the structures were tested; however, it seemed that the analysis was done in a relatively casual way that lacked depth even for middle school students. Getting students to develop a clear grasp of the primary intent of the instruction is paramount to quality education, and this can take place only when students think deeply about the topic. Sometimes, fun activities do not make the transition from amusement to real learning.

Second, Marilyn missed a great opportunity to connect her science class with the capabilities of the technology education program. Assuming that a technology education program exists in Marilyn's school, she could have worked in conjunction with the technology teacher to connect real science with real technology. Students in both programs could have worked together to solve the problems associated with Newton's Third Law by using knowledge constructed in both science and technology classes. By connecting with the technology program, she could have allowed her students to experiment with structures that are more realistic and apply loads to the structures that are more accurate than simply placing a book on the top of the linguini structure. By using a multidisciplinary approach to solving this problem, all students and even the teachers gain a better perspective of the scientific and technological concepts associated with Newton's Third Law.

Making the Most of Limited Computer Technology with At-Risk Middle School Students

David F. Jackson

In this closed case, David describes the experiences of Bridget, a pseudonym for a veteran middle school teacher, who volunteered to try out her principal's plan to stimulate innovative approaches to teaching at-risk students. When challenged by her students' poor academic and social skills, Bridget turned to computer technology for help. Experiences with computers over the school year, which were initially frustrating, became opportunities for students to show their learning capabilities and provided the impetus for Bridget to shift her teaching approach from information giver to learning facilitator. The case is followed by commentary from David, the case author, and Morgan Nolan, a former science teacher with expertise in instructional technology.

Bridget was a sixth-grade teacher at County Central Middle School, located in the center of a small city. A white woman, 39 years old at the time of the experiences described in this case, she had 11 years of teaching experience, primarily in middle school science. For several years she had served as a team leader, responsible for coordinating the efforts of the various content area teachers who work with a common set of heterogeneously grouped students. Widely known at the school as a personally caring teacher, and cited by her principal as an example of one who has particularly effective classroom management skills and policies, she regularly hosted student teachers and practicum students from a nearby state university. In short, although the title does not exist in her district, she was widely recognized as a master teacher.

In this particular year, however, she accepted an unfamiliar challenge. She was one of a handful of teachers who volunteered to try out her principal's plan to stimulate innovative approaches to teaching at-risk students. These teachers were, in principle, given complete freedom in determining the details of the curriculum, although the explicit expectation was that a major goal was to improve the students' performance on standardized tests in the core academic areas of reading and mathematics. Plans called for interdisciplinary classes (in Bridget's case, science and mathematics), with about half the number of students (averaging 15 for each of 3 classes), held during blocks of time twice as long (90 minutes) as was normal.

The students in each middle school grade with the most consistent history of low academic achievement were homogeneously grouped into these classes. Almost all of these students had been retained for at least 1 year at some point during elementary or middle school. A great majority were African American, nearly all were thought to be from disadvantaged socioeconomic backgrounds, and there were approximately equal numbers of male and female students.

Based on very limited experience (2 days) in some recent in-service workshops, Bridget seized on the idea of using computer technology as the primary means of providing new and potentially valuable leaning experiences for these students. The school was in the process of making significant investments in information-oriented computer resources for use in the media center alone (on-line and CD-ROM-based databases). No additional budget for classroom materials (either high or low tech) was provided; but Bridget's resourcefulness allowed her to scrounge a modest quantity of largely obsolete computers and software (salvaged from a lab classroom that was recently broken up and from surplus and loans from the local university). Hardware available in her room included as many as eight Apple IIe computers, a single IBM-compatible (MS-DOS) system, a single Macintosh, a videodisc player, and a monochrome liquid crystal display (LCD) projection panel.

Bridget's initial adjustment to teaching these classes proved more difficult and more central a problem than she initially envisioned. Many of the specific activities and some of the general methods that she was accustomed to using failed her with these students. She was accustomed to approximately 2 weeks of lead time in unit and lesson planning; by the end of the first week, this had been reduced to 12 hours or less as she cast about in many directions for ideas. During the first few weeks, the experience was an especially exhausting but exhilarating one for Bridget:

> Normally at this point in the year, I feel very comfortable but also sort of trapped—I don't want to be anywhere else, but everything is going to be roughly the same. This year I wonder if I'll *ever* be comfortable, but I know I'll never be *bored*. *Right now*, it's a good trade. (September 14)

As a result of her frustration with students' difficulties in understanding basic mathematics facts and algorithmic skills, the first computer application Bridget decided to use was the drill-and-practice software provided with the textbook (*Heath Mathematics: Computer-Assisted Instruction,* 1985), which she discovered in a storeroom, previously unopened. She had tried a conceptual approach to several topics (e.g., place value in addition, subtraction, and multiplication), but as she explained:

> They couldn't even *start* to *think* because the more basic things weren't there. [The software] appealed to me at first because it was something different, but I thought they couldn't mess it up . . . They didn't even have to *read* to know what they were sup-

posed to do next, really, and they just needed to go over and over some of these things. At this point, to heck with if they understand. They can figure out the answer any way they darn well please – fingers, pencil marks, just as long as they get the answer. (September 21)

Bridget quickly perceived, however, that the motivational value and the more independent work that she was expecting from bringing several computers into the classroom were not apparent:

Before, it wasn't *fun*, and that was the problem, but it really didn't get any more fun, and some of them are still confused about what the *point* even was. It *wasn't* something different, really. . . . I mean, just like with a worksheet, they can*not* follow directions . . . so it really takes somebody going over there and saying "Mash this." I'm thinking this is the reason I'm not teaching first or second grade—it's driving me crazy! If they can't read and follow directions any better than that, it's not much different than teaching first and second grade but with larger bodies, *much* larger! (October 15)

As a result, Bridget decided to expose students to some software-based activities that were potentially more entertaining, although less obviously related to the expected curriculum emphasis (the logical problem-solving game *The Incredible Laboratory*, 1984). She decided, however, to run only a single computer herself, displayed on the television screen in the front of the room, because then "I could walk the students through the computer activities step-by-step, because they need a *lot* of specific guidance to have any *chance* of getting it."

Bridget began the year with very low expectations of these students' academic achievement, and this had not changed after the first 2 months of school. She often used the term "slow" (as opposed to "smart") to describe them; she was explicitly resigned to the fact that some of them were "hopeless" in terms of retaining or transferring any learning or making measurable gains in academic achievement:

OK, here's what I think. Number one, the kids enjoyed *The Incredible Laboratory*. Number two, it *did* get them thinking in a scientific way more, during the time that they actually were *using* it. Number three, it is short lived, in several ways. The novelty really does wear off, which I suppose I should have known. The skills that they seemed to develop over 2 or 3 days were not retained. I took it for a grade after 5 days. The other day, they *could* do things by trial and error, most of them even seemed to be doing *some* logical deduction, which I was amazed at. . . . Then yesterday they were *completely helpless*—they had to start from the beginning. They could no more make sense of their notes than. . . . I didn't even try to look at the paper-and-pencil test of logical reasoning, since they didn't even retain the computer skill. At this point, I see this all as primarily for entertainment value. (September 27)

No matter how much we try to spoon-feed them, we're not going to make all the slower kids smart. We can keep them in school, maybe, but we'll not all of a sudden instantly make them smart. You know, there are a few of them that we will help—they'll come out of here with more skills, but they're not going to be real smart kids, *ever* [laughs and rolls her eyes], but they'll be able to survive, and if you . . . you just have to keep looking at it that way. Since I've started thinking like that I don't think *less* of the kids, I just. . . . I'm not nearly as stressed out about "Oh my God, what am I going to do with these kids, what can I do next?" (October 23)

Feeling that she should make the science-oriented software more directly tied to an identifiable content-knowledge goal (as well as to general thinking skills), Bridget next turned to a program that, while it was simple in concept and graphic displays, incorporated modestly artificially intelligent adaptive feedback (*Theory Formation: Reflection and Patterns*, 1986). Even with software that was clearly intended for individual students' interactive use, during the first half of the year, she still felt the need to plan to structure and closely supervise the students' experiences and to provide an extrinsic motivation for them to pay close attention to the tasks:

> I could first have them demonstrate, or have me demonstrate with them helping, about the bouncing the balls, but with a mirror and flashlight, and *then* let them go to the computer. . . . I'd have them do it one at a time, which would take longer, but they'd have to do it at the computer, and once they get it so that it bounces over to the object, they'd have to call me over and show me. In a week's time, if I had to do other stuff, and if I put a time limit on it, given the opportunity that . . . not even extra credit, but have it as an assignment, but have it run for a week. If it's something that's not very difficult, I could have a 10-minute time limit. With each of my classes being 90 minutes long, in a week certainly I could get everybody, if it's timed, get time at the computer. (October 23)

After following through with these plans, Bridget consciously took a break from technology-based activities (or anything else unfamiliar) for several weeks, until the Christmas break. During this time, according to an anecdote that she jokingly related repeatedly later in the year, a colleague noted one day that she looked unusually relaxed and energetic, and she laughed out loud and said "That's because I haven't used the computers this month, and I've just been pulling stuff out of the drawer for 2 weeks!"

Bridget was referring to a series of general science miniunits, which she had always considered largely successful with her sixth graders in previous years. The reason that she had withheld them thus far was based on her previous experience with particularly low-achieving students in heterogeneously grouped classes in the past: They were based on cooperative learning methods, and she had always relied on the phenomenon of, as Bridget put it, "the brighter students carrying the others along, in terms of thinking but *also* just in terms of *working*, and effectively serving as teachers."

Cooperative groups will not work with these kids, she reasoned, because they lack intrinsic motivation and would not be exposed to the model of more successful students. Her change of heart came as a result of a change in her assumptions about the objectives to be addressed by cooperative learning when used with an entire class of at-risk students. She came to see the chief value of cooperative learning as developing social skills rather than academic skills, as of inherent value rather than instrumental value.

After returning in January, Bridget decided to revisit *The Incredible Laboratory*, because she thought that the students had enjoyed it more than most activities, but this time with the students working independently in pairs at the computers. She tried to ease the transition away from a teacher-centered approach by providing students with the structured record-keeping worksheets that came with the program documentation. While she still saw some pairs of students as lost or helpless without direct supervision and oral instructions, she was both surprised and encouraged by the reactions of many of the student pairs. She found that motivation and small-scale cooperation were noticeably enhanced when several pairs of students spontaneously began a *de facto* competition to solve the problems most quickly. She then began to suggest that the students use the challenge function included in the software to "show off" their achievements in front of the class and teach their peers by example.

A backdrop she gave to her students' need for social skills was that they are trying to survive. She elaborated by explaining, "In their environment, survival means taking care of yourself," and therefore cooperative learning was something foreign to the culture of the majority of her students. This viewpoint probably explains why Bridget was so overwhelmed (in a positive way) with one incident in February. She herself put a series of challenge problems on the LCD panel and asked student pairs, in turn, to tackle them while thinking out loud. In a class where she perceived that each student had been "looking out for his or her own needs, they actually applauded other teams when they got it." She saw this affirmation as a major difference in the way her students related with each other and a major achievement of her year.

Bridget also reflected how she sensed at the beginning of the year that low self-esteem was probably a problem with many of her students. She related an incident where a particularly quiet girl, Nicole, knew the answer to a question related to a software-based activity when Bridget was sitting beside her, but couldn't do it at all when Bridget left to help another student. As soon as Bridget walked back to her side, she could do the problem again. Bridget thought this exemplified the student's need for attention, rather than for teaching.

Late in the year, Bridget noted that her students had more self-confidence and their self-esteem had improved. She gave two examples of this improvement. One student, James, begin the year failing all of his subjects. "Now, he's making an A in science and missed an A in math only because he didn't turn in two daily assignments." She felt like the difference was that James was now in an environment where he was hearing, "You're not stupid." She also told about Demitri, who, although he still can't do math or written work, "can see things" intuitively when working with the computer. She described him as somewhat of a class leader when it comes to figuring things out in regard to software-based problems. She said that Demitri comes up with "higher level thoughts than you ever would have guessed existed."

Bridget said that she came to believe a statement that she remembered hearing that a positive self-esteem is 75% of achievement. By the latter part of the year, she was so pleased with the way her students' attitudes and capabilities were improving that she said "I would love to move up with these kids to seventh and even eighth grade, which was talked about at one point last year," to continue helping them grow in this area. She felt that if students continued through middle school as a team that they could move into average-ability high school classes, be successful, and even graduate rather than earning only an attendance certificate:

> James *never, never* did his work, but we've now gotten to the point where we can iden-
> tify. . . . I mean, we *knew* he couldn't read, but it used to be that he didn't even *try*. Now
> James, if he can't read something, he'll come up and say, "What does this say?" and *he's
> a smart kid*, he just *can't read*. Demitri and Milton are really smart, they *are*, [loud sigh
> yielding to a laugh] but their *communication* skills, anything but verbal, and even then
> [shakes her head] . . . sometimes its impossible, but if they *start off* next year feeling
> better about themselves, well, people like those two could go somewhere. (March 19)

When she introduced another computer-based problem-solving activity, *The Factory* (1983), Bridget changed her teaching approach. First, she did not require the students to take any specific notes or fill out any worksheets when they began working with the program. She did not give them any initial hints or guidelines but, rather, just let them try. Her shorthand for this approach was "not shoving it down their throats."

She later described this approach as putting the burden of learning on the students' shoulders. It was students' responsibility to interact with the computer and with each other and to learn. To Bridget, giving responsibility to the students was "a very freeing experience," since "it *forced* almost all of the last of them to get involved, after the leaders like James and Demitri just get started."

The notion of teacher as facilitator was one that Bridget had always found attractive when thinking about gifted students, but "before, I wouldn't have dreamed of doing this with these kids." She credited the shift in her attitude and expectations to the development of students' group work skills during the course of the year. Even though she considered the computer applications used early in the year to have failed miserably in many respects, the use of the computer-based activities eventually served as "the first spur to get them to *try* to actually work together on something."

In April, Bridget introduced "probeware" lab activities (*The Microcomputer-Based Laboratory Project: Motion,* 1987), in a whole-class context but with students rotating the duties of performing the mechanics of the demonstrations in front of the class. This activity

> put some of them right over the top, in terms of their attitude. They didn't want to
> leave class this week, they didn't want to go to lunch, and they would rush through
> lunch to get back to class. . . . They stop me in the hall and ask when it will be their turn
> to be up in front.

Bridget described this time as "a great week. It makes me so excited to see them excited."

By the final days of the year, Bridget used a multimedia-based, four-person "jigsaw" group activity, *The Great Solar System Rescue* (1992) for an entire week and was "amazed at how many of them stayed involved, especially when so many of them, of course, still couldn't read the information booklets." She also recognized in this package a coherently planned example of a hybrid approach to classroom organization, combining aspects of competition and debate on the whole-class scale with cooperation on the small-group scale.

Questions for Reflection and Discussion

1. What were some challenges that Bridget faced in teaching at-risk students? How did she see computer technology as an aid to work through these challenges?

2. Bridget's approach to introducing computer technology into her classroom was to begin with drill-and-practice software and gradually engage her students with more complex software. Do you think this was a wise decision? Explain.

3. Bridget was very resourceful in getting the computers, software, and probeware she needed for her class. If confronted with a situation similar to Bridget's, how would you go about gathering the technology resources you might need?

4. Early in the school year, Bridget thought that cooperative learning experiences would not benefit her students; what caused her to change her mind? What was the role of computers in the cooperative learning experiences Bridget planned for her students?

5. Helping her at-risk students build self-esteem was an important year-long learning goal for Bridget. Why do you think she selected this as a goal for her students?

6. How were computers used, specifically, to facilitate science learning?

■ ■ ■

With a Little Technology, Can At-Risk Students Succeed?

David F. Jackson

Bridget's experience is in many ways a microcosm of the evolution of methods and attitudes about the use of educational software. One example is the desirable but difficult transition from simple drill-and-practice programs to increasingly sophisticated and demanding simulation-based problem solving. Another is the gradual identification of an appropriate middle ground between the extreme views of technology-based materials as either substitutes for the teacher (especially in a multicomputer setting) or as tools to be directly controlled only by the teacher.

The progression of her thoughts also mirrors the confusion attending the appropriate treatment of at-risk students. In many cases, Bridget's reflections have revealed a highly problematic conflict between deep-seated personal and professional beliefs, both negative and positive, and her sincere concern for the well-being of her students: "This is the most just plain lovable group of kids I think I've ever had. . . . I'm sorry, but too many of these kids are just plain slow. . . . I know that some of them hate being labeled and set apart like this, but I want to cry when I think of them getting placed back in regular seventh-grade next year and floundering again."

Prominent policy makers in the field of middle school education often regard affective outcomes in general and students' self-esteem in particular as central concerns for education at this level. While recognizing that much confusion exists about what this means in practice, general principles often cited include the avoidance of either any kind of tracking or any kind of competition, in both of which Bridget found some observable short-term value during the course of this year spent with these children. She valued self-esteem for its presumed correlation with eventual academic achievement, rather than as an end in itself in connection with the functions of schools and teacher *in loco parentis*. What can we make of her experiences and thoughts in trying to make the best of this tough situation?

■ ■ ■

I Faced Bridget's Dilemmas as a Ninth-Grade Teacher

Morgan B. Nolan

In this case, an experienced teacher, Bridget, when teaching at-risk students for the first time, is faced with an array of difficult dilemmas. First, she must adjust her familiar teaching practices to meet the unique needs of these children. Next, she must determine, essentially on her own, how to integrate computer technologies into her daily and long-term goals for her class. Finally, she must acknowledge and deal with her expectations about the children in her classes. For Bridget and for her students, these three dilemmas intersected in a way that brought positive change into their middle school classroom. Not all teachers will face this much change at one time in their classrooms, but every teacher will face each of these dilemmas at some time during their careers. The manner in which Bridget faces these dilemmas illustrates the attributes that have made her a master teacher.

As a ninth-grade science teacher, I found myself facing some of these same dilemmas when I was asked to teach in a new at-risk program at my high school. As I read Bridget's story, I was reminded of the hurdles, both personal and academic, that I and my students faced on a daily basis. For Bridget and me, the seemingly simple task of planning daily lessons became almost overwhelming. Familiar exercises and activities failed miserably or left the students more confused and frustrated than when they started. Each day became a curricular experiment, with the results being used to help improve the next day's activities. What I see in Bridget's reaction to these problems is what I consider a major attribute of a master teacher, the ability and the willingness to act under fire, to try something new, to try again, and to move on to something different. She can neither make her students learn nor learn for them, but she does provide them with experiences that could help them learn.

Bridget's choice to use computer technology to help her provide learning experiences for her students is amazing. Few teachers would choose to combine a new course preparation with a new instructional method, especially with so little experience. Bridget's inventiveness and determination allow her to make extensive use of materials and equipment that others had tossed out as useless. What Bridget found through using the technology, however, was that the technology in itself did not contribute significantly to her students' learning. Initial excitement and motivation quickly faded when the lessons became difficult, confusing, or irrelevant. Bridget's discovery is also a frequently debated issue in the domain of instructional technology: Does media make a difference in learning? Many experts feel that the technology itself is simply a tool or a vehicle and that what really matters in learning is the instructional methodology. New technologies simply provide easier, more inclusive, or more efficient ways of presenting good learning activities. We see evidence of this as Bridget's students showed little interest in software that mimicked worksheets but much greater interest in software that involved problem solving.

Meaningful learning may be enhanced by the use of technology but is not dependent on technology to be successful. If technology is just a vehicle for learning, how do we explain the changes that took place in Bridget's students in terms of self-esteem, cooperation, and social skills? Was this a function of the technology, or was it due to Bridget's shift away from information giver and toward learning facilitator? It is difficult to tease these interactions apart. The meaningful learning activities presented by the technology provided Bridget's students with a way of being successful that they had not experienced previously. As their abilities and self-esteem improved, no doubt, Bridget's expectations improved, as did her confidence in not having to structure every activity. It was also Bridget's willingness to try new methods and shift responsibility for learning to her students that helped this classroom evolve. As the positive impact in this case demonstrates, technology can be beneficial in education. It is just as important, however, to have schools and teachers that are willing to engage in thoughtful and reflective practice to create classrooms that encourage and support all types of learners.

Resources to Consider

American Association of School Librarians. **KidsConnect** [On-line]. Available: http://ala8.ala.org/ICONN/kidsconn.html

When students ask questions that you can't answer, have them contact KidsConnect. KidsConnect is a question-answering service designed to help students use information available on the Internet. Volunteer library media specialists respond to questions usually in 3 days or less. The service can be accessed at the Internet site or via e-mail: AskKC@ala.org.

Bybee, R. (1998, September). **Bridging science and technology.** *The Science Teacher, 65,* 38–42.

How are science and technology different? How are they interrelated? Rodger Bybee answers these questions and offers strong arguments for why technology should be an important dimension of school science programs. He recommends that the natural and design world can be linked in science classes by providing students with opportunities to design and implement solutions to problems and to engage in inquiry-oriented laboraratories. The article also includes examples of learning experiences that support standards-based outcomes of technology.

Ebenezer, J., & Lau, E. (1999). *Science on the Internet: A resource for K–12 teachers.* Upper Saddle River, NJ: Merrill/Prentice Hall.

This 180-page, 4-chapter handbook by Jazlin Ebenezer and Eddy Lau is a great resource for science teachers who wish to realize the potential of the Internet. The first chapter explains what the Internet is, and the second chapter describes how to use the Internet to promote science learning and science teacher professional development. The heart of the book is Chapter 3, which describes numerous science sites and gives their Internet Web site addresses, or URLs (Uniform Resource Locators). Chapter 4 presents information about Internet sites related to science education standards and issues of importance to science educators at all levels. Look for this handbook to be updated regularly to keep step with changes to Internet sites.

Ridgeway, D. (1998, February). **Internet opportunities**. *The Science Teacher, 65,* 20–22.

Physics teacher Dori Ridgeway identifies a number of sources of current science information available on the Internet. Sites she recommends focus on the topics of optics, sound, science and society, and professional development. Ridgeway includes addresses for all sites she describes.

University of Michigan's Digital Library Science Teaching and Learning Project [Online]. Available: http://www.umich.edu/~aaps/fw/print.html

This World Wide Web site provides information about the University of Michigan's Digital Library Science Teaching and Learning Project and its unique approach to engaging students in inquiry-based learning. The learning materials available at the site are intended to support science inquiry through on-line resources. Topics for which project learning materials for high school and middle school students are available on-line include astronomy and science fiction, conservation, natural disasters, oil and water, ecology, weather, waves and vibrations, and women in science.

References

The Factory [Computer software]. (1983). Pleasantville, NY: Sunburst Communications.

The Great Solar System Rescue [Computer software]. (1992). Cambridge, MA: Tom Snyder Productions.

Heath Mathematics: Computer-Assisted Instruction [Computer software]. (1985). Lexington, MA: D. C. Heath.

The Incredible Laboratory [Computer software]. (1984). Pleasantville, NY: Sunburst Communications.

The Microcomputer-Based Laboratory Project: Motion [Computer software]. (1987). Pleasantville, NY: HRM Software.

Theory Formation: Reflections and Patterns [Computer software]. (1986). Irvine, CA: Educational Technology Center, University of California.

Marchionini, G. (1988). Hypermedia and learning: Freedom and chaos. *Educational Technology, 28,* 8–12.

Marx, R. W., Blumenfeld, P. C., Krajcik, J. S., & Soloway, E. (1997). Enacting project-based science. *The Elementary School Journal, 97,* 341–358.

National Research Council. (1996). *National science education standards.* Washington, DC: National Academy Press.

National Science Foundation. (1992). *Materials, development, research and informal science education—program announcement.* Washington, DC: National Science Foundation.

Resources for Technology Education. (1998). [On-line]. Available: http://www.TCNJ.EDU/~teched/te_resources.html#faq

Secretary's Commission on Achieving Necessary Skills. (1992). *Learning a living: A blueprint for high performance.* A SCANS report for America 2000. Washington, DC: US Department of Labor.

University of Michigan. (1998). *Middle Years Digital Library Project* [On-line]. Available: http://mydl.soe.umich.edu/

Veal, W. R., Jackson, D. J., Finnegan, B., Tippins, D. J., & Crockett, D. (1995). Alternative and supplemental definitions of "technology": Science educators' answers to "so what?" In F. Finley, D. Allchin, D. Rhees, & S. Fifield (Eds.), *Proceedings of the third international history, philosophy, and science teaching conference, volume 2* (pp. 1238–1248). Minneapolis, MN: University of Minnesota.

Wallace, R., Soloway, E., Krajcik, J., Bos, N., Hoffman, J., Hunter, H., Kiskis, D., Peters, G., Richardson, D., & Ronen, O. (1998). *Artemis: Learner-centered design of an information seeking environment for K–12 education.* Los Angeles, CA: ACM.

10

Assessment in Science

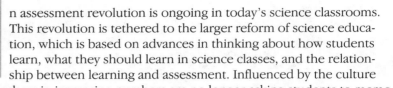

An assessment revolution is ongoing in today's science classrooms. This revolution is tethered to the larger reform of science education, which is based on advances in thinking about how students learn, what they should learn in science classes, and the relationship between learning and assessment. Influenced by the culture of reform, teachers in increasing numbers are no longer asking students to memorize isolated science facts and formulas but to construct new and meaningful science understandings for themselves. To match the sophistication of the science learning expected of students, significant changes are occurring with regard to assessment practices. According to the *National Science Education Standards* (National Research Council, 1996), assessment tasks must make use of a broad array of data collection methods that provide in-depth information about what students are learning. They must be free of bias, have clear purposes, and serve to blur the distinction between instruction and assessment. Assessment in science must also provide students with opportunities to practice problem-solving skills and refine their science understandings in authentic contexts. In addition, data resulting from student assessment may be used by teachers to make decisions about their own instructional practices and by school administrators, policy makers, and government officials to make decisions about issues ranging from next year's science courses offerings to the percentage of the federal budget targeted for science education. When teachers and other individuals interpret or make judgments about assessment data, they are engaging in evaluation (Hart, 1994).

A pressure point for teachers in shifting to more authentic and varied forms of assessment is grading, the practice of sorting students based on their performance. Tension occurs when teachers are called on to produce numeric scores from assessment tasks never intended to yield such data and to justify the objectivity of these scores to students, parents, and school administrators. Also, when the responsibility for grading is shared with students, the teacher must consider alternatives to grades to promote student engagement and learning. There is little doubt of the need to bring assessment practices into alignment with science instructional reform, but moving from that which is easily measured to that which is highly valued presents considerable challenges for science teachers.

The four cases in this chapter highlight dilemmas that science teachers have wrestled with when attempting to use alternatives to traditional assessment methods. In the first case, a chemistry teacher turns to a colleague for help in trying to think of a way to assess what his students have learned from projects without giving a test. The second case highlights the dilemma a teacher faced when trying to explain to a student how she scored his chemistry laboratory report using a scoring rubric. An experienced physics teacher, dissatisfied with traditional assessment, describes his success involving students in the assessment of their learning in the third case. In the final case, a newcomer to a well-established school tells of his personal struggle to deal with a mandate to change his assessment practices to conform to the community's expectations.

■ ■ ■

Making the Grade: What Is Assessment Without a Test?

Carol Brisco

In this open case, Carol shares Dan Mayfield's story about how he is changing his chemistry teaching. Based on his belief that students learn science by doing science, Dan involves his students in open-ended, self-paced investigations. Dan observes their work and products to assess their learning. But the assignment of grades is a high-stakes event for Dan's students, and he worries that his evaluation procedures are not valid and fair to all. Dan's dilemma is captured in the question, Can I ever know what my students are learning without giving tests? Commentary on the case is provided by Mark Templin, a science educator with expertise in classroom-level assessment practices.

For most of his 16 years as a chemistry teacher at Rice High School, Dan Mayfield has used the textbook, the publisher's lab manual, and tests as his guides to formulating the curriculum in his classes. In past years, he has occasionally engaged his students in project work; however, these opportunities for students to explore chemistry on their own were few. This year, though, Dan decided that things were going to be different.

Last summer Dan attended a school district workshop that focused on the new state standards for science education. Mrs. Jenson, a district science teacher who presented the workshop, emphasized that the new state standards suggest that students should be engaged in doing science rather than learning science in more passive ways, like reading or lecture. She suggested that many activities typically done as recipe laboratory assignments could be modified to provide opportunities for students to plan most of the experimental procedures for themselves. During the workshop, teachers were provided with time to examine their own curriculum and plan several laboratory activities that would provide learning opportunities that were consistent with the standards. The types of learning experiences that Mrs. Jenson was recommending were particularly interesting to Dan because they were designed to encourage students to apply their knowledge in real-life situations, rather than simply repeating science facts and principles or using algorithms to solve textbook problems.

Dan had always wanted his students to find ways to use chemistry in their daily lives. Yet, constrained by a traditional approach to teaching chemistry, Dan recognized that his students had little opportunity to construct such relationships. Mrs. Jenson's presentation and the discussion and activities that followed encouraged Dan to provide more opportunities for students to experience authentic ways of learning chemistry. With implementation of the new curriculum guidelines, students would be encouraged to place more emphasis on developing problem-solving skills than on memorizing facts and algorithms. "Perhaps," he thought, "this would be the key to helping my students understand the importance of chemistry." Besides, he liked the idea of being able to facilitate, rather than direct, students' learning experiences.

When the new school year began in August, it was much like any other year; getting to know the students, developing rules for classroom behavior, passing out textbooks, organizing for group work, introducing students to the laboratory, assigning readings, and developing class discussions. But there was also the challenge of implementing curriculum consistent with the vision Mrs. Jenson had presented.

Near the end of September, as Dan is leaving the department meeting, he is joined by Eric Dupree, who teaches physics in the room across the hall from Dan.

ERIC: Dan, how's it going?

DAN: I'm not sure. I've really been thinking a lot about what Mrs. Jenson said, and the activities we did this summer at the workshop. I've been trying some of those open-ended labs with my students, and so far they seem to be going well.

ERIC: What do you mean by open-ended lab? I was at the beach the week of the workshop, remember.

DAN: Well, I've set up some experiments that the students can pretty much explore on their own or together in small groups. I spend my time in class circulating around the room and looking at what they're doing and asking them what they're thinking. I try to avoid telling them if they are right or wrong. Rather, I try to help them clarify their thoughts and maybe suggest some avenues they might explore. It seems that in their groups, the ones who understand help the others. And if nobody understands, they can at least talk about it and try to figure it out.

ERIC: Tell me more. Exactly what kind of experiments are you talking about?

DAN: For instance, this week, I told them to imagine that there'd been a hurricane and, although they can buy water for drinking, the only water they have available for cleaning is from a nearby pond. I made up some dirty water with mud, salt, oil and threw in some garlic juice to make it smell bad. I told them this water had suffered from saltwater inundation and run off from various sources that had added several contaminants they would need to remove. I gave each team some water, and I made available some materials, like alum, filters, charcoal, sand, and a heat source (if they needed it) to use to clean the water up. Most of the groups did a pretty good job of getting their sample of water clear. I didn't have to help them much either. The students really got into it! Next week, I plan to have them study the chemical change that takes place when baking soda and vinegar are mixed. This will involve some library research and some experiments for them to find out how this particular reaction occurs. The students will report their findings during a mock scientific conference in a couple of weeks. Different teams will be responsible for setting up the various aspects of the conference so they can see what it's like to be involved in that aspect of professional life in science.

ERIC: You have really been busy. Sounds great, but it also sounds like more work than I'd want to do. How do you keep track of who's doing what? It's almost time for 6-week grades, how are you managing to keep track of what the students are learning? Are you giving tests?

DAN: You've brought up something that has been bothering me. I really like having the students work in groups, and they seem to be enjoying chemistry, but I'm very uncomfortable with how to grade their work. I can watch them as they work, and it seems as if they are really learning. The experimental designs they come up with and the way they make sense of the data just amaze me. I have them turn in reports of their work sometimes individually and sometimes for the group. Overall, they are very good. But assigning a grade, that's another story. Without a quantitative criterion, I'm kind of lost. I know, there's that business about, "you're a professional, you should be able to tell whether it's an A or a B by looking at it," but how do I know if I'm being fair?

ERIC: What are you doing now when you look at the reports you get that you think might not be fair?

DAN: Well, for example, last week, before I looked at the papers, I tried to think through an answer that seemed reasonable to me. Then, I read their papers to get an idea of what they produced. In scoring, I tried to come to some balance between what they did and what I expected. If the response had some reasonable chemistry in it in relation to the question, right or wrong, I gave at least 1 point, on a scale of 0 to 4. You could tell from what they wrote that some of them really didn't understand the lab. But I didn't feel I should give them a 0 because they had, in a sense, done what I asked them to do—to solve the problem to the best of their ability. I gave zeros to some students who just put something down that had nothing to do with what the

	problem was about. And I gave fours to students whose explanations came very close to mine but maybe had a minor error or two.
ERIC:	That doesn't sound like a bad plan, although I sometimes wonder about giving students full credit when the answer is not completely correct. Besides, you've always done project work and graded it. What's bothering you about it?
DAN:	Yes, I know I've done projects before, but they were only a small part of my overall grading plan. Now the projects are high-stakes work. And when I think about it, the real problem with grading is the consistency. You know if you do a multiple-choice test and you grade it, you've got consistency from one person to the next in terms of how you arrive at the number of right or wrong. If you have to look at each person's answer and make a judgment about it, then ensuring consistency across the group is real hard. I guess that's my concern, that it might not be totally fair in some cases. At the beginning, I may have graded one of them a certain way, and then by 50 papers later, I may have gotten harder or easier. At least if you have a number of right or wrong, you've got some measurable thing, as opposed to just your personal opinion. I just don't know what to do. I can really see a change in my students' attitudes toward chemistry with these kinds of learning activities. If I start testing again, I'm afraid the students will focus on learning the wrong kinds of things. But if I don't test them, I'll never be sure that the grades I'm giving are what students really deserve. To top it off, the other day, Kenny Jacobs, who has always been an honors student, got really upset when I handed back one paper with a grade lower than he is used to getting. He threw it in the trash can as he left class and mumbled "Why can't we just have tests like everybody else?"
ERIC:	Wow. I can see you have thought a lot about this. You want your students to learn chemistry by actively participating in the learning process, and you think that learning and assessment should be intertwined, so you don't give tests. But you haven't found a way to assess students' learning while they are engaged in their various projects that allows you to easily assign grades.
DAN:	That's it! That's my problem.
ERIC:	I'm afraid that right now, I don't have an answer that will help you. I know that testing is a big part of what we do, and we have become so comfortable with this form of assessment, it's hard to think that any other format might be just as good. And it really makes it hard when students, and maybe their parents, fight against change. Give me some time to think about it, maybe I can come up with some ideas to help.
DAN:	I hope so, Eric. I'd really like to be able to say with assurance that my students have learned this or that. Right now, I think they are learning, but I'm not sure. I sometimes think that it's too complicated for us to even know. What do you do?

Questions for Reflection and Discussion

1. Dan experienced at least one student's dissatisfaction with his assessment procedures; what proactive steps might he take to avert one student's reaction from
   spreading throughout the class? To parents and the school community?

2. How might Dan use student self-assessment or peer assessment to alleviate
   some of his concerns about his personal subjectivity in the grading process?

3. Suppose Eric suggested to Dan that he try to develop some sort of a scoring
   rubric to use in assessing his students' work. What features do you think should
   be included in the rubric Dan designs?

4. Dan has tried to blend assessment with instruction in his classes by giving scores
   for student participation and for the products of their work, including laboratory
   reports. What other forms of assessment might Dan find useful to assess his students' chemistry learning?

5. Should Dan include traditional forms of testing as part of the curriculum? Why
   or why not?

6. Suppose that the central dilemma of the case is framed as an issue of authority,
   rather than one of fairness or equity. How might you change your responses to
   questions 1 through 5?

■ ■ ■

Is Testing Appropriate When Authority Is Shared?

Mark A. Templin

Carol Briscoe's open case provides insights into Dan Mayfield's motivations for
changing his instruction and assessment practices and the dilemmas he encountered
in implementing them. In developing the story, Briscoe allows us to eavesdrop on
Mayfield's conversation with fellow teacher Eric Dupree about his concerns over the
lack of apparent fit among student-centered instruction, context-rich assessment,
and traditional grading practices. In responding to this case, I will use my reflections
as a point of entry into the discussion before suggesting a different, authority-based
frame for this case that further deepens this dilemma. I will then conclude by suggesting a different set of reflective questions that I hope will expand on Briscoe's call
for reflection and inquiry into the relationships among science teaching, learning,
and assessment.

In reflecting on Mayfield and Dupree's conversation, I found that Mayfield
identified fairness and equity as important considerations for assigning student
grades. For instance, he was concerned about the consistency of his scoring and the
negative impact of his assessments on certain students. Certainly, these considerations directly impact student grading, and Briscoe takes up these considerations in

the reflective questions, asking the reader to reflect on technical solutions that might alleviate them. Yet, as important as fairness and equity are to the process of grading, I felt that Mayfield had difficulty communicating the underlying issues that made these considerations problematic in his classroom. If fairness and equity were the only concerns, he could have simply warned the students that he would be using an objective test to evaluate their performance, given them review opportunities based on the test, and then followed through with the testing. I believe that Mayfield had an intuitive sense that this was not the solution, but he was unable to articulate the complexities of his dilemma.

I re-read the case several times to search specifically for clues about what Mayfield might see as the underlying issues of his dilemma. From this interpretive process, I discovered that Mayfield's dilemma was tied to the concept of open-ended lab, which he defined for Dupree as, "experiments that the students can pretty much explore on their own or together in small groups." In subsequent discussion with Dupree, he outlined the changes in classroom responsibilities, control, and owner-ship that he and his students had undergone. For example, he spoke of spending his time circulating around the room and asking students questions that provoked thinking rather than instructing them in what to think. He concluded this outline by saying, "And if nobody understands, they can at least talk about it and try to figure it out." In other words, if students can't come to own an answer, at least they can still own the problem.

I like to use the metaphor of shared authority to describe the dynamic give and take among classroom members over these issues in student-centered learning envi-ronments. Based on my interpretation of this case, I believe that issues of authority, rather than fairness or equity, ultimately ground Mayfield's dilemma over classroom-level testing. Framing this case as an authority-based dilemma comes as disquieting news for two primary reasons. First, it suggests that the root of the dilemma lies in the social structure of the student-centered learning environment rather than in the assessments themselves. Thus, piecemeal technical changes to assessments such as new scoring rubrics or changes in assessment formats probably will not be enough to solve this dilemma. Second, it suggests that issues of authority sharing are linked in complex ways to ethical issues of student assessment and grading.

With these concerns in mind, a shared authority frame for this dilemma chal-lenges us to think more holistically about classroom-level assessment change by reflecting on questions such as (1) How can Mayfield change the discourse in his classroom such that students secure greater authority over their classroom work? (2) Should Mayfield negotiate with students to jointly develop classroom assessments and scoring rubrics? (3) If Mayfield negotiates assessments and scoring rubrics with students, what evidence could Mayfield gather to judge the validity of the scores derived from this process? (4) Could Mayfield's concerns about the reliability of his scoring be addressed by periodic student audits of his scoring practices? (5) How can student portfolios facilitate the student auditing process so that Mayfield and his stu-dents could enter into a dialogue about what counts in his assessments?

The Problem with Tyler's Grade

Dava C. Coleman

Teachers are often called on to justify their assessment of students' work. When using an assessment technique unfamiliar to students, even an experienced teacher can have difficulty explaining the process by which a score was derived. In this open case, Dava describes her attempt to explain to a student how she scored his laboratory report using a scoring rubric and the difficulties that arose in the process.

teach in a multiethnic high school of approximately 1,600 students located in a university town in Georgia. My teaching assignment includes three levels of chemistry: average, advanced, and advanced placement (AP). This is my seventh year at Maple Rivers High School. I came to this school almost as a first-year teacher, having left teaching for a state-level administrative position eight years earlier. In both my current teaching and former administrative positions, issues of assessment have frequently been a topic of discussion.

It was fifth period, about 2:35 PM, and the bell had just sounded. I was gathering up materials to get ready for my next class, when I saw Tyler approaching out of the corner of my eye. Oh no, I thought to myself. What now? Tyler had spent the first 4 weeks in my class debating every classroom policy, every assignment, and every test question. While I was praying he would go past me, he didn't.

"Dr. Coleman, may I speak with you about my grade on the last laboratory assignment?"

Here it is, I thought. I smiled and said, "Of course, let's go sit down and look at it."

We moved to a pair of desks and sat down. I opened the conversation with "What questions do you have, Tyler?"

He replied, "I don't understand why you rated my work as 'professional' when Jon's work was 'expert.' We did the lab together, and you made more corrections on his report."

I knew that his question referred to the scoring rubric that I use to assess laboratory work. My first instinct was to say, I don't know. And, to be truthful I really didn't. I had three classes of advanced chemistry, and I had graded 83 laboratory manuals in the past 2 days. My recollection of his report was zero. But, I was saved by the sixth-period bell and a large group of AP students. I told Tyler to leave me his notebook, and I would make specific comments about areas needing improvement.

Lab work is an important component in my chemistry classes. By state mandate, I must provide laboratory experiences for a minimum of 25% of the instructional time. I usually average about 30%. Not only do I enjoy doing laboratory work, I firmly believe that it allows students to understand chemistry. My students are required to maintain a lab manual, which is really a bound composition book. I use these because they are an inexpensive alternative to the real lab books used in colleges. For each laboratory activity, students are required to report the title, objective, and procedure. They must show their data in an appropriate table and provide appropriate data analysis. The report concludes with a discussion of results.

My decision to require a laboratory report for each activity performed is an attempt to keep students thinking and hopefully connecting what we discuss in class to the lab work they perform. At the beginning of school, I show my students how to set up their notebooks. I also give them a copy of the scoring rubric that I use and provide example lab reports for each performance level.

While sitting at my duty station immediately after school, I read Tyler's lab notebook again. The laboratory activity involved the separation of the components of a mixture. It is a standard laboratory activity for an entry-level chemistry course. The rubric that I use assesses student laboratory work on four components: procedure, observations, data analysis, and discussion of results. Performance levels are identified as expert, professional, competent, and novice. Scoring criteria for each level are shown in Table 10.1. This time, through the lab report, I was careful to comment on all strengths and weaknesses in Tyler's work. His performance level was the same on the second grading.

The next morning, Tyler stopped by my room before the first-period bell. "Dr. Coleman did you have a chance to read my lab again?" he asked.

"I did. Do you have a moment to go over it with me?"

He agreed. Armed with his report and my scoring rubric, we proceeded to move through the report section by section. I thought I was doing a good job explaining how his work compared to the expert level when Tyler stopped me and asked, "But, how many points do each of these errors count? I have all the sections that are required." Clearly, Tyler wanted an accounting of his score point by point.

"Tyler, I wish I could give you a point by point account, but I can't. The assessment of a lab report is not a simple minus 2 here and minus 1 there. I have to look at your level of performance overall." I could see that Tyler was not satisfied with my response or his performance level on this report.

TABLE 10.1   Laboratory report scoring rubric.

Expert
- Title and purpose are stated clearly.
- Procedure is recorded in concise numbered steps with enough detail to replicate and is written in the correct verb tense with no errors.
- Observations are recorded accurately, completely, and in the proper place.
- Data table is organized appropriately and contains all data.
- Calculations are accurate and complete with units.
- Responses to questions are written completely and accurately.
- A discussion paragraph is provided that includes the purpose of the lab and a summary of results with percent error, if applicable. Logical sources of error are identified along with how each error affects the results.

Professional
- Title and/or purpose are provided.
- Procedure is recorded in concise numbered steps with minor omissions and is written in the correct verb tense with only minor errors.
- Observations are recorded accurately, completely, and in the proper place with only minor errors.
- Data table is complete but unorganized.
- Calculations are accurate and complete but with missing or incorrect units.
- Responses to questions are written correctly but incompletely.
- A discussion paragraph is provided that includes the purpose of the lab and a summary of results with percent error, if applicable. Identified sources of error are logical but are limited, considering the total lab.

Competent
- Title and/or purpose are provided.
- Procedure is recorded in the correct verb tense but steps may be omitted and detail is missing.
- Observations are recorded accurately with only minor errors.
- Data table is incomplete.
- Calculations are complete but with minor errors.
- Some responses to questions are incorrect.
- A discussion paragraph is provided that includes the purpose of the lab and a summary of results with percent error, if applicable. Sources of errors are identified but are not logical based upon results.

Novice
- No title or purpose is provided.
- Procedure is recorded but is incomplete with significant deviations in verb tense.
- Observations are inaccurate or incomplete.
- Data table is missing.
- Calculations are incomplete or contain serious errors.
- Responses to questions are incorrect, poorly written, or missing.
- A discussion paragraph is not provided.

After a few moments, he looked up. "I understand that you judge my work on each of the criteria, but there are seven criteria for each performance level. How do you decide my performance level when on some of the criteria I am on the expert level and for others I am on the professional level? Does it take four out of seven or what?"

I thought that the "Or What?" was an excellent question.

Questions for Reflection and Discussion

1. What are the advantages and disadvantages of using a scoring rubric to assess performance levels of student work?

2. The chemistry students were provided with a copy of the scoring rubric and example lab reports. What are some other activities that the teacher might have done to help students make the transition to this type of assessment?

3. Suppose you were Tyler. What additional questions would you have asked about the scoring rubric and its use? As a teacher, how would you respond to these questions?

4. Examine the scoring criteria for each performance level listed in Table 10.1. How would you answer Tyler's last question?

Scoring Tables and Rubrics Working Together

David L. Radford

Assessing recall of facts is simple; a standard multiple-choice test will do. Assessing critical thinking, science process skills, and the ability to perform tasks is more complex. Evaluating students' responses to these alternative assessment methods is more difficult than scoring a multiple-choice test. Rubrics can aid in the process. The rubric that Dava constructed has several advantages over traditional methods of holistic grading such as an 85 or the letter B. The rubric provides students with specific criteria for what is expected in their lab reports. Feedback based on the rubric has the potential for guiding students toward improved performance. The problem was not the rubric but with the form in which the evaluation was reported. Tyler's grade was difficult to justify because the manner in which the overall score (professional) was obtained was not clear.

Tyler's concern about how to interpret his grade points out a common problem with many rubrics. How do you decide on an overall performance level when some criteria are met and some are not met in each category? At least three solutions to this dilemma are possible: (1) The overall performance level (expert, professional,

TABLE 10.2   Lab report scoring table.

Criteria	Level of Attainment				Comments
	Expert	Professional	Competent	Novice	
Title and purpose					
Procedure					
Observations					
Data					
Calculations					
Responses to questions					
Discussion					
Total x Value	x 4	x 3	x 2	x 1	
Score					*Total Score =

* 28–26 = expert   25–20 = professional   19–13 = competent   12–7 = novice.

competent, or novice) may be predicated on the student's meeting or exceeding *every* criterion in that category. (2) Or the student may be required to meet or exceed the *majority* of the criteria (e.g., 4 of 7) to be rated at that level. (3) Or point values may be assigned to each level of attainment and the overall score based on the *total points* accumulated in all categories. This last method may be facilitated by constructing a scoring table to be used in conjunction with the rubric (see Table 10.2). Constructing the table will require some extra time initially but has several advantages. Students are given specific feedback in each area being assessed; an overall numeric score will be generated, which allows the assessment to be incorporated into calculating grades for report cards; and the teacher should not have to spend large amounts of time explaining the grade to students like Tyler.

Students benefit from the detailed feedback provided by a rubric, but they must understand the rubric and how it is applied. In this case, Dava provided her students with the rubric in advance and gave them sample lab reports at each performance level. Because of the importance that she placed on lab reports and the frequency of their use, a more detailed introduction to the rubric is justified. A good class exercise would be to provide students with several examples of lab reports and have them work in groups to evaluate each report. Their scores and the scoring process could then be reviewed in a whole class discussion.

■ ■ ■

Against the Grade: Students' Assessment of Learning

Wolff-Michael Roth

This closed case illustrates how Wolff-Michael, an experienced physics teacher, resolves his uneasiness with traditional forms of assessing learning and learning outcomes. By changing his teaching, he allows students greater control over their learning, the learning process, and assessment of learning outcomes. Along the way, his students learn a great deal about electricity and themselves as learners. The experience strengthens Wolff-Michael's resolve to use alternatives to teacher control of students' learning and assessment. The case is followed by Wolff-Michael's reflections on the nature and purposes of assessment.

O ver the nearly 12 years of my teaching in middle and secondary schools, I have become disillusioned with the lack of motivation and control over their own learning older students bring with them to learning situations. I could empathize with my students because I had experienced the disempowerment when my teachers determined what from the myriad of things in chemistry I was to learn and how my learning was to be assessed. My reading of Foucault (1975) confirmed that evaluation and the associated grades are a major factor that make schools so similar to prisons.

Several years ago, I was teaching physics in a private college-preparatory school. The school and its teachers were very conservative; teacher lectures and silent student work were the predominant learning environments across subject areas. Students were from well-to-do homes but comparable in their ability to the students attending several nearby public high schools. Students' parents expected a return for their investments (expensive tuition fees), which the school administration virtually guaranteed by advertising a 99% university admission rate of its graduates. Physics was taught differently from other subjects, in that I provided opportunities for students to structure their own learning, design experiments, do textbook work and problems of their own choice, and engage in many discussions about epistemology. Many students were bewildered when they first came to my classroom, because of the radical change in learning environment; for example, one student reflected that "There is very little supervision and times when there is direct teaching; we are teaching ourselves" (student C.A., April 1992).

At the beginning of the unit on electricity, I communicated to my three junior-year physics classes that the Ontario Ministry of Education prescribed topics roughly equivalent to two chapters (which I specified) from their textbook and that we had about 6 weeks to complete this unit. I suggested that they spend the first week discussing within their self-selected groups of three to four members how they wanted to learn about electricity, how they wanted to demonstrate what they had learned, and what appropriate evaluation criteria were for their project. The framework for the assessment was such that 60% of the unit assessment was to come from peer evaluation, 5% from self-evaluation, and 35% from teacher evaluation.

As a result of the broad curriculum framework, the nature of the activities that students enacted varied widely. The following brief descriptions of four projects provide a sense of the nature of students' activities.

■ One group of two male and two female students decided to learn about electricity by developing a unit for teaching electricity to elementary (grade 5 or 6) students. They wanted not only to develop the unit but also to actually teach the unit to children of the appropriate age level. As they proceeded, the four students developed investigations with circuits, worksheets, overheads, and curriculum outlines. After having completed the unit, the four presented what they had done to their peers and then team taught the unit to one of the grade-5 classes. The four students were very proud of their work. More importantly, they learned not only about electricity but also about teaching. One student said, "We never thought how difficult it is to teach science" (student B.O., May 1992).

■ Another group of four male students was fascinated by superconductivity. After conversations with me during the first week of the unit, the four had planned a series of investigations, the results of which they intended to report to the class in the form of a poster and a compilation in a single (but lengthy) report. The investigations progressed from circuits containing normal carbon resistors, metal resistors, and semiconductors as they are used in computer chips, and culminated in several experiments involving a superconducting material. In the processes of designing their investigation, the students realized that they needed liquid nitrogen. Rather than supplying them with the substance, I asked the group to organize purchase, transport, and storage. With some hints from me, and after several phone calls, the students not only found a place where they could purchase the liquid nitrogen but also found out that they needed special containers (Dewar flasks) for keeping the substance and that they had at best 24 hours before the nitrogen would evaporate. In their evaluations, they wanted to see accounted all the organizational work it took to get the experiments actually off the ground. Furthermore, in a poster session, they presented the different aspects of their work to their peers, which, together with their reports, were the basis of the evaluation.

■ A third group decided to produce a video that would teach viewers about electricity through skits, colorful displays of information, and puppet plays. As they familiarized themselves with the topic of electricity, these students began to write the scripts and design the displays that they would need for their videos. The evaluation of their understanding was to occur during a public playing of the video that they had constructed.

■ Finally, one student with little interest in schooling and with poor grades across all subjects decided to learn about electricity by studying the functioning of the brain, particularly the way electrical charges moved through the different parts of the brain. He decided that he would demonstrate his understanding through a conference presentation with a subsequent questioning period during which the audience (his peers) could ask any questions. Despite my anxieties that this particular student would abuse his freedom, I witnessed the most impressive presentation by any high school student. He spoke freely and in great detail, supported only by his transparency, about the electrical properties of the brain including university-level topics such as the formation of potential gradients and ion transports across synapses.

In the end, the quality of the projects was overwhelmingly high. It was interesting, however, that (with only two exceptions) my own assessment of the projects and students' understanding of electricity was consistently higher than the peer- and self-evaluations. A further benefit of the learning process was that students never came to ask whether they were on the right track. Rather, my relationship with the students, already respectful under normal circumstances, was characterized by consultations and respect for our mutual perspectives on the issues at hand. There were many discussions about the evaluation of particular projects. Evaluations were negotiated and were well supported by participants, with descriptions of the positive and negative elements in the presentations and knowledge about electricity apparent. Typical comments on the experience follow:

> I have learned many things about electricity and also the application of electricity. This project was overall beneficial and was also a challenge given to us. As a group we finished what we aimed to do and therefore we are satisfied and proud. We also learned to trust and rely on each other, to listen to advice and justifications from our partners. It has been fun and I will never forget the nights we spent in the physics lab. I really appreciated that our work was evaluated by ourselves and by our peers. (student J.O., May 1992)

> Working independently was beneficial to me in that it gave me the opportunity to understand and have a knowledge of all the different portions of my experiment. I also proved to myself that I do, in fact, possess the ability to work independently, develop individual thoughts, and evaluate what I have done without the help of the teacher. (student F.R., May 1992)

Interviews with the students revealed that they felt tremendously empowered by this experience. They were in control of their learning environment, their learning, and the assessment frameworks. The students experienced contributions by peers to the evaluation process as positive because, as they suggested, peers were in a better position to assess the difficulties of each project and what it meant to learn about electricity than any teacher (who had long forgotten what it meant to learn a particular subject matter). Overall, the students and I felt that we had successfully dealt with some important issues of learning, particularly those of control and motivation. Their voices were not only heard but in important ways contributed to the construction of learning and achievement. Because the students contributed to assessment by means of self-evaluation (and their reports, posters, etc.), their lived work was also accounted for in their grades. Furthermore, students used their experiences of success in interesting ways to construct new selves:

> I found it interesting that, when questioned, I knew more than I thought I did. Each time someone questioned my work, it seemed I always had an explanation and I was never caught off guard. I believe that this is due to the style of learning we are currently undergoing. (student C.A., May 1992)

In my mind, this case may be considered closed because I was able to resolve my uneasiness and problems with traditional forms of evaluation of learning and learning outcomes. However, it may also be considered open, for while this new learning context and the outcome were evaluated as positive by students and by myself, several major dilemmas arise from our efforts for those who might want to adopt these evaluation practices. My classroom practices violated traditional assumptions about the objectivity of assessment, in that someone who presumably knows considerably more than the students establishes a set of evaluation criteria and judges all students or student groups against the set. Here, the criteria and the rater reliability are taken as constant. However, because of the variability in student projects, neither the criteria nor the evaluating peer group are constant.

Questions for Reflection and Discussion

1. The criteria and the rater reliability are taken as constant. What are the implications of this assumption for the meaning of the grades within contexts outside of the particular class (e.g., school, school district, university)?

2. What are the new roles of teachers if they no longer control delivery of curriculum and assessment of students' learning processes and products?

3. What is the role of assessment when institutional criteria can no longer be designed, such as to stratify students by distributing grades in the form of a Gaussian (bell) curve?

4. What are the potentially deleterious effects when peer evaluations are used to construct differences along the lines of gender, race, or any form of minority?

5. How do teachers have to adapt if they are deprived of their traditional instruments of control, power, and therefore of discipline in their courses?

6. What are teachers' roles when their traditional positions are decentered and when they are no longer gatekeepers? How do students' roles also change?

■ ■ ■

Reflecting on the Change Role in Assessment

Wolff-Michael Roth

Assessment is a thorny issue in school learning. Normally, teachers are responsible for assessment. Because of their position as gatekeepers at obligatory passage points for those who want to go to college, teachers are in the position to exercise power and control over classroom events, particularly the behavior of each individual student (Roth, 1996; Roth & McGinn, 1998). Grades are therefore not only assessment tools but also tools of coercion and discipline; science becomes more a rite of passage with science teachers being stern gatekeepers for access to a university (Brookhart Costa, 1993). This double control that teachers hold over learning and behavior may well be the origin of student passivity, fear of engaging in open inquiry, and constant requests for feedback (right answerism). Evaluation is a particularly insidious tool invented during the beginning of the industrial revolution to create obedient bodies and compliant students (Foucault, 1975; Postman, 1992). Most of those who do not submit to the regimen are shaken out of science and technology-related career paths.

Historically, grades have been used to stratify society and allow opportunities and (university) access to some while refusing it to others. The divide between those who get high grades and therefore access to opportunities often lies along traditional markers of difference such as race, gender, and social status (Lemke, 1990). As Lemke showed, the language and values that we use as references in science teaching and assessment are those of the white middle class (often male), so that those using different forms of English are already handicapped and biased against. To overcome such bias, we must enact more democratic science curricula that allow our students with different backgrounds to participate in the curriculum planning and assessment. My experience was an attempt (in my and my students' view, successful) to create different conditions of learning physics and assessing what students learned and knew about the subject.

Assessment and evaluation are of particular importance, not because they tell us something about how well students cleared a particular hurdle in their academic life, but because they contribute in crucial ways to the construction of identities and careers. In a case study of learning in an Australian grade-12 physics class, I showed how students used teacher evaluations to construct their own identities and contributed (in a negative way) to the construction of their peers (Roth & McGinn, 1998). Sean, an A⁺ student in physics, used Rhonda's C grade to construct her as having little interest and capabilities; he therefore felt obliged to take charge and control all laboratory activities. Rhonda, on the other hand, felt disempowered by her lack of co-participation in the activities and resigned to becoming a mere bystander and onlooker. Her negative experiences led her to abandon her cherished career goal, optometrist, and she selected physics (required for all scientific and technical university programs) as the subject that was not to be counted in the calculation of her grade-point average. For the same reason, her friend Brenda could not co-participate in physics activities and ultimately abandoned her career goal as an X-ray technician.

In my view, teachers (at all levels of schooling) are not technocrats who implement technologies of stratification so that others have easy and legitimate ways of allowing access (e.g., university) to some but not others. As part of the educational system, we can actively work to change the system. Engaging students in the planning of science activities and curriculum, setting of assessment criteria, and in the assessment itself is a small step toward a more democratic way of learning science.

■ ■ ■

Standards Are Needed, But What Should They Be?

Norman Thomson

Teaching as a Peace Corps volunteer in East Africa, Norm finds that his views on assessment are not shared by the school's Headmaster and biology students. Highlighted in this open case is the tension Norm experiences when faced with two competing referents: his worth as a teacher as evidenced by his students' success; and, at the same time, the need to conform to the expectations and acceptable standards set forth by the system. The backdrop for this case is a national examination that drives the educational process.

In retrospect, the introduction to my school in a remote area of southwest Uganda as its first Peace Corps biology/chemistry teacher was a portent to the challenges I was soon to encounter. I learned a lot about East African culture and the country's intertwined inherited British educational system during that first year.

I am the Headmaster here, Sherwood is the name. We will use the African tradition of calling you by your father's last name, so your name is Thomson. So, Thomson, your dossier suggests that you have college preparation in biology and chemistry. You need to know up-front that the rest of the world treats anything but the American Ph.D. with suspicion.

We typically find that American graduates are inadequately prepared to teach and assess the subjects for which they have purported degrees. Their credentials are lacking, and they can not easily teach and assess to the breadth or depth required in our subject-specific educational system, even at the secondary level. It is demanding, has quality, and standards that far exceed the established mediocre expectations we know about in the United States. We require in-depth comprehensive oral, written, and practical terminal examinations for all our students in all subjects. The educational system, to be sure, is assessment driven, and thus the students' success and futures depend upon how well you prepare them for their examinations. To put it bluntly, as an American, you most likely don't have what it takes. On the other hand, you may wish to try to live up to the challenge. You are going to have to learn your tropical biology, especially for East Africa, learn the syllabus, and study past examinations. Remember, practical examinations require familiarity with local flora and fauna. Students and parents will help you to learn, and do not be afraid to ask them for assistance, after all, it is their lives that are at stake. They are the critical stakeholders. As a volunteer teacher, you are a temporary but important medium in their lives.

To be sure, I was interested in meeting the challenges presented to me by Sherwood, so I set out trying to establish myself as a competent tropical biology teacher. I spent time trying to construct lessons that would integrate the syllabus and past examination questions into relevant practical hands-on lessons.

The school year consisted of three terms, and the school day was based on a quasi-block schedule, so laboratory time was built into the time table. Furthermore, students studied biology (and all other sciences) all 4 years in secondary school. Following the British educational system, during years (Forms) 1 and 2, students have three lessons per week: one double laboratory period and one discussion period, and during years (Forms) 3 and 4, four lessons per week: one double laboratory period and two discussion periods. I was assigned to teach Forms 3 and 4 (240+ students), so immediately I was placed in charge of 120 students preparing for their terminal biology examinations.

A serious confrontation with my senior students came at the end of the first term. At the end of each term, each class sits for a week of examinations in every subject. Each examination is comprehensive and includes any topic mentioned in the syllabus for which the students have previously received instruction. My examination, which included two parts called "papers," seemed to go quite well, following the national model and using previously set questions. The theory paper included 40 multiple-choice questions, 8 questions that required short and structured responses, and a choice of two of four essays. The practical paper included three in-depth hands-on tasks, each beginning with observations and drawings to label and ending with inferences and extrapolations.

After marking the papers, I assigned numerical grades based on a typical U.S. scale, awarding 93 and above an A, a low score of about 65 points, and the range providing a bell-curved distribution. I even had the audacity, I later learned, to award some students a score of 100 for their performance. When I announced with pride to my students that they had done exceedingly well and submitted my grades to the office, an eruption occurred not only among the students but from within Sherwood's office. I was called to his office, and an explosion of rebuke poured out as I was, figuratively, having mud flung into my face. He had never seen such outlandishly high scores, and students were protesting that I was misinforming them of their actual performance. It was a form of lying to them and neither treating them fairly nor honestly. I was accused of absolutely lacking any standards.

The students and Sherwood agreed that I should re-mark the examinations and tighten up the marking scheme, developing much more stringent guidelines and expectations. The expectation was that even the best students could achieve a maximum score of 80% with the lowest score being about 25%. Marks above 90% were extremely rare, as such an examination was considered to be nonchallenging and have created a glass ceiling, regardless of whether it was performance or criterion (a preferable standard) based. In addition, it was considered to be an effective examination if performance plotted more to a broad curve (platykurtic) with a balance across the total spectrum of possible marks rather than a bell curve (mesokurtic). Rather than a five-base letter grade (A to F), a nine number-based (1 to 9) grading system was used. A grade of 1 meant "distinction" and was usually a minimum score of 72%, while a grade of 8 was a Pass at about 30%.

I regraded the papers to conform to expectations and acceptable standards but really pondered about the meaning of being a successful teacher with a high rate of externally imposed failures. My revised scores ended up being comparable with those awarded by other teachers, but no faculty member could justifiably explain to me the scoring system. The terminal examination and standards were marked and set in Britain by the Cambridge Examination Board, which administered national examinations throughout the British Colonies and Protectorates. It seemed that that was the way it was, no questions asked.

Questions for Reflection and Discussion

1. Did Thomson have any choice but to conform to the expectations set by Sherwood and his students? Explain.

2. What kinds of assessment instruments and grading practices would you likely find in United States middle and secondary schools? Would you feel compelled to conform to these expectations? Why or why not?

3. What kind of messages does a grading system like the one used in Thomson's school send to teachers about their role in helping students to understand and master the content of their lessons? To students about their ability, self-worth, and potential for future academic success?

4. Should teachers in a school teaching the same subject be required to have similar grading systems? Why or why not?

5. When should assessment be norm referenced? Criterion referenced? What are acceptable ranges and distributions of scores and grade scales for daily work? For major examinations? For final grades?

6. What are the benefits and disadvantages of national or state examinations? If there was a national examination for science in the United States, how would you prepare students for the exam?

7. What can be learned from the educational systems in other countries, including developing nations, that could provide insights into assessment helpful to educational reform in the United States?

Assessment Is Always Affected by Culture

Lynn A. Bryan

Intriguing, thought-provoking issues permeate this case. In this response, I highlight three difficult issues with which Thomson seemed to grapple and for which there are no easy alternatives. Thomson encounters a situation in which his expectations for learning do not match those of his Headmaster, Sherwood, and the community. As a result of differing expectations, Thomson confronts a second issue: the meaning of grades. Finally, within the broader context of this case, Thomson has to take into account cultural influences on decision making.

■ What Expectations Are Appropriate, and Who Determines So?

Grades inherently communicate a message about how well the student met the expectations of the person or system assigning the grade. Thomson had expectations for his students, and his grade distribution communicated that his students met those expectations to varying degrees. Many students were able to meet those expectations in an exemplary manner and received high scores for their performance. The fact that not only the Headmaster but also the students revolted against Thomson's grading scale called into question the legitimacy of the expectations set by Thomson for his students. In describing Ugandan education vis-à-vis education in the United States, Sherwood commented, "It is demanding, has high quality, and standards that far exceed the established mediocre expectations we know about in the United States." However, Ugandans are not alone in their criticisms of U.S. expectations and standards for education. The study "What College-Bound Students Abroad Are Expected to Know About Biology" (American Federation of Teachers and the National Center for Improving Science Education, 1994) depicts the high standards achieved by students in countries other than the United States:

> Approximately one-third to one-half of the age cohort in England and Wales, France, Germany, and Japan take advanced subject specific exams. In sharp contrast, only 7 percent of U.S. 18-year-olds take one or more AP exams. (p. 26)

When one-third to one-half of students in these European and Asian countries are able to meet the high standards reflected in these exams, but only 7% of students in the United States meet such standards, what does this imply about the expectations for academic rigor in the United States? When are standards too low (or too high)? Who determines whether standards are reasonable and acceptable? Do you think that Thomson's expectations were acceptable?

■ The Meaning of Grades

A second issue in Thomson's case is related to expectations and standards as well: the meaning of grades. What does it mean to receive an A, when the same performance in another country would earn one a much lower grade? What does an A mean, when the majority or all of the students in a course make an A? Should students be graded relative to each other's performance? Or, should students be graded against a set of clearly defined criteria? Thomson felt forced to conform to a stringent, externally imposed grading system that allowed only a very small percentage of students to reach the top end of the scale. How did this externally imposed grade distribution change the meaning of grades for Thomson's students? These questions encourage reflection on the use of norm-referenced versus criterion-referenced assessments. What are the roles of these two different measurements? Who decides which is appropriate and for what use?

Another issue concerning the meaning of grades is the match between the grade and the mode of assessment. Assessment procedures used in the Ugandan school appear to drive toward the same aim as assessment procedures in the United States: measuring student achievement (most often in the form of recall of knowledge) and ability to apply that knowledge for solving problems. In addition, the East African assessment practices are concerned with the assessment of students' practical skills in science. Each of these assessments is intended to measure what students know (or have learned) from a course. Consider the fact that in today's high school science classroom in the United States, fill-in-the-blank and multiple-choice exams remain the major form of assessment. What do these assessments measure? What don't they measure? The interpretation of an assessment measure (grade) is meaningful and useful only when the assessment truly corresponds to the type of interpretation to be made. What knowledge and skills are measured in science? How should they be measured? Is the ability to memorize equivalent to learning, understanding, or the ability to apply information? How do assessments allow students to express what they know?

The previous questions raise yet another point that has been contemplated for centuries in different contexts and cultures: What forms of knowledge are most valuable, and who determines so? (see Herbert Spencer's 1859 revolutionary essay, "What Knowledge is of Most Worth?" in Kliebard, 1992, p. 31). Such questions raise a challenge to traditional forms of assessment widely used in the United States. For example, fill-in-the-blank and multiple-choice assessments ignore oral traditions of expressing what one knows. How did the forms of assessment that Thomson used acknowledge or ignore multiple ways of knowing? As classrooms in the United States continue to become increasingly diverse, how can teachers ensure that assessments correspond to what they intend to measure (i.e., what students know)?

■ Cultural Contexts of Decision Making

Aside from the issues of assessment and standards, Thomson finds himself in a difficult decision-making situation. His options for making decisions are influenced not merely by his own view of assessment and standards. This case provides an interesting dilemma in terms of personal interactions within a cultural context different from that of Thomson's own cultural background. Despite the options that may exist for resolving his dilemma, Thomson must be aware of and sensitive to sociocultural factors that influence his interactions, especially with the Headmaster. Not only is the Headmaster Thomson's elder, his position within the school system is superior to Thomson. As Jegede (1994, p. 124) explains, in traditional African society

> the belief is strongly held that the older person, having been exposed to more life experiences, should be in a better position to appraise a situation and pass "correct" judgment. The society frowns at a situation where the elder's point of view is challenged or questioned. Accordingly, the elder asserts authority in decision making. It behooves the younger individual to accept without question the directives passed down by the elder.

It would be disrespectful, and moreover unacceptable, for Thomson to ignore the cultural traditions of the society in which he resides and works. What were Thomson's options if one of his goals was to maintain respect for the traditions and cultural beliefs of the community in which he resided?

The issue of cultural contexts emphasizes the complexity of decision making, the intricacies of interactions among those of different values and traditions, and the necessity of acknowledging sociocultural factors that influence educational decision making. Additionally, this issue is applicable to all teachers, not simply those who may teach within a culture different than their own. The K–12 student population in the United States has become increasingly diverse over the past two decades, and it is projected that schools will become even more diverse in the years ahead. Teachers must become more responsive to the increasingly diverse classroom populations. What are examples of decisions that have traditionally ignored sociocultural influences of culturally diverse science classrooms? Failure to become aware of, be sensitive to, and take into account the cultural contexts in making decisions ignores the principles of equity and social justice on which democratic societies are founded. As a teacher, what is your role in placing sociocultural contexts into educational practice?

Resources to Consider

Barton, J., & Collins, A. (Eds.). (1997). *Portfolio assessment: A handbook for educators.* Menlo Park, CA: Addison-Wesley.

> Edited by James Barton and Angelo Collins, this 113-page book includes a wealth of information about designing portfolios, how they are used by teachers in kindergarten through high school, and the challenges associated with their implementation. Pieces authored by Susan Butler and Angie Williams about using portfolios with middle and high school science classes and another by Susan Pasquarelli entitled "Using Portfolios to Assess Your Own Instruction" may be of particular interest.

Doran, R., Chan, F., & Tamir, P. (1998). *Science educator's guide to assessment.* Arlington, VA: National Science Teachers Association. (National Science Teachers Association, 1840 Wilson Blvd., Arlington, VA, 22201)

> Before developing another multiple-choice test, examine Rodney Doran, Fred Chan, and Pinchas Tamir's descriptions of the latest in science assessment. This 210-page handbook is divided into two sections. Assessment theory, alternative assessment formats, and the development of assessment tasks are discussed in the first section, while the second section contains model assessment examples, including scoring rubrics, grouped by science discipline. The book also includes a glossary of often used assessment terms.

Hart, D. (1994). *Authentic assessment: A handbook for educators.* Menlo Park, CA: Addison-Wesley.

> This publication, authored by Diane Hart, is from the Assessment Bookshelf series and should be a welcome addition to any science teacher's professional library. The handbook begins by discussing standardized testing and moves quickly to providing a rationale for authentic assessment, with most of the 120 pages devoted to demystifying the many strategies of authentic assessment. An assessment glossary is also provided.

Schurr, S. (1998, January/February). *Teaching, enlightening a guide to student assessment. Schools in the Middle, 6,* 22–31.

> Sandra Schurr explains the role of assessment in middle school education and why it is important to realign assessment activities with the needs and characteristics of early adolescents. In addition to highlighting some of the unique benefits of alternative assessment, she describes how grades should be viewed when product and performance assessments are used in combination with traditional assessments.

References

American Federation of Teachers and the National Center for Improving Science Education. (1994). What college-bound students abroad are expected to know about biology: A special report. *American Educator, 18*(1), 7–30.

Brookhart Costa, V. (1993). School science as a rite of passage: A new frame for familiar problems. *Journal of Research in Science Teaching, 30,* 649–668.

Foucault, M. (1975). *Surveiller et punir: Naissance de la prison* [Discipline and punish: The birth of the prison]. Paris: Gallimard.

Hart, D. (1994). *Authentic assessment: A handbook for educators.* Menlo Park, CA: Addison-Wesley.

Jegede, O. (1994). African cultural perspectives and the teaching of science. In J. Solomon & G. Aikenhead (Eds.), *STS education: International perspectives on reform* (pp. 120–130). New York: Teachers College Press.

Kliebard, H. M. (1992). *Forging the American curriculum: Essays in curriculum history and theory.* New York: Routledge.

Lemke, J. L. (1990). *Talking science: Language, learning and values.* Norwood, NJ: Ablex.

National Research Council. (1996). *National science education standards.* Washington, DC: National Academy Press.

Postman, N. (1992). *Technopoly: The surrender of culture to technology.* New York: Knopf.

Roth, W.-M. (1996). Tests, representations, and power. *Journal of Research in Science Teaching, 33,* 817–819.

Roth, W.-M., & McGinn, M. K. (1998). Science education: Lives/work/voices. *Journal of Research in Science Teaching, 35,* 399–421.

11

Student Teaching and Mentoring

Student teaching is a challenging time for most beginning teachers. It is when beginning teachers are expected to apply what they have learned over years of college work in the sciences and education, and it also marks the beginning of a lifelong process of learning and professional development. Often, as the student teaching experience unfolds, beginning teachers come to realize that they must construct a new base of knowledge if they are to be successful in the classroom. This new knowledge base extends far beyond the science content to be taught and classroom survival skills; it includes knowledge of the curriculum, instructional strategies and methods, assessment practices, adolescents and their science understandings, learners' construction of science knowledge, school politics, and community norms and expectations. This knowledge base ties together the intellectual challenges and the practical issues associated with science teaching.

The beginning science teacher needs help to develop this knowledge base and support to deal with the complexities associated with everyday teaching. This assistance is most often provided by a mentor teacher, in whose classroom the beginning teacher first observes and later teaches lessons. Mentor teachers are typically chosen from among teaching veterans who have proven themselves in the classroom; but an excellent science teacher may not have developed the understandings and skills necessary to be a good mentor. Desirable mentors are those teachers who can provide assistance to beginning teachers in the areas of science instruction, curriculum, and the classroom environment, and provide consultation on personal matters that affect the beginning teacher's feelings of belonging and self-esteem (Gold, 1996).

The mentor's analysis of the beginning teacher's lessons and teaching plans is an important vehicle for providing assistance. During mentoring conferences, the beginning teacher's strengths and weaknesses can be discussed and recommendations for future work can be negotiated. The discussions sometimes reveal differences in expectations between the mentor and beginning teacher. These differences are often tied to the conflicting views of learning to teach as an intellectual challenge (college perspective) versus learning to teach as a refinement of practical craft (the school perspective) (Hayward, 1997). Issues surrounding such topics as student teachers' prior knowledge, the benefits of contextual learning, and metaphors used to guide teachers' thought and actions may be contested and negotiated. There is little doubt that what is learned during student teaching has a significant impact on a teacher's career. For this reason, beginning science teachers must have the benefit of working with quality mentors, mentors able to foster the development of the knowledge base and reflective skills needed for quality science teaching.

The cases in this chapter highlight different dilemmas associated with beginning teachers and mentoring. The first case recounts how a middle school student teacher, with the help of his science methods course professor, wrestles with the constraints he encounters when proposing to teach a life science unit. The unit focuses on *Pfiesteria* and the evidence for the possible mechanism(s) of infestation in fish and in humans in the Chesapeake Bay area. In the second case, the authors describe how a student teacher develops her knowledge of teaching by thinking about the nondirective guidance her mentor teacher would have whispered in her ear had she been standing at her side. And the final case illustrates how a high school student teacher turned to personal journal writing in the absence of a university supervisor to grapple with her mentor teacher's insistence that she teach about simple machines in a way contrary to her personal beliefs about teaching and learning.

Walking the Tightrope Between the World
of Academia and the World Of Work

J. Randy McGinnis

In this open case, Randy describes Sam's dilemma associated with engaging students in learning experiences intended to fulfill a school system's environmental health-risk science curriculum requirement. The tension felt by the teacher candidate is associated with balancing his notions of curriculum, instruction, and assessment developed in his college science methods class with the constraints he finds in his middle school classroom. Sam consults Randy, his science methods professor, as he struggles to resolve this dilemma. Following the case is commentary by Ronald Simpson, a university educator with expertise in science education and higher education, and Melissa Warden, a science educator and former middle school teacher.

I am a professor of science methods who specializes in teaching elementary/middle-level teacher candidates how to teach science. I work with undergraduates in a senior-level methods block semester that precedes their final semester as a student teacher. The methods semester consists of classes on campus and a semester-long field placement with a classroom teacher in an elementary or middle-level school.

The majority of my teacher candidates come to me unsure of the elementary/middle-level curricula or appropriate instructional and assessment strategies. This uncertainty is compounded by a misgiving that their knowledge of science is inadequate for them to successfully teach upper elementary/middle-level students science. To lessen their fears and create a classroom climate in which they can begin to positively consider teaching science, my teaching strategy focuses on the teacher's and the learners' co-construction of knowledge in a social setting rather than on the teacher being a transmitter of science content knowledge. On the whole, my students come to believe in their ability to plan and teach engaging science lessons, while simultaneously enhancing their own science content knowledge as they gain teaching experience. My students also express that our state science assessment program for fifth and eighth grades, which uses an alternative assessment system (distinguished by broad categories of performance, e.g., "Exemplary" or "Needs Improvement"), provides them a flexible, yet definable method to gauge their students' science content growth.

I have often wondered, however, how a teacher candidate with a well-developed body of science knowledge would approach learning how to teach middle-level science. What would this type of teacher candidate focus on if the main concern were not a perceived lack of science content knowledge? How would this teacher candidate resolve theory into practice?

I recently had an opportunity to find out answers to these questions when a cohort of undergraduate teacher candidates participating in a National Science Foundation-supported teacher preparation program, the Maryland Collaboration for Teacher Program (MCTP), entered my science methods class. These teacher candidates were distinguished by having taken nearly double the number of science and mathematics content classes required by our typical undergraduate elementary/middle-level teacher candidates. Their level of science sophistication was further enhanced by summer internships in science-rich contexts such as NASA. While each of the MCTP teacher candidates was unique, the case of pseudonymous Sam as he walked what he termed "the tightrope" between his college classes (the world of academia) and his school placement (the world of work) is particularly insightful.

Sam was a nontraditional undergraduate who was a former truck driver. As he often stated, "I have driven long hours, and I know hard work. I am prepared to work hard to learn how to teach kids science. I have little fear of science. I am looking forward to exploring science with my students." Sam's knowledge of science was extensive, as measured on a 75-item content assessment diagnostic I designed to measure middle-level knowledge in the physical, life, and earth sciences recommended by the standards documents. (Sam responded correctly to 52 items, ranking him first in his methods class of 30 teacher candidates.) In addition, his attitude toward science as a discipline distinguished him from my typical students, "I enjoy the sciences and believe they are fun and filled with exciting discoveries about our world and our lives."

Sam's attributes and disposition encouraged me to work closely with him during the semester to develop a science teaching activity for the seventh-grade students in his school placement that relied heavily on his high level of science knowledge. Sam's cooperating teacher requested that he teach a lesson that would fulfill the environmental health-risks topic in her county's curriculum. As a rule, in science methods I teach the science education topic of Science-Technology-Society (STS), so Sam was familiar with the underlying principles of engaging students in a socially relevant science and technology-related issue. I encouraged Sam to design a lesson that focused on a real-world issue, instead of defaulting to a science activity that placed more emphasis on interpreting data in a hypothetical environmental problem. Sam designed a lesson that focused on a recent outbreak of a microbe infestation in the

Chesapeake Bay. The media had identified the microbe *Pfiesteria piscicida* as responsible for the death of several thousand fish in the Bay and for the perplexing illnesses of several humans involving inexplicable memory loss, vomiting, and eye irritation. Sam's job was to teach his students what the scientific community knew about *Pfiesteria* and the evidence for the possible mechanism(s) of infestation in fish and in humans.

Sam approached his topic with confidence that he could readily learn the science associated with *Pfiesteria* by researching the available data base via the university library and the World Wide Web. Sam was not constrained by a lack of confidence in his ability to understand scientific findings in technical reports. In fact, he rapidly became somewhat of an expert on this dinoflagellate organism, knowledgeable of its taxonomy, its complete life cycle, and the mechanism by which it infected hosts. In response to my direction for him to gauge the knowledge level of his diverse students on this topic before designing instruction, Sam interviewed three of his students (representative of high, middle, and low level) and presented his findings in concept webs. With his scientific understanding of the topic, he was able to develop a rich interpretation of his findings and how he anticipated using this information to design instruction:

> The learners have a good base for constructing a better understanding of *Pfiesteria*, its characteristics, how research is done, and how it affects our community. They know of some factors that affect water pollution but do not seem to make the connection between chemical fertilizers and runoff from farmland or that these chemicals could foster growth of an organism that hurts the environment. There seems to be a lack of understanding of what factors might contribute to, or limit the spread of, *Pfiesteria*. They have some knowledge that further study will enable them to see how science is used to help understand and manage modern-day problems. The learners also have a concept of government's role in issues like this, but they may not be aware of the media's role or the scientist's role and their respective effects on society. These learners need to see that there are deeper issues than students' simply defining the problem and reversing the cause. They should understand that science must work with society to find solutions and that the answers are not always easy. This is what I will assess in my evaluation of their growth in this lesson. The current *Pfiesteria* issue is a good platform to use in teaching science, the scientific method, and social responsibility.

I was impressed with Sam's use of science education techniques to assist him in designing instruction. I felt that his sophisticated interpretation of his learners' scientific knowledge base was a direct consequence of his own considerable scientific knowledge base.

From his science methods course, in which Sam became familiar with the tenets of the *National Science Education Standards* (National Research Council, 1996), Sam knew that the world of academia favored an inquiry perspective in teaching middle-level students science. He worked hard to enact this type of teaching perspective in his proposed lesson. His goal was for his students to learn science by doing science.

Sam first wanted his students to share what they knew about this issue in a journal entry. He then wanted his students to work in small cooperative learning groups to generate a testable assertion, such as "Are fish and humans both deleteriously affected by the microbe *Pfiesteria piscicida*?" His students would then examine microbes under the microscope, read some text on what the scientific community knew about the infestation and the microbe, and write their conclusions in a student journal based on their understanding of the scientific evidence on what society should do—in this instance, to solve an environmental risk. He would assess their knowledge gain by examining their journal entries.

When Sam presented these ideas to his cooperating teacher in the world of work, he was told that the curriculum allowed him only 50 minutes to teach this entire lesson. As a result of this great constraint, she advised him to tell students the nature of the problem and not take time for the students to examine microbes under the microscopes. Instead, she advised him to use the majority of the class time to have students individually read summaries of newspaper articles (which he would need to prepare) on the topic. The lesson would end with him summarizing the science content for their note taking. She also advised him to assess the students on his lesson via some multiple-choice items included on an end-of-the-week test.

In a subsequent office hour appointment, Sam shared his bind with me. "I feel like I am walking a tightrope between what is recommended by you and *the National Science Education Standards* (National Research Council, 1996) as exemplary science education and how my cooperating teacher says I need to teach science in the schools." He was pleased that the local curriculum supported the STS initiative recommended by the national standards documents. However, while supportive of the theory of science teaching practice he learned in science methods, he felt great tensions in putting it in practice in his field placement. He wondered how he could resolve this dilemma between the constraints of the workplace and the high ideals of academia.

Questions for Reflection and Discussion

1. What should Randy say in response to Sam's dilemma?

2. What should Sam do to resolve his dilemma? How might he involve both Randy and his cooperating teacher in doing so?

3. How should Sam assess his efforts to resolve his dilemma? What role might Randy play in helping Sam to assess his efforts?

4. Why did Sam find that there is tension between the ideas he developed in his college science methods class and the implementation of those ideas in his field placement?

5. A critical aspect of this case is that both Sam's cooperating teacher and Randy, Sam's university supervisor, believe that their positions are correct. What might Sam do to help both cooperating teacher and university supervisor to see the dilemma from the other's perspective? Propose a negotiated solution that you think might be acceptable to both.

Fundamental Questions of the Science Teaching Profession

Ronald D. Simpson

The problem that emerges in the case entitled "Walking the Tightrope Between the World of Academia and the World of Work" is one of the most realistic and fetching issues in teacher education. Professors like Randy McGinnis teach preservice teachers to examine critically the nature of science and technology and to help students learn in a manner that is consistent with these foundations. These professors teach the use of student-centered techniques that are founded on a constructivist epistemology. This may lead to scenarios where young preservice teachers, with the encouragement of their progressive college mentors, end up in situations where conservative practices in some school systems clash with these newer approaches to teaching science.

Alternatively, many hard-working, experienced teachers learn to cope with reality by using methods of instruction that are not consistent with the epistemologies and learning theories espoused in university classrooms. Often, a lack of materials and equipment, school policies, or local culture interfere with the teaching of science in a way that is consistent with the ideal way to expose students to the learning of science. Furthermore, a teacher of 20 or 25 years may have discovered that to survive the system he or she must revert to simpler instructional strategies that require less preparation and demand less energy.

So the concrete theme of this case and the dilemma of the young, enthusiastic, freshly primed student teacher is that he is "cooking in the kitchen" of a seasoned veteran teacher; this teacher has learned that pacing oneself and keeping things manageable for health and convenience purposes are necessary. In a more abstract sense, however, this dilemma represents a serious professional issue. It deals with fundamental questions such as, Does the preservice teacher have an adequate understanding of the basic principles of science? Does the preservice teacher possess an adequate understanding of how students learn and what is appropriate to teach at various grade levels? Is the supervising teacher up-to-date in his or her subject area? Is the supervising teacher current with respect to important trends and issues in the field of science education? Has there been adequate communication and agreement between the school system and university with regard to appropriate philosophies and methods of teaching and learning in science education?

The important questions that emerge from this case involve three major players: preservice teacher, supervising teacher, and university supervisor. Other important concrete and abstract implications also emerge. This case can serve as an excellent template on which to examine important professional, political, legal, ethical, administrative, and scientific dimensions of science education. By using this case, college students, science teachers, college professors, and school officials can examine together the significant variables that affect all of us interested in improving science education and enhancing the quality of our lives.

■ ■ ■

Play on the Strengths of the Middle School

Melissa A. Warden

Sam's problem is not actually all that unique. Conflicts between the kind of science teaching advocated by his university methods instructor and the kind of science teaching expected by his cooperating teacher are quite common. Many classroom teachers today are unaware of research that provides supportive evidence for using constructivist teaching strategies to improve student achievement and attitudes in science. Those teachers who are aware of such research may still be reluctant to practice these strategies, given the real-world constraints of such things as time and standardized testing. Merely knowing that firsthand experience with topics that have personal and immediate relevance is more likely to result in deeper conceptual understanding and longer retention is sometimes not sufficient to brazenly ignore a local district's curriculum framework and a building principal's instructional expectations. The solution, it seems (for both Sam and his cooperating teacher), is to find a way to keep the planned lessons intact, while, at the same time, working within the existing constraints.

The first thing to take a closer look at is the county curriculum that Sam mentions. If the assignment he has been given fulfills the curriculum's topic requirement for environmental health risks, then perhaps there are other required topics that his lessons may also satisfy. Why not, to use the old adage, "kill two (or, in this case, four or five) birds with one stone?" Spending more time on this particular sequence of lessons can be better rationalized when they are seen in the context of a larger chunk of the official science curriculum. Such topics as the characteristics of marine and freshwater ecosystems, the population dynamics of communities, the flow of matter and energy through a food web, water pollution as it relates to agricultural and farming runoff, and the taxonomy and life cycles of various microorganisms (especially the dinoflagellates) can all be explored via Sam's intended lessons. Also germane to the *Pfiesteria* infestation, of course, are a number of topics associated with habits of mind and the nature of science and of technology, broad themes presented in *Science for All Americans* (Rutherford & Ahlgren, 1990) that take a close look at how scientific knowledge is generated and how the scientific enterprise operates. Given the potential for Sam's lessons to cover more content, his cooperating teacher may very well decide that his effort deserves additional class time to complete.

A second option to consider in solving Sam's dilemma uses to advantage the interdisciplinary nature of the middle school setting. What if science were not the only subject that could be taught using Sam's idea? Because this is an STS problem, social studies is also an appropriate forum for the discussion of its related themes. Students could explore such issues as the existence of overlapping and conflicting local land use priorities, the difficulty of balancing economic growth with a healthy natural environment, and the necessity for governmental regulation and enforcement. Likewise, mathematics could be involved by having students graph exponential growth curves indicative of microbe population explosions or solve ratio and proportion problems associated with the scientific sampling of infected fish in the Chesapeake Bay. In language arts, students could write environmental impact reports using data they collect from various media sources for inclusion in a special edition of the school newspaper. By linking Sam's *Pfiesteria* lessons to other content areas and thus sharing the teaching responsibility among the entire grade-level team, not only is the amount of required science time dramatically reduced, but students also come effectively face-to-face with the complicated and multidimensional nature of the problem.

■ ■ ■

Mentoring Whispers*

Randi Nevins Stanulis and Alice Sampson

When Katie's first attempt to engage seventh-grade students in a laboratory investigation of plant and animal cells failed, she turned to Ms. Lendell, her student teaching mentor, for help. Their planning period discussion led Katie to think about "mentoring whispers," which she then used to guide her thoughts and actions when repeating the laboratory investigation with a second group of students. The critical aspects of mentoring highlighted in this closed case are based on Randi and Alice's experiences in working with student teachers as both mentor teachers and teacher educators. Ms. Lendell and Katie represent composites of teachers and student teachers with whom Randi and Alice have worked over the years. The case is followed by commentary from Julie Gess-Newsome, a science teacher educator with expertise in mentoring for teacher development.

Ms. Lendell's seventh-grade life science class was alive with excitement as the students worked in pairs. The organization, the purposeful activity, the sense that the students knew what was expected and were excited and ready to learn, all helped to lift Ms. Lendell's spirits as she went up and squeezed her student teacher, Katie, lightly on the shoulder. "You're doing *great* work!" she said in an enthusiastic stage whisper to Katie. Katie looked at her for reassurance, then smiled wryly, "Yeah, a drastic improvement over third period. What a disaster! Thanks so much for your honest feedback. It really helped me think about how I needed to improve right away. I keep hearing you whisper behind me, 'Management! Modeling! Expectations! Lab Safety!'"

---

*This case was adapted from research reported in Stanulis, R. N. (1994). Fading to a whisper: One teacher's story of sharing wisdom without telling answers. *Journal of Teacher Education, 45,* 31-37.

As Ms. Lendell moved around the classroom, checking on students' progress and quietly reinforcing positive student behavior, she thought about the relationship she was developing with Katie. She sat down in a chair in the back of her room, her note pad ready to write specific feedback for Katie. Katie had asked her to write down suggestions and to be critical. Since the lab during third period had been less than successful, Katie and Ms. Lendell had conferred during fourth-period planning. Now, armed with new strategies, Katie felt prepared to try again with her fifth-period class.

Ms. Lendell smiled, thinking how refreshing it was to have such a self-assured and capable student teacher as Katie. A student in her mid-20s, Katie was obviously a high achiever and was used to success. Katie had been floored when her third period had many problems with the lab. But she had picked herself up and had asked Ms. Lendell for honest feedback in order to improve immediately. Though Ms. Lendell had worked with many student teachers in the past, she had sometimes felt uneasy about providing critical feedback, worrying that it would upset them during this fragile time. Her instinct was always to protect student teachers, and she felt responsibility and pride in helping them learn to teach. As she thought about Katie's first lab lesson today, Ms. Lendell wondered what role she had played as a mentor in setting Katie up for failure and success.

Ms. Lendell felt her class was pretty typical. She had 26 seventh-grade students of mixed gender and racial backgrounds. Like most of her colleagues, she had a few students with learning disabilities or behavior problems. Through heterogeneous grouping, she was able to provide learning opportunities for each of her students, enabling each one to shine. Ms. Lendell had assured Katie that it takes time to learn to manage such diverse learners and develop sensitivity to their multiple learning styles. Now, as she sat watching Katie, Ms. Lendell acknowledged that students in this class could not handle a lot of movement during lessons. Though it was already January, Ms. Lendell had not yet gone beyond exposing her students to simple lab procedures. Yet, she had not stopped Katie as she planned an active lab in which students would prepare and observe slides of animal and plant cells.

With enthusiasm, Katie had jumped in right away and included hands-on experiences in her first lab lesson. She was excited to hear that Ms. Lendell agreed with heterogeneous grouping and was up-to-date on theories of multiple intelligences, all consistent with Katie's university teacher preparation. During her methods courses, however, Katie was exposed only to lab lessons taught by her peers. This was her first experience doing a lab with a group of real middle school students.

Ms. Lendell thought back to their conversation during fourth-period planning. Katie had talked to Ms. Lendell about how she had presented her lesson to the class. First, Katie had grouped students and instructed them to complete the lab assignment found on the handouts at their stations. Initially, she thought that the students seemed interested and engaged. But as the lab progressed, the level of noise and apparent confusion increased. Katie began to realize that the lab was not going well. Students waved their hands frantically in the air. She didn't know where to turn first, as she heard her name shouted by a chorus of voices. The class period was nearly over; she didn't even have time for closure. Katie kept thinking, "If I can only make it to planning time to talk with Ms. Lendell." After the last student walked out the door, Katie slumped down in a chair and looked at Ms. Lendell expectantly, " That was a total disaster! What went wrong? Please, tell me, what I can do?"

Ms. Lendell asked Katie to take a few moments to jot down her own ideas about what had worked well during the lab and where there was room for improvement. As Katie wrote her own notes, Ms. Lendell thought back to ideas she had learned about mentoring student teachers in a summer workshop. An important idea was not to tell a student teacher too much, because each teacher needs to develop a personal style. Ms. Lendell really didn't want to replicate carbon copies of herself. As she thought about the implications of this belief for her mentoring, Ms. Lendell had considered what good mentors should do in order to really help student teachers grow. Working with Katie provided her with the first opportunity to put the ideas into action.

She began talking to Katie, "Katie, there are a lot of strong teaching qualities that I believe you possess, along with a great intuitive sense about individual kids and their way of learning. I really admire how you wanted to get right in here and do a hands-on lab with the kids. I also think that making mistakes is a part of learning. We can learn a lot if we really take the time to ask questions about the mistakes we make and put together new ways of doing things to make it better."

Ms. Lendell was trying hard to act on her belief that part of a mentor's role in helping a student teacher is to guide him or her in learning to question, think about a lesson, and put new ways of thinking together. At the heart of this philosophy of mentoring is the importance of stepping aside and guiding a student, rather than just giving answers that reflect one way of doing things. "OK, Katie, what are some of the things that you have on your list?"

"Well, I know that I completely underestimated how complicated this lab was for the students. I mean, I didn't give them enough time, I didn't think through what instructions they needed for working with the materials, ugh! What a mess! What could I have done to make the lab better?"

"Katie," Ms. Lendell said softly, "try to think about what you could do to make the lab less complicated. What kind of management issues were problems? What could you do differently? What do you need to think about when considering the use of specific materials, about modeling, and about giving instructions? I know that I could just keep my mouth running and tell you what I might do, but I really want you to think about the main issues you want to focus on and how you would handle them. Let's make a chart of the main issues. You said 'Time,' 'Management,' and then I said, 'Modeling.' Can you think of anything else?"

"Well, I didn't tell them anything about filling out their lab sheets, or when to put away materials, and they left things all over the place."

"OK," Ms. Lendell said comfortingly, "how about if we label one of our columns 'Expectations' in order to cover some of those points. Now, let's talk about how to organize this. What might you talk about under 'Time'?"

"Well, the students needed more time to go back or start over when the tissue samples were too thick or were dyed incorrectly. I'd like for them to know that they can go back again and figure out a procedure that works."

"How could you help them be able to have more success in preparing a slide correctly?" asked Ms. Lendell.

"Oh, let me think," Katie said as she gazed at the chart that she and Ms. Lendell had prepared. She tapped her finger on the column labeled "Modeling." "I guess I could show the class a sample of a correctly prepared slide."

"Yes, great idea!" coached Ms. Lendell. "In my experience, some students become frustrated when they don't have an idea of the end product. Alright, let's look back at this sheet. What kind of management problems did you see? Think about issues of lab safety and cleanup."

Katie put her head in her hands. "This was the worst part for me. OK, let's see. Well, I definitely didn't think about the management problems associated in giving students scalpels for slicing thin pieces of onion skin, or that they would need specific directions when handling raw hamburger." She sighed, "Again, going back to modeling, I could demonstrate the proper use of a scalpel, and talk about safety issues."

"Wonderful thinking," Ms. Lendell chimed in. "And, you should always refer back to the lab rules posted on the wall. It's important to clearly reinforce expectations."

Katie and Ms. Lendell continued this conversation, with Katie taking the lead, framing their discussion around the categories of teaching that together they had created. Ms. Lendell asked Katie if she felt ready to adapt her lesson plan for the fifth-period class that would arrive in just a few minutes.

Katie perked up. "Yes! I know I can do this. Let me try to make some adjustments based on your feedback. Will you watch my lesson and take notes so that I can improve some more?"

"Of course," Ms. Lendell agreed. "Now, summarize for me some things that you will keep in mind during the next class. Pretend like I'm standing behind you, whispering some key phrases to remember. What would those phrases be?"

Katie laughed. "That's a great idea, actually. OK. One whisper would be, 'Did you model what you expect them to do?' Another one would be, 'Did you give the students clear expectations?'"

"Clear expectations about what?" Ms. Lendell probed.

"About lab safety, about completing their lab sheet, and about cleanup."

"Excellent! Any other whispers?," Ms. Lendell asked encouragingly.

"Oh, I think one more would be, 'What management and safety issues do I need to think about when handing out supplies?'"

During fifth period, Katie put her adaptations into action. She demonstrated the proper use of the scalpel and how to handle the raw hamburger, discussed safety components and consequences, and with a twinkle in her eye, referred to the lab rules posted on the wall. She explained that students should replace scalpel covers and drop the scalpels into the empty baby wipe containers when finished with them. She showed students how to carefully peel the onion skin without the use of the scalpel, just by using their fingers. She reviewed the steps on using a microscope. As she looked at the time, she realized that these procedural instructions were taking a lot of time, so she quickly went to ask Ms. Lendell if she could continue preparing students for the lab activity and actually complete the lab the next day. Ms. Lendell thought this was a smart idea, especially since lab procedures were fairly new to her students. She suggested that the students prepare slides for tomorrow.

With a bounce in her step, Katie went back and helped the students review how to use a microscope. Then, the students practiced placing the appropriate amount of water on the slide with a piece of newsprint and correctly situated it on the stage of the microscope. Katie then showed the students the lab sheet and pointed out the directions. She explained that the lab sheet was to be completed as the lab progressed, except when plant and animal tissues were being handled. She discussed cleanup procedures and wrote them on a chart. She assigned the students to teams and discussed their roles for tomorrow's lab.

At the end of the period, Katie looked at Ms. Lendell for encouragement. Beaming, Ms. Lendell went quickly to Katie and gave her a hug. "You are remarkable!" Ms. Lendell said. "I can't believe how quickly you adapted! You certainly have demonstrated flexibility. The students really learned a lot. You were very effective."

Katie smiled widely and sat down. "Thank you so much for all your help. I really heard your whispers as I taught. If you hadn't helped me think through what went wrong during third period and given me specific cues so I could guide myself, I never would have made it!"

"Well," Ms. Lendell said as students filed in for the sixth period, "You get to do it all over again in a few minutes. We'll talk at the end of the day about some important things you learned that can help you even more tomorrow. Great work!" Katie stood up and went to the door, greeting the students as they entered, giving clear directions about her expectations for what they should do first. She had learned a lot already today, thanks in large part to her effective mentor teacher.

Questions for Reflection and Discussion

1. In what ways do you believe that Ms. Lendell was an effective mentor? What is her philosophy of mentoring? What kind of effective teaching skills is she trying to foster in Katie?

2. Student teachers sometimes mimic their mentor teacher's teaching style until they can find their own personal style. How does Ms. Lendell encourage Katie to develop her own style of teaching? What characteristics of teaching are important to Ms. Lendell?

3. Describe the relationship between Ms. Lendell and Katie. What are the shared beliefs on which their relationship is based?

4. What does it mean to be a mentor? Describe the characteristics of a person you would like to have as a mentor.

Bravely Charting Your Professional Growth

Julie Gess-Newsome

So, what do you want in a mentor? Or, more specifically, what type of experience will help you learn the most about teaching? We often believe that having a mentor will solve many of the problems associated with being a new teacher. This belief, while reasonable, is often ill-founded. Mentors come in many shapes and styles. As Ms. Lendell admitted, her first inclination was to nurture and protect a novice teacher from the difficulties of the classroom. While such a response may feel good and inflate your ego, it does little to improve your teaching or prepare you for a life as a professional. Instead, Ms. Lendell chose to mentor Katie by letting her attempt a difficult lesson, fail, and help her learn through the experience. Though I'm sure both Katie and Ms. Lendell were uncomfortable with the lesson's lack of success, both mentor and novice teacher experienced the power of learning from mistakes while in a supportive environment.

I attribute the success of this mentoring episode to one attribute found in both individuals: bravery. Katie exhibited bravery in two ways. First, she took the risk of introducing a lesson format that was unfamiliar to her students, a laboratory, but was in line with her beliefs about teaching. Second, rather than asking for superficial endorsement of her efforts, she asked for honest and concrete feedback that would help her improve in future teaching episodes. These acts of bravery allowed Ms. Lendell to respond in her own courageous manner: She allowed Katie to teach in a manner that was dissimilar to her own, and she allowed her to fail while acting as a supportive and critical friend, encouraging reflection, growth, and future confidence in teaching. The joint bravery allowed Katie to follow a path toward becoming a professional—one who will continue to learn about and improve her teaching over her career.

Several realities affect teaching. First, teaching is an isolated activity. Once student teaching is complete, few teachers have the opportunity to have another individual in their classroom to provide consistent feedback. Therefore, being able to independently analyze your practice, as Ms. Lendell encouraged in Katie, is critical to your continued growth as a teacher. Second, teaching is a complex endeavor. As such, no one is ever fully developed as a teacher. Constantly evaluating and refining our teaching goals and practices both improves our teaching and helps maintain enthusiasm for the profession. Third, as aspects of teaching become routinized, allowing a teacher to conduct some tasks automatically, cognitive space is made available to concentrate on the subtleties of classroom interaction. As a result, teaching gets easier, allowing you to work on goals that are more refined and less central to your survival.

These realities result in a fairly straightforward conclusion: You are responsible for charting your own professional growth. Following are suggestions, emulated by Katie and Ms. Lendell, of how you can continue to improve teaching over a lifetime with or without the assistance of a mentor.

1. *Know who you want to be as a teacher.* The teaching models you saw as a student may exist in stark contrast to the teaching expectations you were encouraged to examine and embrace in your teaching methods courses. These images, in turn, may have little resemblance to the teachers you observe in the public schools. What kind of a teacher do you want to be? What teaching practices are in line with your views of science, teaching, and student learning? Be brave. Take risks. Be willing to implement practices that are consistent with your teaching beliefs while you continue to examine those beliefs.

2. *Carefully identify areas for improvement.* As much as we would like to, it is impossible to improve every aspect of teaching at once. Select a few concrete aspects of teaching on which to concentrate your improvement efforts. The following list reflects many of the concerns of novice teachers, potentially in order of more to less immediate concerns:

   > Classroom management
   > Subject matter presentation
   > Monitoring student understanding
   > Constructing appropriate responses to student comments and
   >   questions
   > Establishing conceptual connections within lessons and across the
   >   curriculum
   > Tailoring materials to meet the needs of individual students
   > Accurately portraying the nature of science
   > Teaching in line with the national science reforms
   > Emulating teaching goals to practice (Reynolds, 1992; Gess-Newson,
   >   in press)

3. *Help yourself while you enlist the help of others.* Write down your goals for teaching improvement. As you plan each lesson, think about what you can do to make progress toward these goals. Create your own "mentoring whispers." Evaluate each lesson, both while you are teaching it and at its conclusion. When possible, enlist the assistance of others to act as a critical mentor. Request honest feedback and strategize, individually and together, methods to improve practice.

4. *Use opportunities to improve your practice.* As a secondary teacher, you probably have the unique opportunity to teach the same lesson several times in a given day. Use each teaching episode as an opportunity to improve on your previous lesson delivery. At the conclusion of each day, reflect on the lessons learned and record these "whispers" for future reference. And congratulate yourself on your continuing commitment to and success in improving your teaching practice.

When It's My Turn,
I'll Be Able to Teach My Way!

Lynn A. Bryan and Belinda Gibson

Student teaching is most commonly relied on to provide prospective teachers with their first professional experience. What kinds of experiences in student teaching facilitate prospective teachers' development of professional knowledge? In this open case, Lynn and Belinda describe a dilemma Emily faced while student teaching that stems from differences in teaching philosophies: her own philosophy versus that of Mrs. Simmons, her cooperating teacher. On proposing to teach her ninth-grade physical science class about simple machines using inquiry-based lessons, Emily is told that she must follow the more restrictive and didactic curriculum and methods favored by Ms. Simmons. The central issue raised in the case is, When a cooperating teacher and a student teacher, who lacks support from a university supervisor, are at odds about how to teach a class, what should the student teacher do? Emily is a pseudonym for a former student teacher known to both Lynn and Belinda. The case is followed by commentary from Barbara Crawford, a university science educator with extensive experience in matters of student teacher mentoring.

As the familiar ring vibrated through the hall, signaling the end of another school day, Emily could hardly wait for all of the students to pack their book bags and scurry off to catch the buses. Her eagerness was not because she was tired and certainly not because it had been a particularly challenging day. Emily excitedly awaited the end of the school day because she was going to meet with Mrs. Simmons. The time finally had come in student teaching when Emily was going to be able to teach the class the way she thought was best. All of those years taking courses, reading books, writing papers, observing classrooms, and designing lesson plans finally were going to pay off. The moment Emily had been waiting for was quickly approaching, and she and Mrs. Simmons were meeting to work out the details.

As the last student filed out of the room, Mrs. Simmons motioned for Emily to take a seat next to her at a lab table.

"So, Emily, were you able to write your plans for the next 2 weeks? I'd love to see what you have done."

Quite pleased with the work she had been doing on her lesson plans, Emily responded with both confidence and anticipation, "Oh yes, I made a copy for you. I have some really great ideas that I think you'll like.

"First, I designed some activities that I think our students will learn from and enjoy. I know that hands-on activities tend to be frowned on at Medlock because the students can get a bit rowdy. But, I really think our students can do the activities I have planned. I believe that our students can learn physical science best when they explore the concepts with real, everyday materials. In fact, I don't see how they will really understand pulleys, levers, and inclined planes without actually using these simple machines. And, I think once they figure out for themselves the force–distance trade-off for the simple machines, they will be able to explain it in their own words. That is what real learning is all about."

Emily had carefully crafted details of her lessons including goals, objectives, lists of materials, procedures, and time lines. She planned to have students examine each of three simple machines individually and then determine general relationships that hold true for all the machines. For each simple machine, Emily planned the following series of events: Each group will explore with the equipment; take systematic measurements and record data; discuss patterns in the data; and write a consensus explanation of their findings. After completing the individual simple machines investigation, Emily planned to have the students compare and contrast the different machines, determining the relationships that apply to all of them. As a culminating activity, the class would construct a Rube Goldberg contraption in which all three simple machines had to be used. As she proudly displayed her lesson plans, Emily thought to herself, Mrs. Simmons is going to be impressed.

"Well, this looks really good, Emily," Mrs. Simmons said almost without emotion, "but I think that we had better stick more closely to the teachers' guide concerning the video materials and the worksheets for this unit. As a rule, the students don't do well with these kinds of activities. They won't be able to handle working in small groups and messing with all of this equipment. We have a routine with the students, and I would hate to try something different from what we all are used to and not have it work." Trying to lend an encouraging word, she continued, "But, it looks like you have put together a good unit."

Emily felt the wave of disappointment permeate her body. Repressing her instinct to react, Emily gently pursued Mrs. Simmons's comment, "I thought that during these next 2 weeks, I would be taking over and teaching the science." Continuing to plead her case, "I have tried these activities myself, and they're really great. I checked the manual, and I'll still be covering the same material that is in the video. But this way, instead of just watching the video, the kids will be able to measure and feel the difference in force and see the differences in distances. Plus, by having these hands-on experiences, they will be more likely to engage their minds, ask questions, and see the relevance of science in their everyday lives. In the final project, they will even design something based on what they learned. I want them to talk to each other about the science, use what they know, and not just listen to me or the video."

Emily continued, "The activities are really fun and interesting, and I know they are appropriate for ninth graders. I am sure that they will do very well and learn a lot if we allow them to participate in these activities. Our students are capable of conducting investigations, but I realize they may not have much experience in doing so. And, I know you think they might get a little out of control if they are let loose. But, I have given a lot of thought to grouping the students; I have collected all of the materials; I have questions prepared to get them to think about what they will do in the activities. And as you can see, I have even developed an assessment plan that I think will cover the same points as the video. I really have my heart set on trying this out."

Mrs. Simmons listened intently but could not be swayed, "I think these students will learn best with the materials we have been using. Remember, Emily, that these students are not on the college-prep track. They aren't Medlock's brightest students. And, they only have 2 weeks to learn about simple machines. I think you have done some great work here, but I don't feel that we can afford to do things differently right now. If the activities don't work, the students will be at a disadvantage. They need to know these facts and definitions not only for next year but for the state exam in the spring."

With an exasperated breath, Emily proposed a compromise that she felt was reasonable. "Maybe I could start by trying just one of the lessons. How about doing the inclined planes activity with them? We can see how that goes. I think they will respond really well. If it goes well, if they seem to learn from it, and if I manage their behavior well, then maybe we can discuss the pulleys activity. If it doesn't work, I'll go back to the video and worksheets for the rest of the unit. I just think we should give these students more credit. They have the ability to do these activities and understand simple machines. I think these activities will motivate them."

Mrs. Simmons shrugged off the suggestion and maintained her position. "Like I said, I think these students learn best using the routine we have established. Routine is really important for kids like the ones we have in physical science. We should stick with what we know works. This doesn't mean I don't like your plans. As I said, you have done a good job, Emily. I think you're well prepared for the next 2 weeks. Now, let's take a look at the teachers' manual for the video lessons. Let's see what it says about simple machines."

Feeling dejected, Emily pulled out the teachers' manual. It was difficult to concentrate. Her mind was swimming with thoughts: "But the *routine* does not work. The students aren't learning, and they're not motivated. They are memorizing facts, definitions, words. They are searching for answers to fill in the blanks and are not curious about how things work. This is not science. This is not learning. And this is not how I want to teach. I want a chance to practice with my ideas and my plans. Is this really how student teaching is supposed to be? Will I have to continue emulating Mrs. Simmons's way of teaching? Will the next several weeks be the same old thing? What am I going to do? How will I get through this?"

Emily, the Science Enthusiast

As long as she could remember wanting to be a teacher, Emily had always been eager to teach science. She loved working with youth, and she loved science, so what better way could she combine the two than to become a high school science teacher? She believed that students loved to learn science and were always eager to get their hands into equipment and mess around. Although Emily had not always had great experiences as a science student herself, she knew that the few great experiences she did have influenced her career decision. She had always wanted to teach young adolescents because her own ninth-grade teacher had made such a powerful impact on her. Emily remembered how Mr. Smith always had lots of investigations for students to do, and science class was constantly bustling with activity. When she wrote in her journal about her science experiences, memories from Mr. Smith's class took center stage:

> One of my fondest memories was working with circuits. We broke into groups of four and experimented with lightbulbs, batteries, wires, and switches. I absolutely loved it! I never thought I would understand how circuits worked, but that experience taught me that I could learn anything. I never realized that learning could be so much fun, and from that point on, I loved science.

Emily recognized that both the positive and negative experiences that she had in science classes influenced her idea of what school science should be like. She wanted to be a great science teacher. She wanted to inspire and encourage her students to ask questions and seek their own answers to those questions. She envisioned an abundance of investigations in her classroom with students discussing, debating, thinking, and problem solving. The last things she wanted to do were stand in front of a class lecturing and hand out worksheet after worksheet. Emily wanted to use science journals and try portfolios as a means of assessing her students' understanding. She wanted to use the textbook as a resource but not as a centerpiece for her instruction.

Emily also knew that her vision of teaching science would not be easy to implement, especially in her first years of teaching. She had countless practical questions that she hoped to begin to answer when she started student teaching. Her personal journal served as an outlet for her to reflect and to document the questions that she wanted to pursue in her student teaching.

> How should I group students so that they work together well? How can they contribute to the planning of our activities? What ideas do they already hold about science? How will I know if an activity is too hard or too easy for them? What kinds of questions should I ask to foster their discussion of the results of their activities? Will I be able to encourage them to ask good science questions? How should I grade the journals that I want to use? Do I determine what should go in portfolios or should the students?

Emily could hardly wait to finish her university coursework and get into the classroom. She had so many ideas, so many questions! In Emily's eyes, student teaching was the beginning of a lifelong journey of learning to teach: a journey on which she was more than ready to embark.

◼ Emily's Journey Begins

As she drove into the parking lot on that first day at Medlock County High School, Emily was a little nervous but excitedly so. This school was much different from the high school she had attended in Indianapolis. Medlock was in a small, rural community about 30 minutes away from Emily's university campus. Most of the students came from working-class families. Many of the students had attended Medlock County Schools since their primary years and knew each other well. Emily knew from her many phone conversations with Mrs. Simmons that there were 20 students in the ninth-grade physical science class and that students taking physical science as ninth graders were usually below average in ability and relatively unmotivated. Approximately one-third of the students in Ms. Simmons's class had failed the course at least once in the past. Some were behavior problems, but Mrs. Simmons had told her that the community's parents were actively involved in the educational lives of their children.

The first 4 weeks of student teaching had fallen short of Emily's expectations. It became clear early on that she and Mrs. Simmons held very different philosophies about science teaching. Mrs. Simmons had been teaching for nearly 20 years, all of those years spent at Medlock County High School. Two years ago, the school district adopted a new videodisc-based physical science curriculum. In lieu of a textbook, Mrs. Simmons followed this curriculum, consisting of videodisc lessons and a teachers' guide. Typically, when covering a topic, the students watched a series of video episodes that explained the science concepts student were expected to understand. Then, Mrs. Simmons asked questions from the teachers' manual and called on students to answer the questions. Sometimes the students were allowed to do a short experiment, or Mrs. Simmons performed a demonstration. There were always worksheets for students to work on quietly at their desk. On the day before a test, Mrs. Simmons reviewed the questions from the multiple-choice test with the students in a practice session.

This way of teaching science was markedly different from what Emily had envisioned. Emily recognized that some students would be more challenging to teach than others. However, after being in Mrs. Simmons's classroom for 4 weeks, it came as no surprise why these students seemed unmotivated. Their role in the physical science classroom was so passive. Nonetheless, Emily was not in the position to challenge Mrs. Simmons' years of experience and the class routine. So, she just went with the flow. Eventually, Emily figured, Mrs. Simmons will give her more autonomy.

"After all," Emily thought, "the first 4 weeks are really just meant for me to get to know the students, become familiar with the schedule, learn some management techniques, and get used to planning. When it is my turn, I'll be able to teach my way."

In the meantime, Emily assisted in instruction using the video materials, asking questions from the script in the teachers' manual, handing out worksheets to reinforce the concepts, and reviewing for the unit tests. It was frustrating, but Emily felt it was better to lie low. She would have her chance to teach soon.

One week before Emily was scheduled to take over Mrs. Simmons's class, she began preparing for the upcoming science unit. Great! The topic would be on simple machines, an area of physical science Emily felt she knew fairly well. She collected resources, dug through her boxes of university notes, and grabbed a pad of paper. Making herself comfortable and cozy for a couple of hours of work on the couch, Emily started to write down the myriad of ideas for teaching simple machines. Work, energy, force, distance, pulleys, levers, and inclined planes. There would be so much to accomplish, but it would be fun, and more importantly, motivating for the students.

She thumbed through a large, somewhat battered notebook from the first of several physics courses she had taken over the last 3 years. What great labs there were in this course! It was a special course, intended for middle and secondary education majors, and the professor was one of Emily's favorites. Like Mr. Smith, Professor Braxton somehow managed to make science fun and interesting for prospective teachers. Unlike other science classes that she had taken in college, this particular course was based on a philosophy of teaching that Emily believed in: Students learn science best by engaging actively in meaningful investigations; the students' role is to explore, experiment, and discover, while the teacher's role is to guide, facilitate, and ask questions. Emily fondly recounted some of the laboratory experiences she had experienced in the class. One in particular, the lab on pulleys, proved to be particularly helpful now, since Emily would be teaching about pulleys in the unit. She pulled the lab report out from her notebook and began sketching out a plan for how she was going to approach teaching simple machines. Before long, an outline for 2 full weeks of lesson plans was ready for typing in the computer.

The Aftermath

After a long day at school and a less than satisfying conversation with Mrs. Simmons, Emily sank back into her favorite place on the couch and comfortably positioned herself to write. Thoughts had raced through her head on the drive home as she reflected on her meeting with Mrs. Simmons. Her journal now offered a place of solace, an outlet for the frustrations and ambiguities that she was encountering in her student teaching.

> I do not agree with Mrs. Simmons's philosophy of teaching. I feel like I am feeding students answers. I have seen their exams, and all they require are for the students to memorize facts. Through discussions with the students, I have come to realize that they are storing all of this information into short-term memory, and in a couple of hours, they forget it. One day they understand, and the next day they cannot recall anything. They are not learning, and they are not asking questions!
>
> Mrs. Simmons says this is the mandatory curriculum. We can't deviate from it, because the district says it is what we're supposed to do. I am afraid to use any of my ideas because it would be going against Mrs. Simmons's wishes. On the other hand, I

know the activities that I have planned are consistent with the curriculum that I am supposed to teach. They fit perfectly with the video materials, and I know the students would learn so much more this way. They can formulate questions and do the activities. I know they are capable of doing this. I think that doing these activities would be a great experience for them, and I just want the chance to try.

This is not at all what I thought student teaching would be. I want to try some of the things I have learned. I want to get some answers to the questions I have about teaching. Should I approach Mrs. Simmons? Should I override Mrs. Simmons and prove her wrong? How can I show her that the activities will result in student learning? I always thought that when it is my turn, I'll be able to teach my way!

Emily encountered a significant student teaching dilemma and struggled to find a satisfactory resolution for both parties. In addition, she lacked a human support system, individuals from whom she could seek advice or simply talk through issues. During her 16-week student teaching experience, the university supervisor only twice visited her classroom. Emily yearned to interact with someone who would be honest about her failures, yet offer her the expertise needed to help her analyze and learn from those failures. Although Emily conscientiously planned and reflected on her teaching, these activities were essentially solo endeavors; she couldn't help feeling like a boat afloat in stormy weather.

Questions for Reflection and Discussion

1. What would you do if you were Emily? Would you teach all or part of your planned lessons? Or would you continue to pursue the issue with Mrs. Simmons? What would you stand to gain and lose by your decision?

2. Can dilemmas like the one that confronted Emily be avoided? If so, how?

3. What makes a student teaching experience meaningful? What constitutes your ideal student teaching experience for science and how can that ideal be achieved?

4. If a student teacher proposes a plan that would, in the eyes of the cooperating teacher, disrupt an established classroom atmosphere, should the student teacher be allowed the freedom to teach as planned? If not, what would be a reasonable compromise?

5. Who bears the responsibility (and for what) in the process of a student teacher's professional development with respect to science teaching and learning?

6. In the absence of a critical friend, how might strategies such as journal writing and self-talk be used to facilitate a student teacher's professional development? What other strategies could be used to nurture reflection?

Early Communication Can Help

Barbara A. Crawford

This case describes a common problem encountered by student teachers: how to gain approval to try out innovative, untested ideas that are in direct opposition to those of the cooperating teacher. In many cases, the student teacher is caught in a squeeze-play pleasing two masters: her cooperating teacher and her university supervisor. Often, the university supervisor expects the student teacher to design reform-based lessons that differ considerably in style and content from those used routinely by the cooperating teacher. The cooperating teacher may view her role as mentoring the student teacher in how to carry out the activities "honed to perfection" over the years. Or, the cooperating teacher may view keeping her classes together and following the departmental program as a high priority.

In Emily's case, the student teacher appears alone in her struggle to convince her cooperating teacher that using hands-on activities will motivate students and enhance their understandings of physical science concepts. The first issue in this case is that replacing the videodisc-based lessons with these new hands-on lessons does not fit the cooperating teacher's image of what seems best for her students. The second issue is the minimal, almost nonexistent role played by the university supervisor. In fact, there is little evidence of any support for Emily or feedback to Emily's journal writings or draft lesson plans.

Ideally, Emily should never have been put in a situation where her cooperating teacher and university supervisor had different expectations for her. The cooperating teacher should be knowledgeable of what is being taught in university classes and of the university's expectations for its students before agreeing to host Emily. In many locations, classroom teachers work cooperatively with university faculty to develop the desired science teacher education program. If this had been the case at Emily's university, her cooperating teacher should have been more supportive of what Emily was attempting to do. In addition, university faculty who serve as supervisors should be available for their students and should see the support of student teachers like Emily as an important mission of their work. It would have been helpful had Emily's supervisor negotiated expectations with the cooperating teacher before Emily entered the teacher's classroom. If differences over expectations for Emily could not be satisfactorily resolved, then a more suitable cooperating teacher should have been identified.

Given that Emily's student teaching situation is less than ideal, a possible solution to the problem that she faces may center on increased and early communication between Emily and her cooperating teacher and university supervisor. First of all, the responsibility for review and feedback of unit plans should rest equally with the university supervisor and the cooperating teacher. However, research indicates a lack of consensus about the university supervisor's role and that many cooperating teachers have little training in supervision and skills in conferencing (Glickman & Bey, 1990).

Effective growth in teaching develops from the ongoing communication between members of the triad: cooperating teacher, university supervisor, and student teacher. Since Emily appears to be operating as one of a dyad with her cooperating teacher, she needs to be proactive in presenting her ideas to her cooperating teacher during the 4 weeks preceding her unit. Emily should have requested feedback from her university supervisor as well. Emily might have prevented her unexpected disappointment of not being able to carry out her plans if she had submitted an outline of her unit and a rationale much earlier. Citing support from national reform documents and research on student learning could have strengthened her argument and given her cooperating teacher opportunity to weigh the risk of letting Emily try out activities against the potential for enhanced student learning and motivation. Instead, during the first 4 weeks, Emily remained passive about her ideas and acquiesced to the teacher-centered style of Mrs. Simmons. When Emily does get her turn as a first-year teacher and begins to teach her way, she will have missed perhaps the best opportunity for mentoring and support she will ever get.

Some additional questions to consider regarding Emily's situation include: What other ways could she have presented her ideas to Mrs. Simmons? What recourse does Emily have if her cooperating teacher flatly refuses to allow her to try out new ideas? What is more important, trying out new ideas or keeping peace with your cooperating teacher? What other support could Emily enlist to enable her to use some different lessons from those designed by Mrs. Smith?

Resources to Consider

Allsop, T., & Benson, A. (Eds.). (1997). *Mentoring for science teachers*. Buckingham, UK: Open University Press. (Open University Press, Celtic Court, 22 Ballmoor, Buckingham, UK, MK181XW)

This handbook, edited by Terry Allsop and Ann Benson, contains eight chapters authored by experts on science teacher mentoring. The chapters are presented as cases in action and are of particular value to teachers seeking insights into critical issues associated with mentoring beginning science teachers. Issues addressed include the conditions for student–teacher learning in schools; the distinctive knowledge, skills, and attitudes required of mentors; the relationship between the university and school in science teacher education; and student teachers' theorizing about how to learn to teach.

Jacobowitz, R. (1997) **30 Tips for effective teaching**. *Science Scope, 20,* 22–25.

Roberta Jacobowitz presents some great suggestions for energizing any middle school or high school science class. Beginning teachers should find the suggestions particularly helpful. They can serve as a reminder of important teaching and learning ideas addressed during methods courses. Among the suggestions Jacobowitz discusses are use community resources, allow students to experience success, and don't expect to finish the book by the end of the year.

Motz, L., & Madrozo, G. (1988). *Third sourcebook for science supervisors*. Arlington, VA: National Science Teachers Association. (National Science Teachers Association, 1840 Wilson Boulevard, Arlington, VA 22201)

Edited by LaMoine Motz and Gerry Madrazo, this book contains 24 chapters on topics concerning supervision in science. Topics addressed in the book of particular value to mentors of beginning teachers include supervisory skills and responsibilities, managing change, teaching and safety in the laboratory, and important teacher characteristics.

Wong, H., & Wong, R. (1991). *The first days of school*. Sunnyvale, CA: Harry K. Wong Publications.

This book is a must read for beginning teachers. Authored by Harry and Rosemary Wong, it is full of suggestions about how to become an effective teacher. The book's five units identify the characteristics of an effective teacher and address the how-to's of establishing positive expectations for students, managing the classroom, designing lessons to help students learn, and becoming a professional educator. Dog-eared copies can be found in the professional libraries of many successful science teachers.

References

Gess-Newsome, J. (in press). Secondary teachers' knowledge and beliefs about subject matter and their impact on instruction. In J. Gess-Newsome & L. G. Lederman (Eds.), *Examining pedagogical content knowledge: The construct and its implications for science education*. Kluwer: The Netherlands.

Glickman, C., & Bey, T. (1990). Supervision. In W. Houston (Ed.), *Handbook for research on teacher education* (pp. 549–566). New York: Macmillan.

Gold, Y. (1996). Beginning teacher support: Attrition, mentoring, and induction. In J. Sikula (Ed.), *Handbook of research on teacher education* (2nd ed., pp. 548–549). New York: Macmillan.

Hayward, G. (1997). Principles for school focused initial teacher education: Some lessons from the Oxford Internship Scheme. In T. Allsop & A. Benson (Eds.), *Mentoring for science teachers* (pp. 11–26). Buckingham, UK: Open University Press.

National Research Council. (1996). *National science education standards*. Washington, DC: National Academy Press.

Reynolds, A. (1992). What is competent beginning teaching? A review of the literature. *Review of Educational Research, 62,* 1–35.

Rutherford, F. J., & Ahlgren, A. (1990). *Science for all Americans*. New York: Oxford University Press.

12

Science Teacher Education: Exploring the Paradoxes and Possibilities of Case-Based Instruction

Many of the dilemmas of science teacher education are characterized by the paradoxes of what is and what ought to be. Often described as the theory/practice gap, these paradoxes are evident in the perceived lack of epistemological fit between university-espoused philosophies and those of classroom teachers. Tensions surround notions of critical reflective practice advocated in many science teacher preparation programs and actual opportunities for reflection within the everyday realities of the classroom. These tensions are also apparent in a view of professional development as a challenging intellectual endeavor, which stands in stark contrast to experiences designed to reflect a practical, skills-based orientation. Cases, when used with care, are one potential avenue for exploring the urgent questions that surround these educational conundrums.

Early education experiences often reinforce the notion that problems can be resolved by applying a correct formula. Thus, it is not surprising that prospective teachers may at first view the dilemmas of practice in terms of simplistic solutions that lack a sense of history or ethical overtones (Kagan & Tippins, 1991). For prospective and practicing teachers alike, case-based pedagogies may represent a radical departure from traditional approaches to recognizing and considering the dilemmas that are inherent in science teaching and learning. While not advocating a single approach to case-based instruction, we share some recommendations and guidelines that have proved beneficial in our own experiences and educational contexts.

Creating Your Own Cases

Classroom cases can serve many overlapping purposes within a science teacher education program or professional development setting: as exemplars, as opportunities to practice analysis, or to stimulate personal reflection. While these varied contexts provide opportunities for teachers to frame and view dilemmas and challenges from multiple perspectives that reflect the complexity of school life, we must ensure that the use of cases does not resemble what Sacken (1992) has described as the "kitchen sink" approach to constructing multiple meanings and analyses. Dilemma-based cases by their very nature may reflect issues with no right answer. However, a systematic approach to incorporating case-based instruction within curricula and professional development experiences may enhance its usefulness as a pedagogical tool. One possibility for addressing this issue is through the use of guidelines that support the development of written cases and responses. Our own experience has shown that introductory guidelines can help teachers better understand the processes involved in writing and interpreting cases.

In many ways, the process of developing a written case resembles that of baking a cake. Both processes depend on a variety of ingredients that are added in varying amounts and different sequences; just as no two cakes are ever the same, teachers' case narratives will reflect great diversity in their representation of classroom dilemmas. We have adapted some guidelines initially developed by Kagan and Tippins (1991) as a template for introducing case writing to prospective and practicing teachers. We ask teachers to develop written cases using open or closed formats. Teachers exchange these narratives with colleagues, who write solutions or responses that examine the issues highlighted in each case. We emphasize our belief that no case is ever really closed.

■ Writing an Open Case

Initial Considerations

1. Establish a safe environment for the writing of cases. New and experienced teachers alike are vulnerable when sharing sacred stories of the classroom. Care must be taken to ensure that their written case materials will not be used without permission.
2. Emphasize the importance of the writing process and not just the final case product.
3. Cases should reflect a realistic view of the complexity of teaching that does not oversimplify the messy nature of classroom dilemmas.
4. Mundane, everyday experiences should not be overlooked as potential source materials for cases (Hansen, 1997).
5. Written cases should emphasize the human dimensions of teaching and learning that invoke intentions and feelings that are often at the heart of classroom dilemmas.
6. Cases should be of reasonable length to facilitate opportunities for group discussion.
7. A summary or abstract of the case can be useful in orienting the reader.

Guidelines

Use a real or imaginary classroom situation as the basis for developing your case. You may choose to enhance a real situation with imaginary details. Your case should include *a clear description of the dilemma or challenge*. Your case may include any or all of the following components:

■ Description of the teacher
■ Teacher's background and/or experiences
■ Description of the classroom, school, or community
■ Description of the students

- Teacher's feelings and intentions
- Students' feelings and intentions
- Actual or imaginary dialogue
- Description of other relevant parties (e.g., parents, principals, other teachers)

Do not include a solution, outcome, or morals with your case. You may use as many or as few of these components, and you may arrange them in any order. There is no correct way to write an open case.

Writing Solutions to an Open Case

Guidelines

Exchange open cases with colleagues who teach similar subjects or grade levels. Write a response to the case in which you comment on any of the following:

- Your interpretation of the dilemma or challenge
- The solutions you recommend
- An explanation of why you think your solutions are viable
- Any morals or lessons you think you can draw from your reading and interpretation of the case

Your response may include any, all, or none of the following elements:

- Theories about science teaching and learning
- Theories about human behavior
- Your own experiences as a student, teacher, or parent
- Experiences of friends or colleagues
- Common sense
- Reference to any component of the case itself

There is no correct way to write solutions to an open case.

Writing a Closed Case

Guidelines

Use a real or imaginary classroom situation. You may choose to enhance a real situation with imaginary details. Your case should include the following components: *a clear description of the dilemma or challenge* and *a clear description of the solutions.* Your case may include any or all of the following components:

- Description of the teacher
- Teacher's background and/or experiences
- Description of classroom, school, or community
- Description of students
- Teacher's feelings and intentions
- Students' feelings and intentions
- Dialogue
- Description of other relevant parties (e.g., parents, principals, other teachers)
- Outcome(s) (How did the solutions work?)
- Lessons or morals that can be drawn from the case

You may use as many or as few of these components as you like, and you may arrange them in any order.

Writing Responses to a Closed Case

Guidelines

Exchange closed cases with a colleague who teaches similar subjects or grade levels. Write a response in which you comment on any of the following:

- Your interpretation of the dilemmas and/or challenges (Do you agree or disagree with the case author?)
- Your evaluation of the solutions
- Your justification of the solutions
- Your opinion concerning the viability of any morals or lessons drawn by the case author

Your response may include any, all, or none of the following:

- Theories about science teaching and learning
- Theories about human behavior
- Your own experiences as a student, teacher, or parent
- Experiences of friends or colleagues
- Common sense
- References to any components of the case itself

There is no correct way to write responses to a closed case.

■ Facilitating Group Discussion of Cases

Equally important as the writing of cases is the opportunity for teachers to engage in discussions that facilitate critical reflection, analysis, evaluation of possible solutions, and the recognition of underlying assumptions and issues. These discussions take place within science teacher education programs as well as interactive professional development contexts. The role of the facilitator in structuring meaningful case discussions is crucial. Miller and Kantrov's (1998) *A Guide to Facilitating Cases in Education* serves as an excellent resource for potential case facilitators. We have found the following guidelines to be useful in facilitating case discussions that shed light on teachers' underlying assumptions and beliefs.

Guidelines for Facilitators

1. Case discussions should encourage dialogue rather than debate.

2. Discussion groups should be small enough to encourage participation of all members.

3. Prospective and practicing teachers should be provided with ample time to read and prepare for case discussions.

4. Group facilitators should analyze and articulate in advance the issues and concepts that are most relevant to their instructional goals.

5. Group facilitators should be open to considering the viability of conflicting alternatives.

6. Group facilitators should encourage conversation that expands the discussion beyond the text of the case itself and situates the case dilemma in a larger context (Miller & Kantrov, 1998).

7. Facilitators should be sensitive to the dynamics of the group, making sure that no one subgroup dominates the conversation.

8. Group facilitators should cherish the multiple perspectives of teachers and, at the same time, seek to build common understandings.

In addition to teachers' personal narratives as a source for case materials, science teachers and science teacher educators may find other sources of case-based teaching collections suitable for their intended purposes. A sampling of the growing number of case-based teaching resources now available is listed at the end of this chapter. Most of these materials include cases of a general nature that cut across disciplines and explore a range of issues; only occasionally is a case with specific relevance to science teaching and learning included in these collections. While casebooks are becoming more commonplace in the educational literature, the need for cases with particular significance to science teaching and learning remains. We look forward to the secondary science casebook being developed by John Wallace and his Australian colleagues and the elementary science casebook project that is close to the heart of colleagues Anne Howe and Sharon Nichols.

Case-Based Teaching Resources

Granwood, G. E., & Parkay, F. W. (1989). *Case studies for teacher decision making.* New York: Random House.

Harvard-Smithsonian Center for Astrophysics. (1997). *Video case studies in science education.* Burlington, VT: Annenberg/CPB.

Kleinfeld, J. (Ed.). (1989). *Teaching cases in cross-cultural education.* Fairbanks: University of Alaska.

Kleinfeld, J., & Yerian, S. (Eds.). (1995). *Gender tales: Tensions in the schools.* New York: St. Martin's Press.

Kowalski, T. J., Weaver, R. A., & Henson, K. T. (1990). *Case studies on teaching* (and Instructor's Manual). New York: Longman.

Kowalski, T. J., Weaver, R. A., & Henson, K. T. (1994). *Case studies of beginning teachers.* New York: Longman.

Schifter, D. (Ed.). (1996). *What's happening in Math class? Vol. 1: Envisioning new practices through teacher narratives.* New York: Teachers College Press.

Shulman, J. H., & Colbert, J. A. (1987, November). *The mentor teacher casebook.* Eugene: University of Oregon, ERIC Clearinghouse on Educational Management; San Francisco: Far West Laboratory for Educational Research and Development.

Shulman, J. H., & Colbert, J. A. (Eds.). (1988, July). *The intern teacher casebook.* Eugene: University of Oregon: Far West Laboratory for Educational Research and Development.

Shulman, J. H., & Mesa-Bains, A. (Eds.). (1993). *Diversity in the classroom: A casebook for teachers and teacher educators.* Hillsdale, NJ: Research for Better Schools and Lawrence Erlbaum Associates.

Silverman, R., & Welty, W. M. (1993). *Primis case studies for teacher problem solving.* New York: McGraw-Hill Education.

Silverman, R., Welty, W. M., & Lyon, S. (1991). *Case studies for teacher problem solving.* New York: McGraw-Hill.

Wasserman, S. (1993). *Getting down to cases: Learning to teach with case studies.* New York: Teachers College Press.

References

Hansen, A. J. (1997). Writing cases for teaching: Observations of a practitioner. *Phi Delta Kappan, 78,* 398–401.

Kagan, D. M., & Tippins, D. J. (1991). How teachers' classroom cases reflect their pedagogical beliefs. *Journal of Teacher Education, 42,* 281–291.

Miller, B., & Kantrov, I. (1998). *A guide to facilitating cases in education.* Portsmouth, NH: Heinemann.

Sacken, M. (1992, February). *Using cases in the education of educators.* Paper presented at the Annual Meeting of the American Association of Colleges for Teacher Education, San Antonio, TX.

Index